THE ESSAY FILM

The Essay Film

FROM MONTAIGNE, AFTER MARKER

Timothy Corrigan

OXFORD
UNIVERSITY PRESS

OXFORD
UNIVERSITY PRESS

Oxford University Press, Inc., publishes works that further
Oxford University's objective of excellence
in research, scholarship, and education.

Oxford   New York
Auckland   Cape Town   Dar es Salaam   Hong Kong   Karachi
Kuala Lumpur   Madrid   Melbourne   Mexico City   Nairobi
New Delhi   Shanghai   Taipei   Toronto

With offices in
Argentina   Austria   Brazil   Chile   Czech Republic   France   Greece
Guatemala   Hungary   Italy   Japan   Poland   Portugal   Singapore
South Korea   Switzerland   Thailand   Turkey   Ukraine   Vietnam

Copyright © 2011 by Oxford University Press, Inc.

Published by Oxford University Press, Inc.
198 Madison Avenue, New York, New York 10016

www.oup.com

Oxford is a registered trademark of Oxford University Press

Library of Congress Cataloging-in-Publication Data
Corrigan, Timothy.
The essay film : from Montaigne, after Marker / Timothy Corrigan.
   p.   cm.
Includes bibliographical references and index.
ISBN 978-0-19-978169-0 (hardcover : alk. paper) — ISBN 978-0-19-978170-6 (pbk. : alk. paper)
1. Experimental films—History and criticism. I. Title.
PN1995.9.E96C67   2011
791.43'611—dc22   2011006312

Printed in the United States of America
on acid-free paper

Contents

THE ESSAY FILM

Introduction: Of Film and the Essayistic

WHEN I BEGAN to work on this book in the 1990s, the phrase *essay film* was a fairly cryptic expression that normally required more than a little explanation. Since then, both the phrase and the films have become increasingly visible, and although for many the notion of an essay film remains less than self-explanatory, this particular mode of filmmaking has become more and more recognized as not only a distinctive kind of filmmaking but also, I would insist, as the most vibrant and significant kind of filmmaking in the world today.

Some versions of the essay film arguably extend back at least to D. W. Griffith's 1909 *A Corner in Wheat*, a sharp social commentary on the commodity wheat trade, or, more convincingly, to the 1920s and Sergei Eisenstein's various cinematic projects, such as his never-completed film adaptation of Marx's *Capital*. Especially since the 1940s, however, more and more filmmakers from Chris Marker to Peter Greenaway have described their own films as essay films, joining numerous film critics, theoreticians, and scholars who, since Hans Richter and Alexandre Astruc in the 1940s, have hailed the unique critical potentials and powers of this central form of modern filmmaking. Whereas Richter and Astruc can be considered two of the earliest filmmaker/critics to identify and argue the specific terms of the essay film, critical attention by critics and filmmakers alike has continually expanded and accelerated: from André Bazin's comments in the 1950s and Godard's in the 1960s through the work of contemporary scholars such as Nora Alter,

Christa Blümlinger, Suzanne Liandrat-Guigues, Catherine Lupton, Laura Rascaroli, Michael Renov, and others.[1]

In the last thirty years, essay films have followed this growth of attention and moved decisively from the margins to the center of film culture, capturing headlines (Michael Moore's 2007 *Sicko*) and Academy Awards (Errol Morris's 2003 *Fog of War*). Often with the look of a documentary filtered through a more or less personal perspective, these sometimes perplexing movies have always been difficult to classify, sometimes difficult to understand, and often difficult to relate to each other. Many of the challenges they pose and misunderstandings they provoke, however, can be mitigated or overcome, I argue, by locating these films specifically within the long and varied tradition of the essay.

Part of the reason for the lack of attention to these films—compared to both narrative fiction films and traditional documentary cinema—is the more general suspicion about the essay itself. More often than not, essays have been considered "eccentric," "a degenerate, impossible genre, not very serious and even dangerous" (quoted in Bensmaïa 96–97); for many filmgoers, essay films have the confusing distinction of suggesting Jean-Luc Godard's goal of combining the "personal" with "actuality." While other forms of writing and filmmaking elicit a certain respect associated with their privileged value as aesthetic or scientific practices, essays are usually (and not necessarily incorrectly) associated with mundane or quotidian activities such as school assignments and newspaper commentaries. Presumably, anyone can write an essay on any topic, and because of their broad and often indiscriminate reach, essays have sometimes been perceived as a merely "prosaic" activity. Indeed, precisely because of the tendency of the essay to respond to and depend on other cultural events that precede them—commenting on or criticizing a political event or a theatrical performance, for instance—essays have frequently been viewed as a parasitic practice, lacking those traditional forces of originality or creativity that, since the late eighteenth century, valorize works of art like paintings or poems.

Part of the power of the essay, however, lies precisely in its ability to question or redefine these and other representational assumptions (frequently enlisted with Romantic aesthetics) and to embrace its anti-aesthetic status. The difficulties in defining and explaining the essay are, in other words, the reasons that the essay is so productively inventive. Straddling fiction and nonfiction, news reports and confessional autobiography, documentaries and experimental film, they are, first, practices that undo and redo film form, visual perspectives, public geographies, temporal organizations, and notions of truth and judgment within the complexity of experience. With a perplexing and enriching lack of formal rigor, essays and essay films do not usually offer the kinds of pleasure associated with traditional aesthetic forms like narrative or lyrical poetry; they instead lean toward intellectual reflections that often insist on more conceptual or pragmatic responses, well outside the borders of conventional pleasure principles.

Besides the centrality of essay films in contemporary film culture, two overarching motifs inform this study: the importance of differentiating the essay film from other film practices and the importance of recognizing an overlooked literary heritage in this particular film practice. First and most prominently, I contend that the essay film must be distinguished from broad models of documentary or experimental cinema and must be located in a more refined historical place that does justice to its distinctive perceptions and interactions. Documentaries, especially experimental documentaries, such as Jean Vigo's *A propos de Nice* (1930) or Luis Bunuel's *Land without Bread* (1933), are clearly important precursors.[2] Yet, despite the many attempts to fold essay films into those longer traditions, these attempts to see film history as a continuity with variations are limited in their ability to fully acknowledge the critical intervention that the essay film makes in the history of cinema. Just as important, essay films must be distinguished from the multitude of more conventional or differently innovative contemporary documentaries, reality television, and other measures of the recent fascination with and resurgence of a documentary tradition.

An abundance of recent labels attempt, for instance, to recover the essay film in categories such as "meta-documentaries," "reflexive documentaries," or "personal or subjective documentaries." None of these, however, strikes me as entirely adequate (although Bill Nichols's notion of performative documentary suggestively intersects with some of the central features of my argument).[3] With their understandable emphasis on a documentary tradition, these categories tend to exclude a large body of essay films that are well outside that tradition, such as Helke Sander's *Redupers: The All-Round Reduced Personality* (1978) or Raoul Ruiz's *The Hypothesis of a Stolen Painting* (1979). Along with the many self-proclaimed documentary essayists (from Marker to Orson Welles), many other filmmakers far from the documentary tradition have comfortably applied the term *essay* to their more fictionalized films, including Greenaway, who describes *A Zed and Two Noughts* (1985) as a kind of essay, "a theoretical observation on the relation between humans and animals" and *Belly of an Architect* (1987) "as an essay on the responsibility of contemporary architects to history and their relation with it" (Gras and Gras 52–53). While those other categories and terminologies properly align recent documentaries with the reflexive tendencies of so many different kinds of modernist cinema, they tend, I believe, to generalize and reduce the strategies and accomplishment of the essay film and to miss or underestimate its distinctive address and achievements.[4]

This study thus aims to explore more exactly the "essayistic" in and through film, where the essayistic indicates a kind of encounter between the self and the public domain, an encounter that measures the limits and possibilities of each as a conceptual activity. Appearing within many different artistic and material forms besides the essay film, the essayistic acts out a performative presentation of self as a kind of self-negation in which narrative or experimental structures are subsumed within the process of thinking through a public experience. In this larger sense, the essay film becomes most important in pinpointing a practice that renegotiates assumptions about documentary objectivity, narrative epistemology, and authorial expressivity within the determining context of the unstable heterogeneity of time and place.

With my second motif, linking the essay film with its literary heritage, I argue that the essay film focuses key issues in the historically varied and multidimensional relationship between film and literature. A prominent measure of cultural shifts in the aesthetics and industry of the cinema for over 100 years, the interchange between the literature and film has usually been mapped across the interaction of film and narrative fiction, dramatic theater, and sometimes poetry. Investigating the literary heritage of the essay that informs and is transformed by the essay film not only broadens the field of that interchange but also introduces distinctive questions, prerogatives, opportunities, and strategies in that relationship. Having virtually nothing to do with the usual fidelities and infidelities of textual adaptation, the literary heritage of the essay film illuminates, most importantly, a unique engagement between the verbal and the visual that has emerged from a long history of self-articulation in a public sphere.[5] From Marker's self-conscious rapport with Henri Michaux to Derek Jarman's baroque linguistics, the literary tradition of the essay film thus becomes a crucial point of departure and often a visible figure in the shape and address of the essay film.

The richness, growth, and variety of essay films in recent decades have made it virtually impossible to attempt a comprehensive survey if one is to respect the diversity of the practice. As a companion piece to retrospectives on the essay film, the 2007 *Der Weg der Termiten: Beispiele eines Essayistichen Kinos 1909–2004* offers a useful historical and cultural panorama that extends from the 1909 *Corner in Wheat* and Dziga Vertov's films of the 1920s to Argentine filmmaker Fernando Birri's *Tire dié* (1960), Thom Andersen's *Los Angeles Plays Itself* (2003), and Thai filmmaker Apichatpong Weerasethakul's *Mysterious Object at Noon* (2003), including along the way films by Leo Hurtz, Peter Nestler, Imamura Shohei, Chantal Akerman, Michael Rubbo, Jean-Pierre Gorin, Kidlat Tahimik, Patrick Keiller, and many other well- and less well-known filmmakers. While wide perspectives such as this highlight the scope and variety of this practice, here I argue for the stricter historical boundaries of 1945 to the present and provide particular readings of individual films that draw out not only the common ground of these films but also their individual distinctions. With this extended focus on single films, many important essay films and filmmakers will not get the attention they deserve here, but for me the benefits of close readings are preferable to the attempt at a broad survey of essay films. Besides, expanding and contracting my ideas around particulars seems to me to be truer to the spirit of the essayistic. My aim is not to canonize certain films and filmmakers within this tradition but to demonstrate the intricate varieties of the practice and to follow the movement of my own thinking through those practices. The result is a study that mixes well-known and lesser-known films, from Marker's *Letter from Siberia* (1958) and Agnès Varda's *The Gleaners and I* (2000) to Alan Clarke's *Elephant* (1989) and Lynne Sachs *States of UnBelonging* (2006).

In addition, my focus here is on the essay *film*, more so than its other visual and media incarnations. As the first two chapters make clear, the essay film has a long historical and theoretical pedigree. While it is crucial to provide this background, I am primarily interested in the modern and contemporary essay film (which sometimes appears through televised venues). Moreover, although the essay film has more recently found some of its most intriguing contemporary transformations through the Internet, other electronic media, and even museum installations,[6] this study concentrates primarily on the cinematic essay—not photographic, video, or Internet essays—between 1945 and 2010. Although virtually every country around the world produces essay films, moreover, my focus is largely Western, in large part because of the historical and cultural origins and evolutions of the essay, a heritage that is clearly changing quickly as a consequence of global and digital shifts in media production.

I have chosen a somewhat generic organization of essay films as way to champion both their many differences and their inevitable overlappings. While attending to the textual specifics of certain films, my study organizes those analyses according to particular modes within the larger history of the essay, as they configure different experiential encounters or experiential concepts linking subjectivity and a public domain. As a base for my argument, chapter 1 distills the pragmatic and conceptual shapes of the essay as it has been practiced and discussed since the late sixteenth century, while chapter 2 investigates the historical emergence of the essay film from earlier documentary and avant-garde traditions, precursors leading to its full visibility in the the 1940s and 1950s. In this first section, my emphasis is on the French tradition, which, while not the exclusive foundation for these films, is the most prominent and influential in those early years. In fact, except for

Jean-Luc Godard, I emphasize the Left Bank school of modern French cinema where the literary underpinnings of essay films by Marker, Varda, and Alain Resnais is much more apparent than in the films of the *Cahiers du cinéma* group of Francois Truffaut, Claude Chabrol, and others. The second section of the book then investigates five different experiential modes informing essay films: In chapter 3, portrait essays describe representations of the self and self-expression; in chapter 4, travel essays map encounters with different spatial geographies; in chapter 5, diary essays depict different temporalities and velocities of modern life; in chapter 6, editorial essays reshape the news of world events; and in chapter 7, refractive essay films critically engage art objects, films, and other aesthetic experiences. Within each mode, essays represent a spectrum from didactic or sermonic positions to parodic and comic positions. Within this organization, as I indicated, it is unfortunate that my choices of films to signal—some canonically important, some historically important, some my personal favorites—can only implicitly acknowledge a vast number of significant essay films that deserve critical attention.

Categorizing essay films according to these modes is, admittedly, a slippery strategy since essay films invariably overlap and mix several of these modes or figures. I believe this overlapping is partly to do with the "unmethodical method" that, according to Adorno, is the fundamental form of the essay and helps explain one of the central paradoxes and challenges of the essay: It is a genre of experience that, as Reda Bensmaïa has pointed out, may be fundamentally antigeneric, undoing its own drive toward categorization.[7] If "genre boundaries" are the staple of one wing of film studies, essay films require the acknowledgment of a defining overlapping whereby these films may participate in a variety of figural or modular crossings, as well as "boundary crossings" of more conventional distinctions, such as narrative versus nonnarrative forms.[8] If Marker's *Sunless* (1982) represents one of the widely acknowledged triumphs of the practice, it represents the triumph of an amalgamation and orchestration of modular layers, as a travelogue, a diary, a news report, and a critical evaluation of film representation. Besides providing a useful heuristic framework, however, isolating these five modes is important in drawing attention to the broader backgrounds that essay films so productively and explicitly engage as part of an archeology that includes sermons, philosophical dialogues, epistolary narratives, diaries, scientific reports, lectures, editorials, art criticism, and other forms of public discourse.

Writing about the essayistic and essay films requires, I found, more self-consciousness than is typical of scholarly and historical writing. My tactics have been to mobilize theoretical and scholarly positions as ways of turning ideas and films around each other, as strategic interventions rather than as blueprints for certain interpretations. To dramatize this movement, I typographically emphasize disjunctions and shifts between the constellation of ideas and arguments in each chapter and the analysis of specific films as my readings respond to and develop those ideas. Partly because of the nature of the essay, partly because of the shifting multiplicity of the material, and partly because of the demands these films make on an actively reflective engagement, these chapters thus act out specific engagements in my experience of certain films and intellectual positions. Indeed, the choices of particular films to emphasize, as well as the choices of certain scholarly and theoretical positions to mobilize, might be described as following the essayistic practice that trusts the richness of "thoughts occasioned by" certain films.

Many have contributed mightily to my thinking through presentations at the University of Florida, University of Pittsburgh, Harvard University, Bryn Mawr College, Drake University, University of Pennsylvania, University of Vienna, the Center for Cultural Analysis at Rutgers University, the Society for Cinema and Media Studies conferences, the 2005 Werner Herzog conference in London, the 2009 conference on "Short Circuits in Contemporary Cinema" at the University of Bologna, and the 2009 Association of Adaptation Studies conference at the British Film Institute. One particularly notable meeting on "Der Essayfilm" at Leuphana University in Lünenberg, Germany, in 2007 provided a rich opportunity to discuss the topic with Hito Steyerl, Sven Kramer, Thomas Tode, Catherine Lupton, Raymond Bellour, Christa Blümlinger, and Bernard Eisenshitz. This book also owes much to the comments and encouragement of Ivone Margulies, Eric Rentschler, Timothy Murray, Dominique Bluher, Michael Renov, David Rodowick, Dudley Andrew, Jonathan Kahana, Yoram Allon, Dina Smith, Ann Friedberg, Lynne Sachs, William Galperin, Tina Zwarg, Bob and Helen Buttel, Ruth Pertlmutter, Kevin Harty, Eric Faden and Greg Flaxman. The work and support of Nora Alter appears so ubiquitously in this book that it would be impossible to detail her many contributions, while my sometimes co-author Patricia White has been, as in all matters cinematic, my inspiring interlocutor in more ways than I can acknowledge. I am grateful to the University of Pennsylvania for a research leave and research support, including the assistance of Maggie Borden and Sara Brenes-Akerman. My colleagues in the Penn Cinema Studies program, Karen Beckman, Peter Decherney, Meta Mazaj, and Nicola Gentili, have been the ideal community for thinking about film as a public endeavor; they have also been my faithful companions in so many other matters. At Oxford University Press, Shannon McLachlan energetically supported this project for several years, and Brendan O'Neill gracefully managed its publication. Earlier versions of parts of this book have appeared in the journal *Iris: A Journal of Theory on Image and Sound, Still Moving:*

Between Cinema and Photography (Duke University Press), *A Companion to Werner Herzog* (Blackwell), *The Geopolitics of Art Cinema* (Oxford University Press), and *Corto Circuito: Il Cinema Contemporaneo Nella Rete* (Archetip Libri, Bologna).

No acknowledgment here can measure the support and contributions of Marcia Ferguson, who knows about the complexity and richness of experience.

PART ONE

Toward the Essay Film

1

"On Thoughts Occasioned by . . ." Montaigne to Marker

FROM ITS LITERARY origins to its cinematic revisions, the essayistic describes the many-layered activities of a personal point of view as a public experience. Anticipated in earlier memoirs, sermons, and chronicles, the most recognizable origin of the essay is the work of Michel de Montaigne (1533–1592), whose reflections on his daily life and thoughts appear, significantly, in the French vernacular of the streets rather than the Latinate discourse of the academy. With the term *essays* emphasizing their provisional and explorative nature as "attempts," "tries," or "tests," Montaigne's writings are views of, comments on, and judgments of his faltering memory, kidney stones, love, friendship, sex in marriage, lying, a "monstrous childe," and a plethora of other common and uncommon questions picked almost haphazardly from a mind observing the world passing before and through it. Imagined, to some extent, as an active intellectual exchange with his deceased friend Étienne de La Boétie, these essays describe a bond between a personal life and the surrounding events of that life in sixteenth-century France, and, in revision after revision that characterize these essays (1580, 1588, 1595), they testify not only to the constant changes and adjustments of a mind as it defers to experience but also to the transformation of the essayistic self as part of that process.

Since Montaigne, the essay has appeared in numerous permutations, inhabiting virtually every discourse and material expression available. Most often, the essayistic is associated with the literary essays whose historical prominence extends from Montaigne to Joseph Addison and Richard Steele in the eighteenth century to contemporary writers like James Baldwin, Susan Sontag, Jorge Louis Borges, and Umberto Eco. From its literary foundation, the essayistic also moves through the nineteenth century in less-obvious practices, such as drawings and sketches, and by the twentieth century, it appears even in musical forms, such as Samuel Barber's *Essay for Orchestra* (1938). Through the twentieth and twenty-first centuries, the essayistic has increasingly taken the shape of photo-essays, essay films, and the electronic essays that permeate the Internet as blogs and other exchanges within a public electronic circuitry.

Aldous Huxley describes the essay as moving among three poles:

The essay is a literary device for saying almost everything about almost anything. . . . Essays belong to a literary species whose extreme variability can be studied most effectively within a three-poled frame of reference. There is the pole of the personal and the autobiographical; there is the pole of the objective, the factual, the concrete-particular; and there is the pole of the abstract-universal. Most essayists are at home and at their best in the neighborhood of only one of the essay's three poles, or at the most only in the neighborhood of two of them. There are the predominantly personal essayists, who write fragments of reflective autobiography and who look at the world through the keyhole of anecdote and description. There are the predominantly objective essayists who do not speak directly of themselves, but turn their attention outward to some literary or scientific or political theme. . . . The most richly satisfying essays are those which make the best not of one, not of two, but of all the three worlds in which it is possible for the essay to exist. (330)

To map and distinguish the essay in its evolution from Montaigne to the essay film, I employ a variation on Huxley's three poles as not separable kinds of essays but as, in the "most richly satisfying essays," interactive and intersecting registers. While one or the other of these three registers may be more discernible in any given essay, my three variations on Huxley's versions of the essayistic describe the intersecting activity of personal expression, public experience, and the process of thinking. Other definitions and models of the essay tend to emphasize one or the other of these features as, for instance, the role of a personal voice or the search for documentary authenticity. For me, however, the variable ratio and interactivity of these three dimensions creates a defining representational shape that emerges from the literary heritage of the essay and extends and reformulates itself in the second half of the twentieth century as the essay film. If part of the power of the essayistic has been its ability to absorb and mobilize other literary and artistic practices, such as narrative or photographic practices, film, since the 1940s, has become one of its richest terrains.

While no single definition of the essayistic will probably ever be sufficiently malleable for its many variations, following this framework as it emerges from its literary foundation (and later adapted to the photographic essay) clarifies and formulates, I believe, the distinctive terms of the essay film. Across the history of its shifting practices, the essayistic stretches and balances itself between abstracted and exaggerated representation of the self (in language and image) and an experiential world encountered and acquired through the discourse of thinking out loud. If Montaigne introduces the literary beginnings of this practice, tracing this history and its emerging priorities leads almost climatically, for André Bazin and others, to Chris Marker's 1958 essay film *Letter from Siberia* and, subsequently, to Richard Roud's prescient characterization of Marker as "1:1.33 Montaigne."[1]

Often cited as the modern or even postmodern descendent of Montaigne, Roland Barthes is, for me, the preeminent literary essayist of the twentieth century, a protean writer of the everyday, fully and concomitantly dedicated to and resistant to the contemporary image and the power of the cinema. Arriving in the 1950s, contemporaneous with the films of Marker, Barthes's work stands out as both commentaries on and representations of the power and singularity of the essayistic: his writing tests the limits and possibilities of the essay (from his collection of encounters with public artifacts in Mythologies *to his meditation on photography in* Camera Lucida*) and, more theoretically and explicitly than most, this work frequently locates the tensions of essayistic expression in that central twentieth-century play between the verbal and the visual.[2] In his "Inaugural Lecture, College of France," he claims, "I have produced only essays, an ambiguous genre in which analysis vies with writing" (457) and proclaims for this kind of writing what I argue is more specifically the province of the essayistic, a discourse of "loosening," "fragmentation," "digression," and "excursion" (476).[3] Throughout his essays, he identifies and gravitates toward textual features—of novels, photographs, or other social texts—that speak to the power and prevalence of a personal voice and experience that articulate and disperse themselves through a vast cultural landscape in an active struggle to make meaning. Appropriately, one of Barthes's most celebrated and important essays, "The Third Meaning," makes famous an "obtuse meaning" which he discovers in Sergei Eisenstein's* Ivan the Terrible *(1947) and which, like the "punctum" he locates in photographs or the "suspended meaning" he finds in the best films and texts, describes an exceptionally personal engagement with a detail, texture, or moment that, in their resisting definitive meanings, dramatizes thought.*

Of his many passing and extended commentaries on film, his essay "Leaving the Movie Theater" reflects on a kind of cinematic encounter whose dynamics adumbrate how an essayist and an essay film might reconfigure the filmic experience. Just as the experience rather than any particular object becomes the primary concern of an essayist, Barthes writes here of a "cinema situation" as both a private and public encounter with his own self, "two bodies at the same time." On the one hand, there is "a narcissistic body which gazes, lost, into the engulphing mirror" (345, 349). On the other, the situation surrounds and counterpoints the "lure" or hypnotic capture of that imagistic mirror, creating "a perverse body, ready to fetishize not the image but precisely what exceeds it" (348–349). The cinematic situation becomes then a "site of availability" that allows the self to be there and elsewhere. Subjectivity now drifts through an "urban dark" where "the body's freedom is generated" (3) in "the sound's grain, the theatre, the obscure mass of other bodies, the rays of light, the entrance, the exit": the "inoccupation of the body" becomes "that of the big city" (346).

This drift across two bodies—a private self and public self, a narcissistic image and an image of the surrounding world as "the Cinema of society" (348)— becomes a suggestive metaphor for the essayistic that begins with Montaigne and continues through essay films today. Creating a verbal drift between the film image and the image of its surroundings (the street, the twilight), Barthes both inhabits the cinematic image and "must also be elsewhere" (347), and so complicates his fascination with his "relation" to the image as a verbal mapping of the "situation," "taking off" from that image in the rhetoric of thought (348). As Barthes spins the visual-verbal tension of this private-public encounter, essayistic encounters situate themselves and find their place in an intellectual and erotic twilight zone between the cinematic image and the street, the one an illusory place and the other, like a photograph, a "mad image, rubbed by the real" (La chamber claire 181). Between them, the subject drifts in a "double space, dislocated, spaced out," the space that locates the essayistic movement of thought (Roland Barthes par Roland Barthes 90). Little wonder that in the evolution of the essayistic and in the evolution of Barthes's body of work, the photogram, as the image halfway between the photograph and film, offers an almost utopian place between the intense privacy of the written word and overwhelming publicity of the cinematic image.[4]

From Montaigne to Barthes to Marker, the history of the essay offers a lengthy list of examples of a personal, subjective, or performative voice and vision as the definitive feature of the essayistic. Best exemplified by the "familiar essay" of nineteenth-century writers like Charles Lamb or Ralph Waldo Emerson, this connection between the essay and personal expression identifies, however, a much more complicated, dynamic, and often subversive position than is often acknowledged in the assumption that essays cohere around a singular self.[5] The history of the essay demonstrates, in fact, that the essayistic is most interesting not so much in how it privileges personal expression and subjectivity but rather in how it troubles and complicates that very notion of *expressivity* and its relation to *experience*, the second cornerstone of the essayistic. If both verbal and visual expression commonly suggest the articulation or projection of an interior self into an exterior world, essayistic expressivity describes, more exactly I think, a subjection of an instrumental or expressive self to a public domain as a form of experience that continually tests and undoes the limits and capacities of that self through that experience. At the intersection of these two planes, we find in the best essays the difficult, often highly complex—and sometimes seemingly impossible—figure of the self or subjectivity *thinking* in and through a public domain in all its historical, social, and cultural particulars. Essayistic expression (as writing, as film, or as any other representational mode) thus demands both loss of self and the rethinking and remaking of the self.

Montaigne's renowned combination of stoicism, skepticism, and Epicureanism consequently plays itself out across the movement from a self-expression undoing itself in the process of thinking through the dynamics of the world "as perennial movement" ("Of Repentance" 610). Aiming to be "an authority on myself" (822) and studying "myself more than any other subject" (821), Montaigne's motto "que-sais-je?" ("what do I know?") calls into question the security of his own authority. It is one of many succinct phrases in his work that describes a principal drive in the writings as an investigation into the terms of one's self and how an individual might discover a certain knowledge of the world through the individual's unsystematic experience of that world. Throughout this work, however, this drive continually rattles the terms of its own articulation, suggesting a self whose thinking through experience becomes a measure of the limits of its own capacities. While freely celebrating thinking about all details of his life, he acknowledges that "I speak freely of all things, even those which perhaps exceed my capacity" ("Of Books" 298).

In his monumental essay "Of Experience," Montaigne affirms "human igno-rance" as "the most certain fact in the school of the world" (824) yet insists repeat-edly on his goal to be "intellectually sensual, sensually intellectual" (433). Since "our life is nothing but movement," essayistic expression becomes that material-ized place for a provisional self and its thoughts, free of method and authority: "For lack of a natural memory I make one of paper" (837), he quips, claiming that "all the fricassee that I am scribbling here . . . record the essays of my life. . . . It's instruction in reverse . . . not corrupted by art or theorizing" (826). Unlike system-atic or formulaic approaches to knowledge, he learns "from experience, without any system," so presents "my ideas in general way, and tentatively" (824). While Francis Bacon's more social, more advisory, and more structured essays (published in 1597, 1612, 1625) serve as a parallel beginning of the modern essay, Montaigne's shifting and layered assertions and denials of passing thoughts on the world become the acknowledged background and touchstone for many of the first essay films, as Roud would explicitly remind us in his description of Marker as "a kind of one man total cinema . . . a 1 to 1:33 Montaigne" (Roud "The Left Bank" 27).[6]

On the foundation of Montaigne, essay writing accelerates and broadens considerably in the eighteenth and early nineteenth centuries when it begins to take a more distinctive shape as a public dialogue between a self and a visible world, often urban and sometimes natural. Eighteenth-century England is a prime example of where both the industrial and democratic backdrops of the essay come into high relief as a function of major shifts in the public sphere: Notably, through the vehicle of new periodicals ideally suited for essayistic interventions in coffee-house culture and propelled forward by the development of the iron press in 1798, the notion of an individual becomes reconfigured in the significantly broader commercial terms of social observation, communication, and interactivity. One of many well-known examples, Addison and Steele's essays, published in *The Tatler* and *The Spectator* as early as 1709, map the changing rhythms and geographies of industrialized urban spaces through the eyes of fictional personae Issac Bickerstaff and Sir Roger Coventry. These essays wander the streets of London as a distinctly self-effacing "looker-on" (Addison 3) whose perspective focuses and disperses across a club of social types (a country squire, a military man, and so on) and whose comments and observations, entwining spectacle and spontaneity, record the social variety and bustle of daily life.

Following this emphatic attention to the public sphere (and urban life), the eighteenth- and nineteenth-century essay tends to refine the moral and political voice of the essay. With nineteenth-century essayists from S. T. Coleridge to Matthew Arnold and Walter Pater, essayistic practice spreads itself more dramatically among autobiography, social report, and art criticism. Coleridge's abundance of essayistic writing from the 1790s to the 1830s thus ranges from politics and theology to literary criticism and philosophy, often underpinned by the pronounced autobiographical current, culminating in his celebrated *Biographia Literaria* (1817). Somewhat typical of many nineteenth-century forays into public life, the *Biographia* ultimately settles for and celebrates the inevitable fragmentation and incompleteness of an essayistic self, materially dramatized in the unfinished conclusion of that famous work.

What I find most suggestive in these historical reformulations of the essayistic—particularly as they help ground and anticipate the essay film—is precisely *not* the usual understanding of them as the coherently personalized expression of an authorized subjectivity, typically associated with some version of the Romantic or modern ego. While virtually every representational and artistic practice might be said to dramatize encounters between a self and the world, the dynamic and balance of that encounter seem to me to be significantly differentiated in the essayistic as a kind of fragmentation that dramatically troubles subjectivity and representation. Whereas representational practices such as those of the novel or lyric poetry, generally speaking, recuperate and organize public space through the finished frameworks of a coherent and determining subjectivity, essays tend willingly, and often aggressively, to undermine or disperse that very subjectivity as it becomes subsumed in the world it explores. This is less an oppositional distinction than a significant distinction in a representational ratio that in part reflects historical changes (mapped in the increasing importance and prevalence of the essay through the nineteenth and twentieth centuries) and in part reflects authorial choices and experiments with different representational relations (seen commonly in a writer's choice to move between traditionally authorized practices, such as poetry or novels, and the essayistic).[7]

Essays are thus most indicative of the form, I believe, when they act out of the subjection of that self within or before a natural space or, as with the essays of Charles Lamb, Virginia Woolf, and Roland Barthes, a public urban space, dispersing or transforming that self within that space and, often and more exactly, its visibility.[8] In Woolf's essay "Street Haunting" (1927), for instance, London becomes a panoramic of sights, where the "eye is sportive and generous; it creates; it adorns; it enhances" (260), and instead of the coherency of seeing oneself as "one thing only," the self becomes a reflection of the visual plenitude of a modern city, "streaked, variegated, all of a mixture" (261), a self "tethered not to a single mind," but a self that puts "on briefly for a few minutes the bodies and mind of others" (265). Just as essayists from Thomas De Quincey to Walter Pater create a certain poetic urgency in a prose aimed at describing the fleeting images of the world around them, Woolf's essayistic self in "Street Haunting" finds her quest for an instrument of self-expression, specifically a pencil, ecstatically waylaid by the a "velocity and abundance" (263) of the London streets.[9]

As a pronounced anticipation of many essay films, many twentieth-century literary essays dramatize this destabilizing encounter between a visual world that resists or troubles its verbal assessment, producing a linguistic struggle with a visual world that continually undermines or subverts the subjective power of language. From explicit cases like William Gass's extended essay *On Being Blue* or any of Jorge Luis Borges's essays to the more naturalized tactics of writers like James Baldwin, this linguistic drama emphasizes the limitations of language as the vehicle for thinking a self in public images and the necessity of reinventing that language to compensate for its inadequacies before the world. In Baldwin's

"Stranger in the Village," for instance, the "sight" of an African American by the local villagers in a small Swiss town produces Baldwin's complex inquiry into American racial history and the struggle to "establish an identity" (*Collected Essays* 127). Throughout this essay and many others, including his long reflection on the Hollywood film industry, "The Devil Finds Work" (*Collected Essays* 477-576), Baldwin develops a rhetorical stance searching for new words that could sufficiently act as an interface between his personal experience and the images of the world that he sees and that sees him. Or, as he puts it in 1999 ("I'll Make Me a World"), "I will not take any one's words for my experience." In the most demanding essays and essay films, this interactive confrontation destablilizes not only the authorial subject but also the resulting text and the reader/viewer's apprehension of it.

If the essay film inherits many of the epistemological and structural distinctions of the literary essay, especially as it plays itself out as a dialogic tension between the verbal and the visual, a key transitional practice linking these two forms of representations is the photo-essay, in which the visual itself begins to acquire the expressivity and instability associated with the verbal realm of the literary voice and now often becomes not oppositional to but an alternative mode of expressivity. Part scientific investigation, part educational sermon, part ethnographic tour, Jacob Riis's 1890 *How the Other Half Lives* figures prominently as an early transitional essay between the verbal and the visual. Here, Riis investigates New York tenements in the 1880s as a public place defined as "the destroyer of individuality and character" (222), and the novelty and power of this work spring directly from its use of shocking photographs of the deplorable living conditions to counterpoint the melodramatic voice of the commentary.[10] The 1930s later become the heyday of the photo-essay, and during this period a heightened dialogic tension between verbal texts and photographic images define a transitional period that would lead to the first discussions and practices of the essay film in the 1940s. This verbal-visual dialectic is most famously witnessed in James Agee and Walker Evan's 1939 essayistic collaboration *Let Us Now Praise Famous Men*, in which the literary privileging of the verbal against the pressure of the visual is reversed as a fundamental doubt about the adequacy of a verbal text to express the fragmentary mobility of images: "If I could do it," Agee writes, "I'd do no writing at all here. It would be photographs; the rest would be fragments of cloth, bits of cotton, lumps of earth, records of speech, pieces of wood and iron, phials of odor, plates of food and of excrement" (13).

As a supplement for the subjective voice in the photo-essay, a verbal or literary text often dramatizes and concretizes a shifting subjective perspective and its unstable relationship with the photographic images it counterpoints. In other cases, the structural formulation of the photo-essay, as the linkage of separate photographs whose implied relationship appears in the implicit gaps or "unsutured" interstices between those images, becomes itself analogous to the shifting and aleatory voice or perspective of the literary essay as it attempts, provisionally, to articulate or interpolate itself within the public spaces and experiences represented. In 1937, Henry Luce, founder of *Life* magazine, suggests, in his "The Camera as Essayist," just this ability of the image to mimic or usurp the verbal subjectivity of the literary essay when he describes the photo-essay as part of a historical evolution that links practices from the seventeenth century to Riis and the heyday of the photo-essay in the 1930s. Here, the construction of images can itself assimilate the role and language of the essayistic commentator since the camera "is not merely a reporter. It can also be a commentator. It can comment as it reports. It can interpret as it presents. It can picture the world as a seventeenth-century essayist or a twentieth-century columnist would picture it. A photographer has his style as an essayist has his" (quoted in Willumson 16). Whether with an explicit or implicit voice or text, the essayistic tension between a verbal register and a visual order that resists and troubles the verbal thus creates, in W. J. T. Mitchell's words, "dialectic of exchange and resistance between photography and language," making it "possible (and sometimes impossible) to 'read' the pictures, or to 'see' the text illustrated in them" (289). Complimenting German writer Christa Wolf's claims that "prose should strive to be unfilmable" (33), Alexander Kluge would later extend this logic when he remakes the tradition of the photo-essay as the contemporary essay film in which, like his *Blind Director* (1985), "Language in film may be blind" ("Word and Film" 238).

Against this historical background, the essayistic has become increasingly the object of theoretical and philosophical reflections and self-reflections, starting especially in the early twentieth century. Well before this point, many essayists themselves reflected on the practice as a particular kind of writing. Yet, during the twentieth century attention to the essay as a unique representational strategy flourishes as a distinctive aesthetic and philosophical question, perhaps in anticipation of Jean-Francois Lyotard's provocative claim that the essay is the quintessential form of postmodern thought in the latter half of the twentieth century (81).

Anticipating key dimensions and strategies of the essay film, several celebrated positions are especially important for theorizing its heritage, its status as a form of knowledge, and its subversion of aesthetic unity. Published in 1910, Georg Lukacs's "On the Nature and Form of the Essay" is one of the earliest and most celebrated accounts of the essay in terms of a dialogic idealism that envisions essayistic experience as "an event of the soul" (7). For Lukacs, successful essays are "a conceptual reordering of life" (1), "intellectual poems" (18) that either address "life problems" (3) or re-create that vitality as a critical engagement that becomes itself a work of art. Even within this framework, Lukacs identifies, however, the essayistic experience as an active "questioning" that asserts the primacy of a subjective "standpoint" (15) and works to discover through that questioning the "idea" of a "life-sense" (15). In this mobile activity, the essayist becomes "conscious of his own self, must find himself and build something out of himself" (15) and so becomes extended through the conceptual revelations of this dialogue with real or aesthetic experience. Pinpointing what will be a central dialogic structure in essay films, Lukacs sees Plato as "the greatest essayist who ever lived" (13), and "Socrates is the typical life for the essay" since Socrates "always lived in the ultimate questions . . . to comprehend the nature of longing and to capture it in concepts" (13–14). All essays are "thoughts occasioned by" (15) and lead to his famously pronounced motto of a self suspended in the experience of thinking through the core of life: "The essay is a judgment, but the essential, the value-determining thing about it is not the verdict (as is the case with system) but the process of judging" (18).

Contrasting Lukacs's focus on the essay's Platonic heritage, midcentury discussions of the essay in Germany and Austria evolve around questions of the essay's unique epistemological resources. Significantly, the essay now begins to distinguish itself not as an aesthetic or idealistic experience but as an intellectual activity and form of knowledge that resists the lure of an idealism often perceived as an aesthetic experience. In Robert Musil's monumental 1930 essayistic novel *The Man Without Qualities*, the essay refigures thought as an experiential engagement with the world: It "explores a thing from many sides without wholly encompassing it—for a thing wholly encompassed suddenly loses its scope and melts down to a concept . . . an essay is . . . the unique and unalterable form assumed by a man's inner life in a decisive thought. Nothing is more foreign to it than the irresponsible and half-baked quality of thought known as subjectivism" (I, 270, 273). In 1947, Max Bense refines the argument in postwar terms that would be especially important to the multilayered form of film by noting: "The essayist is a combiner, a tireless producer of configurations around a specific object. . . . Configuration is an epistemological arrangement which cannot be achieved through axiomatic deduction, but only through a literary *ars combinatoria*, in which imagination replaces strict knowledge" (422). Like the configuration of fragments in a kaleidoscope or cinematic montage, the essay offers, for Bense, a creative rearrangement and play "of idea and image" (423–424), comparable to Benjamin's "constellations" of knowledge in *The Origin of German Tragic Drama*, in which "ideas are to objects as constellations are to stars" (34).

Especially as it describes the conceptual and formal activities of the essayistic, T. W. Adorno's "The Essay as Form" offers one of the most resonant models of the essay as it looks forward to the essay film. Here, Adorno argues that the distinguishing strength of the essay is its ability to subvert systemic thought, totalities of truth, and "the jargon of authenticity" (7) through "methodically unmethodical" (13) strategies through which essay's "innermost formal law is heresy" (23). Fragmentary and "noncreative," the essay represents "reciprocal interaction of concepts in the process of intellectual experience" (13), and the essayistic subject becomes a "thinker" who "makes himself into an arena for intellectual experience" (13). Configured as "force fields" (13), essays celebrate "the consciousness of nonidentity" and the emancipation from the compulsion of identity (17), simultaneously exploring a subjective activity that realizes "nothing can be interpreted out of something that is not interpreted into it at the same time" (4). "The essay is concerned with what is blind in its objects," according to Adorno. It wants "to use concepts to pry open the aspects that cannot be accommodated by concepts, the aspect that reveals, through the contradictions in which concepts become entangled, that the net of their objectivity is merely subjective arrangement. It wants to polarize the opaque element and release the latent forces in it" (23). Coincidentally and appropriately, Adorno's essay appears the same year, 1958, as Chris Marker's *Letter from Siberia* and Bazin's landmark description of that film as an essay film.

Few films modulate the play between voice and visuals as a personal and public experience more eloquently and playfully than Ross McElwee's Bright Leaves *(2004). Almost a parody of a Romantic essay, the film begins with a dream of "prehistoric" tobacco fields that draw McElwee back to his childhood homestead, where the romantic aura of a bucolic North Carolina countryside quickly becomes a troubled homeland defined by the tobacco industry. As with many versions of the essayistic, a highly personal and potentially narcissistic subject, McElwee's persona, enters the public arena of nature and culture as a journey of self-discovery that ultimately requires abandoning and remaking of that self within the history of tobacco in North Carolina.*

Following these shifting identities, McElwee and his film then make a third move to locate this strain between the personal and public in a Hollywood film. In what seems like a random, incidental discovery, McElwee encounters a cinephile cousin, John McElwee, who collects films and related movie paraphernalia and who shows McElwee a 1950 Michael Curtiz movie called Bright Leaf, *featuring Gary Cooper, Lauren Bacall, and Patricia Neal. Both McElwee and his cousin suspect the film is a fictionalized documentary about their grandfather and his financial and industrial collapse when his Bull Durham tobacco formula was supposedly stolen by the powerful Duke family and their industry. Searching for a lost grand-father, the film appears as an almost traditional essayistic meditation on self, fathers and sons, and families, which then becomes entangled in an odd reflection on the power and danger of tobacco. Through a series of deft and seemingly random maneuvers held together by McElwee's colloquial voice, the film ultimately becomes a wry theoretical commentary on how film itself binds and unbinds those different motifs and their representational histories.*

The film explores identity across different North Carolina places and spaces, homes, and homelands where McElwee's personal history has persisted, faded, or disappeared. Specifically, he finds himself positioned between two patriarchs, his grandfather and the grandfather's rival, John Buchanan Duke, and McElwee struggles to discover his place between the heritage of those two figures. Homes and other architectural sites are the cultural and institutional frameworks for that heritage, within which McElwee, awkwardly and comically, attempts to place himself. He visits the massive Duke mansion, the parking lot where his great-grandfather once had a mansion, and then his own modest family home around the corner, which his friend Charleen describes as "Buck Duke's outhouse." A historical preservationist shows him former McElwee factories that had been suspiciously set afire at different times in the past and which now store old furni-ture. At one point, he sits alone in the tiny, empty, weedy McElwee Park wonder-ing about the different history—and identity—that would have been his if his family had triumphed. [fig. 1.1] Through the places and histories of two patri-archs, McElwee becomes a self spatially undone by a rival's empire and a history defined by personal loss.

As the luxurious close-ups of that opening dream make clear, the sensuality and abundance of tobacco leaves are the emblem of a complex natural and cultural world that suffuses McElwee's life and history. Most prominently, the film weaves his personal quest for the roots of an identity into a public commentary on the politics and commerce of the tobacco industry, past and present. Here and there throughout the film, McElwee's observations about tobacco fluctuate between soci-ology, psychology, science, and politics, with a tone that moves from the satirical to the tragic. Following the trail of tobacco appears at times to be a documentary exposé of the dominating family of James Buchanan Duke, whose tobacco empire destroyed his great-grandfather's rival business but ironically created an "agricul-tural, pathological trust fund" for generations of McElwee doctors that followed. McElwee visits the Duke University hospital, interviews chain-smoking students at a beautician school (in a building that formerly functioned as a tobacco ware-house), and elicits opinions on tobacco from a small-town parade with an endless array of increasingly smaller beauty queens.

FIGURE 1.1   Undone in McElwee Park (*Bright Leaves*)

Less obvious, tobacco also becomes a peculiar bond for communities and rela-
tionships throughout the film in a way that suggests a complex need for others that
simultaneously implies a metaphoric and real loss of self. Through the second half
of the film, for instance, McElwee returns regularly to a couple struggling to stop
smoking before their marriage and after their marriage, smoking acting as a con-
tinual manifestation of their relationship but one that will eventually, they know,
physically destroy them. In Bright Leaves, *addiction to cigarettes is an addiction*
to nature, family, and community, drawing the individual along a path that is
always shadowed by death and dispersal. Even the central relationship in the film,
between McElwee and his son, intersects with this reality when he takes "his son
to work with him" to interview a woman being treated for cancer, which, he admits,
is "an unusual place for a father/son outing." [fig. 1.2] Indeed, this last scene
becomes an especially disturbing and dramatic visualization of how private and
public realities can jarringly intersect across the essayistic as the film frame reveals
the usually invisible place of the son operating a sound boom, a now visible place
where the privatized relationship of father and son is, in Barthes's sense, "outed"
to the other world of tobacco and death.[11]

Oddly like Barthes's relationship with the movie theater, McElwee's encoun-
ter with tobacco becomes about the seduction and destruction that is also about his
relationship with filmmaking. Toward the end of the film as he plays with his lenses
and frames, he notes, "Sometimes I feel it's such a pleasure to film, especially down

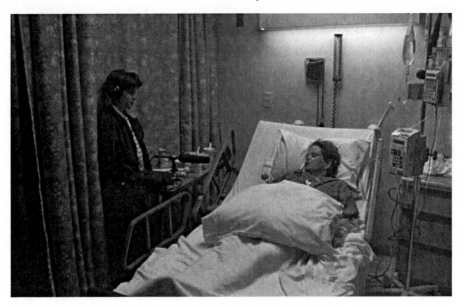

FIGURE 1.2   An unusual place for a father/son outing (*Bright Leaves*)

south, it doesn't matter what I'm filming. . . . Even just shooting around a motel
can be an almost narcotic experience. . . . For me filming is not unlike smoking a
cigarette." It consequently makes a kind of essayistic sense that McElwee's pas-
sionate addiction early in the film is to the Hollywood movie Bright Leaf. *Just as*
his cousin who introduces him to the film pursues his cinephilia as the collector's
passion to find movie people and documents that link films to a public history,
McElwee pursues links that would make this feature film evidence of his own fam-
ily's lost glory so that the Hollywood movie would become a "cinematic heirloom"
and "surreal home movie" in which private life would reveal a public epic. Speaking
over a sequence from the film in which Cooper falls down the staircase of his
burning mansion, McElwee describes the film, with typically muted wit, as "a ver-
sion of my great-grandfather's rise and subsequent fall." He convinces himself that
the performances of the actors in Bright Leaf *reveal "truthful aspects of their real*
lives"; in this pursuit, he identifies an on-screen gesture, Neal's left hand reaching
up to Cooper during a kiss, that, for McElwee, speaks of their off-screen affair now
surreptitiously captured on the screen as "a secret home movie nestled inside a Hol-
lywood production."

Yet, while Bright Leaves *seems to offer the possibility of a utopian salvation*
of that subjectivity through the public images of Bright Leaf, *ultimately the film*
describes the dispersal and loss of the personal in the public images of a film. Most
pointedly, the more profoundly philosophical aspirations of the film transform into

a comic essay as McElwee's (and his interlocutors') often-urgent voice are redis-
tributed through the contingencies of the everyday that continually intrude as
visual disruptions, turning his addictive fascinations into quotidian distractions.
As Charleen explains her childhood memories while gazing at the Duke mansion,
for instance, she suddenly cries out, "There's a black cat in the grass," and the cam-
era flash pans around to find the cat and then quickly pans awkwardly back as
Charleen returns to her more serious memories. Later, McElwee himself becomes
drawn away from his focus on a shot he is filming by contingencies that appear
like comic versions of Barthes's punctum: "When I look through a viewfinder . . . a
kind of timelessness is momentarily achieved. . . . Just fooling around here playing
with exposures, depths of field. . . . [discovering] how many special effects can be
created without the use of special effects. . . . I mean I don't even notice the large rat
that's about to slip by the background there." [fig. 1.3] Able to finally interview
Patricia Neal about Bright Leaf, *he and Neal are distractedly drawn to bags of*
garbage on a roof of a building neighboring her hotel. At this point, McElwee's
project and quest falter: He realizes that Neal "can't just accept my theory about
home movie content residing in a Hollywood production," and when the widow of
the novelist who wrote the story, Foster Fitz-Simmons, completely debunks his
theory, telling him that the story has, most definitively, nothing to do with his fam-
ily, McElwee and his film begin to brilliantly fall apart. "How I can this be?" he says
as an unexpected dog races across his shot, "I suddenly find myself adrift, dogged

FIGURE 1.3   Addiction to filming and the contingencies of the everyday (*Bright Leaves*)

by doubts of my family's cinematic legacy. . . . This small hound that came out of nowhere has ruined the shot."

Encompassing McElwee's two overlapping efforts (to find a lost home and to recover that loss through the cinema), Bright Leaves *might be considered a reflection on the critical blind spots of film, including documentary film, an almost theoretical musing on essayism itself. Hoping film theoretician Vlada Petric will call* Bright Leaf *a "minor classic," McElwee is placed in a wheelchair by Petric, who tells him that "only from unnecessary things in art can you expect something . . . special." [fig. 1.4] As Petric wheels him around in a medium close-up that mimics an intimate conversation with the filmmaker, he quickly deflates McElwee's grandiose expectations by pointing out that "Curtiz simply doesn't have a cinematic vision" or the ability to shoot "a fiction film becoming a documentary, a kind of home movie film" as historical epic. Here, Petric poses a version of an essential question behind the essay film when he asks, "How will you integrate a feature fiction film into a documentary?" Later, sitting in his tiny family park, McElwee stretches the question to identify the theoretical challenge of an essayistic encounter with thought: If documentary film is capable of "transcending the mere photographic recording of reality . . . then what do you do with it?"*

In the end, McElwee and his film must relinquish his binary sense of identities and his coherent narrative of history as tragic loss. In the end, the institutions of the world—from family to film—must give way to the vicissitudes of subjectivity, history, and cinematic representation itself. His family fades across old home

FIGURE 1.4   Vlada Petric and the art of the unnecessary (*Bright Leaves*)

movies that form the backdrop of McElwee's realization: *"I say I wish I had movies of my mother, but in another way I wonder what difference would it make. My father is becoming less and less real to me in these images. Almost a fictional character . . . the reality of him slipping away."* Similarly, the integration of the personal life into that public epic film collapses into a blurred identity in which, as McElwee finally accepts, the movie Bright Leaf *transforms the real subjects of history into the single fictional image that combines McElwee's grandfather and his Duke rival,* "probably melded them into a single character" *as, in McElwee's arch words and voice, a* "McDuke."

Against old home movies of his son, Adrian, playing years earlier at the beach where McElwee himself once played as a child, he acknowledges that film cannot preserve even his relationship with his own son or even the singularity of their separate identities: *"As if the weight of all these accumulated images could keep him from growing up so fast . . . [or] slow the process down. But, of course, filming doesn't slow anything down."* A concluding sequence shows Adrian as a boy moving a small fish from the beach to the ocean, where he releases it, *a release into the world that mirrors McElwee's release of self into the place and time of the future of history. [fig. 1.5] For essayists like McElwee, film is part of public histories and social places where the final question returns as a question to be thought:* In the words of the historical preservationist in the film, *"What exactly is being preserved here . . . what's being passed down?"* Like his son's release of that fish and

FIGURE 1.5   Releasing selves into expanding worlds (*Bright Leaves*)

Montaigne's imaginary dialogue with Étienne de La Boétie, the essayistic self invariably comes undone in an expanding world of continual and changing reflection: "When I'm on the road shooting I sometimes imagine my son, years from now, when I'm no longer around, looking at what I'm shooting. . . . I can almost feel him looking back at me from some distant point in the future . . . through the film I leave behind."

From the numerous literary and philosophical frameworks that precede it, a variety of definitions and descriptions of the essay film have circulated in recent years, including those in the important work of Nora Alter, Paul Arthur, Laura Rascaroli, and Michael Renov. Following the autobiographical and personal emphasis of McElwee's film, many of these positions foreground the role of the subjective voice or perspective in these films: some the mixing and matching of styles, genres, and aesthetic materials and still others a documentary heritage refashioned through a contemporary reflexivity on the epistemological assumptions of that heritage. Building on these and extending them in light of the history and theory of the literary essay, I return to my formulation of the essay film as (1) a testing of expressive subjectivity through (2) experiential encounters in a public arena, (3) the product of which becomes the figuration of thinking or thought as a cinematic address and a spectatorial response. In the following paragraphs, I briefly unpack and describe the three parts of this definition.

An expressive subjectivity, commonly seen in the voice or actual presence of the filmmaker or a surrogate, has become one the most recognizable signs of the essay film, sometimes quite visible in the film, sometimes not. Just as the first-person presence of the literary essay often springs from a personal voice and perspective, so essay films characteristically highlight a real or fictional persona whose quests and questionings shape and direct the film in lieu of a traditional narrative and frequently complicate the documentary look of the film with the presence of a pronounced subjectivity or enunciating position. When lacking a clearly visible subjective voice or personal organizing presence, this act of enunciation can also be signaled in various formal or technical ways, including editing and other representational manipulations of the image. The agency and activity of this subjectivity thus appears in many permutations: from McElwee's self-dramatizations in *Sherman's March* (1986) and *Bright Leaves*, to Kluge's intertitles in *The Patriot* (1979), to the restrained ironic banter of Patrick Keiller's Robinson and his interlocutor in *Robinson in Space* (1997). If Michael Moore's *Roger and Me* (1989) makes unmistakable the centrality of Moore as the subject of the film, *Waltz with Bashir* (2008) partially effaces and diffuses that subjective expression through its distinctive use of animation, while a film such as Chantal Akerman's *News from Home*

(1977) obliquely repositions that enunciator through letters read by a mother and strict imagistic framings.

Often, moreover, essays and essay films anticipate these shifting enunciators with topics and subjects that are analogously fragmented and unstable, such as Errol Morris's estranged mad scientist Fred Leuchter in *Mr. Death* (1999) or Jean-Luc Godard's housewife/prostitute/actress Juliette Janson/Marina Vlady in *2 or 3 Things I Know about Her* (1967). Through this interaction of a fragmented subject and a shifting enunciation, these films work, in turn, to destabilize the subject position of its reception by creating or directly addressing an equally shifting and unstable spectator position, as in Derek Jarman's *Blue* (1993), with its single scintillating blue screen or in Lars Von Trier's *The Five Obstructions* (2003), in which points of identification are continually rejected or deferred. Subtending the instability of these essayistic enunciations, a central rhetorical structure is then a second-person address to a "you" that is (or becomes) disembodied and depersonalized.

If both verbal and visual expression can commonly suggest the articulation or projection of an interior self into an exterior world, essayistic expressivity describes, as evident in *Bright Leaves*, a subjection of that instrumental or expressive self to a public domain, often personified as a shifting and disembodied "you." Essayistic subjectivity—in contradistinction to many definitions of the essay and essay film—refers then not simply to the emplacement or positioning of an individual consciousness before and in experience but to an active and assertive consciousness that tests, undoes, or re-creates itself through experience, including the experiences of memory, argument, active desire, and reflective thinking. Embedded within the textual action of the film, the essayistic subject becomes the product of changing experiential expressions rather than simply the producer of expressions. Following Musil's claim "Nothing is more foreign to [essayism] than the irresponsible and half-baked quality of thought 'known as subjectivism'" (1,273), Walter Benjamin was hyperbolic but correct in identifying the radical potential of the essay as an expression made entirely of quotes (Lopate 246), thus implying a form of subjective expression that inhabits and reformulates itself constantly as the expressions of another or an other. In this context, improvisation, as a commonly recognized essayistic figure, refers to a primary structure in which subjectivity tries out different positions within the world as ways of trying out different selves. Fittingly, Godard's essay *2 or 3 Things I Know about Her* begins exactly on this note with actress Marina Vlady/character Juliette telling the camera that in this film she will "speak as though quoting the truth," and in his *Notre Musique* (2004) an early commentator crystallizes the essayist subject as "Now 'I' is someone else."

More than simply foregrounding the organization of subjectivity as topic, enunciation, and reception, essayistic practices have been most innovative, complex, and defining, I believe, in how they have troubled and complicated subjectivity and its relation to public experience, that second cornerstone of the essay. Those public experiences—as encounters with places, people, and events—are what commonly align essay films with documentaries in which those public realities commonly take precedent as the referent to be revealed.[12] Yet, essay films fundamentally distinguish themselves from other documentary strategies as a form of expression and representation that necessarily relinquishes a self to events, actions, and objects outside the authority of her own subjective expressions and representations.[13] Here, the key essayistic encounter with "the everyday" as an arena of public experience describes both a temporal and a spatial experience notable for its presumed ability to resist public institutionalization and personal formulation. As Maurice Blanchot puts it, "The everyday is platitude, . . . but this banality is also what is most important. It brings us back to existence in its very spontaneity and as it is lived. . . . It escapes every speculative formulation, perhaps all coherence, all regularity" (13). The essayistic subject becomes—instantly, retroactively, or proleptically—a public figure who in contradistinction to more conventional "public figures," such as journalists or politicians, is made and remade within the incoherent potential of the everyday.

Amidst the vast amount of debate and description of what defines a "public" or a public sphere, two assumptions are important here: public life as multiple and changing domains of various registers and as a place of contestation through experience. Discussions of a public sphere often start with Jürgen Habermas, who locates its modern formation in the eighteenth century when literary essays reached a heyday,[14] but even more suggestive for discussions of the essayistic is Hannah Arendt's description of public life as "the world" which, "like every in-between, relates and separates men at the same time" (52). Later, film essayist Kluge and Oscar Negt offer an alternative public sphere precisely filtered through the concept of experience. Negt and Kluge's remaking of this public sphere as competing positions draws attention to the literary terms of Habermas's model and proposes alternative perspectives born more from a variegated "social horizon of experience" than from a cultural hegemony, more from below than from above. Experience here suggests, to put it succinctly, the interface between different individuals and social groups, involving the many dimensions along that interface (the sensual, the emotional, the ideological, the local, the global, and so on). Or, in Michael Warner's characterization in *Publics and Counterpublics*, public experience occurs as "scenes of self-activity of historical rather than timeless belonging, and of active participation rather than ascriptive belonging" (89). Built on the work of

Kluge and Negt, Miriam Hansen sums it up this way: "Experience is that which mediates individual perception with social meaning, conscious with unconscious processes, loss of self with self-reflexivity; experience as the capacity to see connections and relations . . .; experience as the matrix of conflicting temporalities, of memory and hope, including the historical loss of these dimensions" (*Babel & Babylon* 12–13).[15]

As testings of subjectivity within a public domain, the representation of modern experience in the essay film often becomes culturally associated with "risk" and "doubt," moving within and through a cultural "intermediary zone" of contested territories. That the watershed years of the essay film are 1940–1945 also reminds us that failure, crisis, and trauma often become the experiential base of the essayistic. That many of the most charged essay films regularly return to the experience of the colonial and postcolonial historically broadens and builds on those crises as the often-dangerous and fragile base of the essayistic, a questioning and rethinking of self that partly explains the attraction of the essay to politically, sexually, socially, and racially marginalized persons, demonstrated most explicitly by films as different as those of Trinh T. Minh-ha and Derek Jarman and perhaps less so in the films of Raoul Ruiz and Abbas Kiarostami. In this sense, the essayistic almost invariably practices, regardless of the subject matter, a distinctive form of politics, a politics quite different from the ideological and political strategies of narrative fiction films or conventional documentaries. In essay films, the subversion of a coherent subjectivity within the public experience of the everyday may not always be an easily decipherable and clear politics but is, perhaps always, a politics whose core is ideological instability.

As a key dimension of the politics of essay films, the encounter between an open and protean self and social experience produces the activity of essayistic thinking as the third distinguishing feature of these films, an activity that Montaigne early on identified as the testing of ideas. Both subjectivity and experience are of course the products of discourse, and rather than stabilize and harmonize the encounter between these two discourses, the essayistic creates clashes and gaps in each and across their meeting with each other as a place that elicits, if not demands, thought. Thus, an essential part of the essayistic encounter, as Graham Good has characterized it, "aims . . . to preserve something of the *process* of thinking" (20). The essay film, in Godard's words, is "a form that thinks" (1998, 54–57), or according to Phillip Lopate, the essay film "tracks a person's thoughts. . . . An essay is a search to find out what one thinks about something" (244).[16]

Large, speculative, impressionistic, and determined arguments about the way movies think or might think are as varied and old as film history itself. Among numerous others, Hugo Münsterberg, Rudolph Arnheim, Sergei Eisenstein, and

Walter Benjamin have all suggested different versions of a "visual thinking" specific to cinema. More recently, contemporary scholars and film theorists have continued these inquiries into different models of cinematic thinking.[17] Most famously, Gilles Deleuze has become an icon for a thinking cinema, mainly through his extended reflections in *Cinema 1* and *Cinema 2*. While the formidable complexity and reach of Deleuze's positions have been widely analyzed and debated, what interests me here is the practical and specific insistence that film can be understood as a dynamic forum and framework that produces ideas and a process of thinking that extends subjectivity through an outside world. "Thinking belongs to the outside," according to Deleuze (*Foucault* 93), or as he suggests in other terms about film specifically, cinematic thinking becomes a way of restoring our belief in the world (*Cinema 2* 181–182): "The [modern] cinema must film, not the world, but belief in the world" (172). If modern cinema is widely and intricately implicated in the essayistic, Deleuze's motto would work especially for the essay film: "'Give me a brain' would be the other figure of modern cinema. This is an intellectual cinema, as distinct from a physical cinema" (204).[18]

That ways to think through cinema are so central to the essay film is one reason, I think, these films have become so prominent in current film practices and current debates in film theory in which notions of passive identification and cognition are regularly challenged. The essay film requires, however, a more specific model for cinematic thinking suited to its nonnarrative and nonfictional forms and adequate to its particular configuration of subjectivity and experience. In "Toward a Phenomenology of Nonfiction Film Experience," Vivian Sobchack provides a sharp but flexible framework for such a model, bringing cinematic thinking much closer to the essayistic dynamic of experiential subjectivity. Building on the work of Jean-Pierre Meunier, Sobchack examines how different modes of identification operate across documentary films, subjectively modified by the cultural knowledge that a viewer brings to films ranging from home movies to narrative fiction films, with documentaries occupying an intermediate position between those two practices. For Sobchack, the film experience of a documentary offers various degrees of *"constitutive actualization"* (247), subjective modifications of images and sounds, by which we look "both *at* and *through* the *screen*" (246). If home movies more emphatically engage a "longitudinal consciousness" in which "the intentional object is not the specificity of the image itself, but the whole ensemble that the person or event it represents evokes," documentaries usually draw out a more "lateral consciousness" in which knowledge becomes "structured as a temporal progression that usually entails a causal logic as well as a teleological movement" (250). As part of the viewing process of a documentary, "the specific information in each image is retained and integrated with subsequent images to form our cumulative knowledge of that general reality we know exists or has existed 'elsewhere' in our life-world" (250). Most important for my argument, the difference between the longitudinal consciousness of home movies and the lateral consciousness of documentaries is not oppositional but a matter of different ratios between the subjective and objective engagements within and with the film, a kind of dialogic tension of seeing through the eyes and mind of a specific subject as that subject struggles to learn a world elsewhere. Adapting Sobchack's argument to the essayistic, essay films initiate a process conceived broadly as straddling and wavering between the longitudinal positions of home movies and lateral activities of documentaries, between a knowledge accessed through a performed subjectivity and a knowledge acquired through a public experience as "an 'apprenticeship' learning process" (251).[19]

Essayistic thinking is modeled on the question-answer-question format initiated as a kind of Socratic dialogue. Seen in the second-person direct address of many essay films, the dialogic activity of essayistic thinking can also be seen in the way the essayistic assimilates and thinks through other forms, including narrative, genres, lyrical voices, and so on. If activity infers unsettled movement, rather than formal structure, and implies various kinds of effect (on oneself, on the world, and so on), the activity of essayistic thinking here describes a consciousness of reflection and decipherment that distinguishes it from other mental activities (pleasure, fantasy), although these are often the very subjects of that essayistic perspective.

Essayistic thinking thus becomes a conceptual, figural, phenomenological, and representational remaking of a self as it encounters, tests, and experiences some version of the real as a public "elsewhere." Essayistic thought becomes the exteriorization of personal expression, determined and circumscribed by an always-varying kind, quality, and number of material contexts in which to think is to multiply one's selves. Eliciting a particular hybrid of the bond of identification or the activity of cognition, essay films ask viewers to *experience* the world in the full intellectual and phenomenological sense of that word as the mediated encounter of thinking through the world, as a world experienced through a thinking mind. The viewing subject inhabits partially the unstable subject position foregrounded in the film itself (as if, figuratively, a home movie) and partially the expanding position of participating in other ideas and worlds (as if, figuratively, a documentary).[20] Not only does that subject become made and remade through the pressure of the resistant reality of the film but also the lack of a single, dominant, or sometimes even coherent discourse disperses that viewing subject through its pastiche of forms, its mix and subversion of generic structures, and its cannibalization of narrative teleologies or lyrical voices. Essayistic thinking becomes the necessary recasting of subjective experience in the shifting interstices that define worldly experience itself.

For many viewers and scholars, Chris Marker's films define and exemplify the essay film. Not only do they describe a central historical thread in the emergence of this practice from the 1940s to the end of the 1950s, but also, placed in the context of Marker's wide and varied efforts across different fields and disciplines, his work becomes a rich demonstration of how this cinematic practice inherits and remakes the earlier essayistic traditions of the literary essay and photo-essay, as well as anticipating new traditions. Marker is one of the most relentless and innovative essayists working in film and new media, with his 1982 Sunless *rightly considered one of the landmarks of modern cinema. It is, however, at the early crossroads of the photo-essay and the essay film, between his 1959 photo-essay entitled* Koreans *and his 1958 essay film* Letter from Siberia, *in which one finds most visibly his complex engagement with the possibilities of creating a space and time between the images, experiential interstices in which to locate thoughts of the world. As Marker demonstrates in his work just after the war, the photo-essay would provide a transitional paradigm that allows film to discover its capacity to explore those critical conceptual and intellectual spaces between images.*

Best known for his 1962 film The Jetty, *his futuristic "photo-roman" of still images, and the 1982* Sunless, *his extraordinary essay film about a cameraman traveling the globe between "the two extreme poles of survival," Marker has created a multi-media body of work that ranges through novels, literary criticism, museum installations, and the CD-ROM* Immemory *(1998). As different as his subjects and media practices are, however, his concerns have remained remarkably consistent: memory, loss, history, human community, and how our fragile subjectivity can acknowledge, represent, surrender, and survive these experiences. Across the continual undoing and redoing of expression in different forms and places, Marker's work becomes a concomitantly rigorous, witty, and poignant effort to document the human experience as a struggle to understand itself in an increasingly smaller, fragmented, and accelerated global space. If the literary appears as a consistent mode within his early experiments with expression (including a 1949 novel,* The Forthright Spirit), *in 1952 Marker recognizes a new cultural dominant in the public domain. Concluding a book-length literary essay on Jean Giradoux, he acknowledges that now it is the technological image and specifically the cinema that will recapture the "miracle of a world in which everything is at once absolutely familiar and completely strange" (43).*

At these personal crossroads of the literary and the cinematic, for Marker the photo-essay becomes a critical articulation. Just after the completion of his second

short film, the 1953 Les Statues meurent aussi *(codirected with Alain Resnais),*
he edits a series of photo-essays for Edition du Seuil, *produced from 1954 to 1958,*
an experience that lays the groundwork for his own photo-essays. In her book
Chris Marker: Memories of the Future, *Catherine Lupton describes this first*
venture into the photo-essay in a way that suggests the larger concerns that would
permeate all of Marker's work:

> *A potent sense of the prospective disorientation of world travel informs Mark-*
> *er's announcement of the Petite Planete series, which appeared in the Editions*
> *du Seuil house magazine 27* Rue Jacob. *He pinpoints a growing sense that the*
> *post-war world has come within reach as never before, but that as a subjective*
> *experience this prospect of increased access seems confusing and elusive: "we see*
> *the world escape us at the same* time *as we become aware of our links with it."*
> *To combat this disorientation, Seuil is launching a series of books that, to adapt*
> *one of Marker's metaphors, are intended to be user manuals for life on a small*
> *planet. He proposes that each volume is "not a guidebook, not a history, not a*
> *propaganda brochure, not a traveller's impressions," but is intended to be like a*
> *conversation with an intelligent and cultivated person who is well-informed*
> *about the country in question. (44)*

Marker would bring his own distinctive voice to that conversation with his 1959
photo-essay entitled Koreans, *an essay fittingly published as the only volume in*
Edition de Seuil's Court métrage *("short film") series.*[21]

Koreans *is a meditative travel essay about extremes and oppositions but*
mostly about lists and inventories—and the spaces made visible by all these
organizations. Shadowing the images and text are the cold war politics dividing
North and South Korea,[22] *yet oppositions such as this are less central than the*
categorical abundance found in the experience and fabric of everyday Korean life,
the multiplicity of things that, to borrow a phrase from Sunless, *quicken the*
heart. "I will not deal with Big Issues" (135), the commentator concludes in an
address to his cat. Rather, it is the daily routines, legends and myths, conversa-
tions, relics of history, a "list of the spirits and stars that govern human life"(85)
and fragments of a developing industrial future that are photographed and
observed from numerous angles at passing moments. Even the seven-part organi-
zation of Koreans *is a set of numerical categories, "The Six Days," "The Two*
Orphans," "The Seven Wonders," "The Five Senses," "The Three Sisters," "The Nine
Muses," and "The Four Corners," that weave together lists and inventories of par-
ticular historical, imaginative, relational, emotional, and sensual experiences.
"The Seven Wonders" mentions explicitly only the "wonder of ginseng" and, as a
free association, "the seventh wonder . . . the work of builders" who took "fifty

years to complete a ginseng plant" (51–53). The other wonders appear in the mar-
kets and street scenes that come in and out of view as a series of ten photos:

> *A great deal of Korea strolls by on Koreans' heads. . . . Baskets, earthenware*
> *jars, bundles of wood, basins, all escape the earth's gravity to become satellites*
> *of these calm planets, obeying exacting orbits. For the Korean street has its*
> *cycles, its waves, its rails. In this double décor, where hastened ruins and build-*
> *ings still balancing themselves in a second of incompletion, the soldier who buys*
> *a civilian's sun hat, the worker leaving the construction site, the bureaucrat with*
> *his briefcase, the woman in traditional dress and the woman in modern dress,*
> *the porter carrying a brand new allegory to the museum of the Revolution with*
> *a woman in black following step by step to decipher it—all have their route and*
> *precise place, like constellations. (Koreans 44)*

In Adorno's words about the essayistic, here the "elements crystallize as a configu-
ration through their motion" becoming a constellation or "force field, just as every
intellectual structure is necessarily a force field under the essay's gaze" (13).

   These lists, inventories, and oppositions are primarily fading scaffolding that
constantly draws attention to the conjunctive intervals that hold them together:
the "and" that momentarily connects without a teleological logic. They create con-
tinual movement, a recollection and anticipation as a serial activity whose accu-
mulations are endlessly generative and open-ended. If the fundamental structure
of all photo-essays tends to approach that of a spatial categorizing of images, for
Marker this inventory of images always approximates a photogrammatic series of
film frames. In Koreans, *he notes that "A market place is the Republic of things. . . .*
It all went by as quickly as a forgotten image between two shots" (39), a barely
visible conjunctive place where the "and" opens potentially as the space of intelli-
gence. As Deleuze notes about the cinema (and Godard's films specifically), through
this conjunctive "and," categories are "redistributed, reshaped and reinvented" and
*so become "problems which introduce reflection on the image itself" (*Cinema 2
185–186). "The whole undergoes a mutation . . . in order to become the constitutive
'and' of things, the constitutive between-two of images" (180). No episode in Koreans *dramatizes the poignancy and power of this conjunctive place better than an*
encounter at the theater where the experience of a celebrated play based on the
well-known legend of Sim Chon suggests both a mythic categorization and the
emotional and intellectual energy within anticipatory conjunctives: Marker
encounters a female friend crying during an interval over the plight of the heroine,
despite her having seen the play 200 times, and when he tries to assure her that all
will be well in the end, she replies in bewilderment, "How could I be so sure of the
future?"

Several key sections of Koreans are especially dramatic illustrations of that wavering line between the photo-essay and essay film, places in the book where the photos become virtual photograms that draw attention to the space between the images as an interpretive "void" for the photographer/viewer/commentator. In these instances especially, the writer's voice as "expressive subject" documents the experiential expressions around him as faces "literally embodied [as] a smile that melts away, a face that comes undone" (25). At one point, a series of nine photos depicts a woman looking out of the frame telling "her life story." Or "more exactly," the text fills in, "she told us that there was nothing to be told, really nothing" (21–24). [figs. 1.6, 1.7, 1.8] Immediately following, one of the most dramatic conjunctions in the book presents just two shots of two expressions. First, there is a woman's smiling face answering questions about her personal life (her boyfriend, her prospects for marriage), but when asked about her parents, the second photo captures the ruptured transition between the two images as she explains that her parents were killed during the Korean War: "At that moment," the commentator remarks:

> I was sunk in my [Rolleiflex] camera. It was on the Rollei's ground glass that I saw the metamorphosis, the smile vanishing into pain like water drunk by sand . . . and now the young woman's face was covered in tears, but she did not lower her head, and the hands that had hidden her laughter lay immobile on the table.

FIGURES 1.6, 1.7, 1.8   Three of nine photos in which there is "nothing to be told" (*Koreans*)

FIGURES 1.6, 1.7, 1.8   (continued)

The instant was hers. . . . The extraordinary hymn of hate and will power that followed would need more than a story and an image to do it justice. (25–26)

Here, the camera lens itself becomes both a physical and metaphoric interface on which the commentator engages a radical shift in the expressions of the self and its relation to a world and a history. In the "vanishing" that marks the space between his experience of her experience is precisely where he relinquishes himself, his

*images, and his stories—that is, his thoughts—to the unrecoverable reality that
"was hers." [figs. 1.9 and 1.10]*

*In a later sequence, the centrality of this subjective space in its encounter with
the world reappears as a typically askew or inverted exchange. In this case, two
photographs of construction cranes operating over an urban site show first a relatively empty lot and then the shapes of emerging buildings: "All night long, the
aurora borealis of welding torches, spotlights on cranes, reflections of the moon
and the headlights on the great glassy facades of new buildings"(53)," the commentator observes about the two photos. Yet, comparative images such as these and
the interval they document, he quickly notes, are not about that scene and the
temporal passage it records, but about the experiential space from which they are
seen, from which subjectivity and thought have ventured forth to test themselves:*

FIGURES 1.9 AND 1.10   The vanishing in the space between two shots (*Koreans*)

FIGURES 1.9 AND 1.10   (continued)

"I don't care much for propaganda photos in the style: 'Yesterday. . . . Today.' But I still took these pictures of what I saw out my window, at fifteen days distance. In order not to mistake the room" (53–55).

Koreans *follows a temporal and spatial journey through these conjunctive spaces between numerous faces, things, activities, and images, searching those "forgotten image[s] between two shots." As he notes early in the text, "There are many ways of traveling" (16), and one way to view the photographic and photo-grammatic travels might be as a mimetic attempt to represent the dynamic conti-nuity of these active and changing people and places. The journey of* Koreans, *however, is better characterized according to the ambitious model offered by Henri Michaux's surrealist travel memoir* Plume, *in which, according to Marker's essay, the traveler embraces the transitions in time and place as disorderly "rhythms,* waves, shocks, all the buffers of memory, its meteors and dragnets" (16). The opening photo on this trip is thus appropriately a woman descending from a plane, described as the "first Korean girl descended from heaven with the 'gift of transitions'" (10).

The textual commentary that documents these personal experiences of a vibrant and changing world becomes then a string of insertions or interpolations into these rhythms, waves, and shocks. In Koreans, unlike the consistent voice of some traditional photo-essays, the text is multivocal, mobile, scattered, and both historically and geographically layered. Weaving together poetry, photos, ancient maps, quotations from historical reports, literature, reproductions of paintings, Korean tales and legends, and comic book images, the commentary sometimes precedes the photos; sometimes, it follows or is interspersed in the spaces between a series. It recounts parables, historical events, personal reflections, observations, and reminiscences of other places, melding myths with daily observations, anecdotes about ginseng, profoundly serious commentaries on the atrocities of war, and self-debunking and whimsical humor about the commentator's own efforts. Sometimes, it describes the photos; sometimes, it gives voice to the images. Each becomes a way of speaking/seeing as a different representational encounter with a world that resists denotation. As Marker would later insist in his photo-essay Le Depays (Abroad): "The text doesn't comment on the images any more than the images illustrate the text. They are two sequences that clearly cross and signal to each other, but which it would be pointlessly exhausting to collate" (quoted in Lupton 62). Like the images to which it responds, the intense, inquisitive, and reflective subjectivity of this traveling voice and text dissolves into the fissures between the different representational materials they struggle to occupy, as moments of reflection and thinking, in the space between the photographic images.

These doubled fissures—between the textual commentary and the images and between that "forgotten image between two shots"—become in one sense a version of what Mitchell calls a "site of resistance," produced in the photo-essay through its leanings toward nonfictional subjects, its subjective anchoring in a personal point of view, and its "generic incompleteness" (287): "The text of the photo-essay typically discloses a certain reserve or modesty in its claims to 'speak for' or interpret images; like the photograph, it admits its inability to appropriate everything that was there to be taken and tries to let the photographs speak for themselves or 'look back' at the viewer" (289). Signaled throughout Koreans with faces and eyes looking directly at the camera, this spatial resistance is dramatized most poetically in one exchange featuring five sequential photos of six children playing and staring back at the camera, watching the author "watching them. A mirror *game that goes on and on where the loser is the one who looks down, who lets the other's gaze pass through, like a ball" (43). As he quickly acknowledges, "My third eye was a bit like cheating" (43). In this exchange and in the photo-essay in general, according to Sobchack, temporality itself becomes necessarily remade according to a spatial dynamics in which a "temporal hole" appears as a "gap" or "arena" opening up and staging the possibility of meaning:*

> *The lack of depth and dimension in the still photograph seems less a function of the phenomenal thickness of the subjects and objects that it displays than of the temporal hole it opens within the world in which we gaze at it. Indeed, the most "dynamic" photojournalism derives its uncanny power from this temporal hole, the transcendence of both existence and finitude within existence and finitude. . . . The photograph, then, offers us only the possibility of meaning. It provides a significant gap that can be filled with every meaning, any meaning, and is itself meaningless in that it does not act within itself to choose its meaning, to diacritically mark it off. Like transcendental consciousness, the photograph as a transcendental structure posits the abstraction of a moment but has not momentum—and only provides the grounds or arena for its possibility.* (Address of the Eye 60)

For Marker, however, the resistances and holes created in his photo-essays, in which language and subjectivity lose themselves in images of the world, might be best understood with the cinematic framework used by Deleuze. Here, thinking and "intelligence" occur when comprehension and understanding encounter the world on its own terms—in what Deleuze labels "a void" or an "interstice" in the time and spaces of representations: "What counts is . . . the interstice between images, between two images: a spacing which means that each image is plucked from the void and falls back into it" (Cinema 2 179). This creates neither spectatorial "identification," a position of a familiar emplacement in the world, nor a version of Brechtian "alienation," a position of unfamiliar exclusion from that world represented. Rather, this is a suspended position of intellectual opportunity and potential, a position within a spatial gap where the interval offers the "insight of blindness," where thought becomes the exteriorization of expression.

If Marker's photo-essay opens a space, a changing geography, in which thinking may pitch its tent, the essay film must aim to retrieve the possibility of that active intelligence within the continuous landscape of film.[23] *Bridging these different forms of the essayistic, the photogram describes a conceptual borderline between the photography and film, a kind of "stop action," since it pinpoints the transformation of film's moving image into the suspension of "real movement and time" as a series of overlapping photographic images. No doubt,* The Jetty *represents this reflexive merging of the photographic series and film form most famously (also constructed only of still images except for a few seconds when those series of photograms become a brief continuous movement), but enlisting the narrative framework of a science fiction tale rather than an essayistic framework,* The Jetty *creates a significantly different viewing position from the essay film, one based in identification, memory, and desire, rather than observation, reflection, and belief.*[24] *Also constructed of a series of still images but less well known than* The Jetty, *Marker's 1966* If I Had Four Camels *(and later the 2001* Remembrance of Things to Come*) more clearly and fully resists that pull of narrative to appropriate cinematically the full essayistic activity of the photo-essay to explore those interstitial zones as "a photographer and two of his friends look through and comment on a series of images taken just about everywhere in the world between 1956 and 1966."*

Despite the canonical prominence of The Jetty, *the majority of Marker's films are best understood within the framework of the essayistic.*[25] *Partly because of its historical proximity to* Koreans *and its place at this historically formative stage of the essay film and partly because it eschews the narrative logic of the more renowned* Jetty, *I concentrate here on the 1958* Letter from Siberia,[26] *which represents an early paradigm for the essay film for Marker and for the practice in general. Writing about* Letter from Siberia *in 1958, André Bazin has the first and most prescient word:* Letter from Siberia *"resembles absolutely nothing that we have ever seen before in films with a documentary bias." It "is an essay on the reality of Siberia past and present in the form of a filmed report. Or, perhaps, to borrow Jean Vigo's formulation of* A propos de Nice *('a documentary point of view'), I would say an essay documented by film. The important word is 'essay,' understood in the same sense that it has in literature—an essay at once historical and political, written by a poet as well" ("Bazin on Marker" 44).*

Even more explicitly than Koreans, Letter from Siberia *presents itself as an epistolary travelogue whose voice-over begins with lines appropriated from that exemplary traveler in* Koreans, *Michaux: "I am writing to you from a far country. . . . I am writing you from the end of the world." Here, too, cold-war, East/West, oppositions linger in the background, and here, too, a traveler commentator, now a disembodied voice rather than a printed text, negotiates and reflects on serial inventories and oppositional categories: Lists of Siberian plants and animal life alternate with descriptions of daily activities, and the film concludes with the commentator reflecting on the polarized journeys of underground scientists burrowing to the center of the earth while their colleague-cosmonauts launch themselves into outer space. Digressions into an archeological past jump quickly forward to the industrial future: from Yakut tribal rituals and drawings of the wooly mammoths that once populated Siberia to the construction of new highways and telephone lines. [fig. 1.11] The representational heterogeneity of* Letter from Siberia *also parallels that of Marker's photo-essay as the film mixes black-and-white and color film, still photographs, archival footage, and animation to underline, here also, how the bond between experience and representation is the fault line between the world and our knowledge of it. Unlike the efforts of the photo-essay to inhabit the spaces between these images, however, this essay film opens a second dimension to its travels, that particularly cinematic dimension of the temporality of the moving image. Together with the rhetorical and spatial gaps found in the photo-essay, the film thus also depicts and examines the continual dynamics of movement captured on film, from the vertical ascents of flying airplanes to horizontally racing reindeer, through a visual syntax of continual tracks and pans capturing those temporal rhythms with a similar array of directional movements. Early in the film, dramatically different materials create dramatically different forms of temporality as a fabricated image of the past, a realistic transparency of the present, and a visual rhetoric of a desired future: Animated drawings of mammoths precede a transition to documentary shots of the Lena River bustling with its industry and commerce, and shortly after, the film offers a "spot commercial" spoofing the market value of reindeer as pets, transportation, clothing, and food. Bazin goes so far as to identify these constructions as a "new notion of montage" that he calls "horizontal" or "lateral," in which, unlike the traditional "sense of duration through the relation of shot to shot," "a given image doesn't refer to the one that preceded it" (44). Comparable to the spatial*

FIGURE 1.11   The fault lines of knowledge: an animated encounter with the woolly mammoths of Siberian history (*Letter from Siberia*)

openings mapped in The Koreans, *in these instances* Letter from Siberia *pries open the temporal "presence" of the moving images as an interstice (both spatial and temporal) containing multiple time zones ranging from past memories to future fantasies. As the commentator remarks in his conclusion, this Siberia is the image of a temporal vertigo: "Between the Middle Ages and the twenty-first century, between the earth and the moon, between humiliation and happiness. After that it's straight ahead."*

Two sequences stand out in this effort to open the cinematic image as planes with different temporal zones. The most famous is a single shot of a Yakutsk town bus passing an expensive car as workers repair the road, shown four times with four different types of commentary. [fig. 1.12] The first is silent, the next a Soviet panegyric, the third an anticommunistic denunciation, and the last the description in the voice-over of the commentator's own impressions. Each commentary not only creates a very different interpretation of the street scene but also directs the perspective toward different details and activities in the shot: For one, the Zim luxury car dominates the scene; in another, the voice-over points out a man's injured eye. For the commentator, this series of judgments without verdicts most immediately questions the impossible notion of objectivity regarding a landscape "with huge gaps and the will to fill them." Indeed, a major problem with "objectivity" is that it "may not distort Siberian realities but it does isolate them long enough to be appraised." Instead, the four different commentaries here offer four interpretive planes or zones that describe the street scene and direct our attention in a way that maps the temporal fullness of a short interval during which "what counts is the variety and the driving momentum."

FIGURE 1.12   Workers repair the same Yakutsk road through four contrasting sequences (*Letter from Siberia*)

The second, considerably longer, sequence follows these four shots to suggest that even this layering of a cinematic present is inadequate. "A walk through the streets of Yakutsk isn't going to make you understand Siberia," the commentator admits. "What you might need is an imaginary newsreel shot all over Siberia" in which "the commentary would be made up of those Siberian expressions that are already pictures in themselves." Locating and measuring its own voice in "those Siberian expressions" it aims to document, the commentator literally evokes images of those expressions by opening a second frame within the center of the image of the street scene, which then expands to fill the entire frame and become a collage of winter images. As the collage proceeds, this "imaginary newsreel" assumes a future conditional voice developing through a series of conjunctive "ands": "And then I'd show you" the snow, the Yakut, the spring festivals, and so on.

As these sequences suggest, the voice-over in Letter from Siberia *is that of a time traveler and guide through a world that will always elude him and us temporally and spatially. Whereas the text/image relationship in* Koreans *identifies a fissure or gap, the audio commentary offers a more temporally mobile relationship with the fragmented chronologies of the film image. The changing voices, incorporated quotations, and music and sound recordings—from the lyrical, to the bemused, to the pedagogical—describe a series of shifting subject positions surrounding and intervening in the visuals. This address of the voice-over can even be dramatically insistent as an ironic and overdetermined attempt to direct the viewer according to a specific chronology: at one point, the commentator anticipates the contrast between the past and present in the image of a large truck passing a horse-drawn cart and quickly reminds the viewer, "[This is] the shot you've been waiting for." The unusual mobility of this voice exploring time between images creates, in Bazin's words, a "montage . . . forged from ear to eye" ("Bazin on Marker" 44). Through it,* Letter from Siberia *insists "that the primary material is intelligence, that its immediate means of expression is language, and that the image only intervenes in the third position, in reference to this verbal intelligence" (44).*

It seems to me a curious paradox that Deleuze says nothing about Marker's films in his monumental Cinema 1 *and* Cinema 2, *for few writers have theorized the cinema in terms so sympathetic to Marker's essayistic films and their aim to elicit a "cinematic thinking." Although Deleuze's perspective on "thought and cinema" casts a much wider net than the essayistic, it accommodates Marker's work and essayistic cinema in general in a manner that few theoretical models can— which is the justification for my selective appropriation of Deleuze. For Deleuze, thought is "the essence of cinema" (Cinema 2 168), and it can be discovered in various orders throughout film history, beginning with the "movement images" of Eisenstein, Abel Gance, and Alfred Hitchcock.[27] Of a different order, however, is* "the modern cinema," the cinema of the "time-image" (169) and, for me, the essay-istic. In these films, of which there are no better examples than Marker's, thought in the cinema "is brought face to face with its own impossibility" (168), where "the suspension of the world" "gives the visible to thought, not as an object, but as an act that is constantly arising and being revealed in thought" (169). Just as the essayistic subjects personal expression to the public domain of experience, "thought finds itself taken over by the exteriority of a 'belief,' outside any interiority of a mode of knowledge" (175). For Deleuze and Marker, encountering the interstices and time zones between film images is thus the pathway to "belief" in a world always eliciting and refusing thought.

Although the genealogical relationship between the photo-essay (and the literary essay) and the essay film is not a difficult argument to make, few writers, photographers, or filmmakers demonstrate their intricate and compelling connec-tions better than Chris Marker, a writer and photo-essayist who can deservedly be characterized as one of the most consistent, earliest, and most articulate practi-tioners of the essay film. Essay films are arguably the most innovative and popular forms of filmmaking since the 1990s, producing a celebrated variety of examples from filmmakers around the globe. However extremely they may vary in style, structure, and subject matter, the best of these, I believe, work in the tradition of Marker, a tradition that draws on, merges, and re-creates the literary essay and the photo-essay within the particular spatial and temporal dynamics of film. With-out assuming that one practice anticipates or prepares for the other in Marker's career, it seems certain that, in his early essayistic encounters with words and pho-tographic images, Marker discovers an essentially modern territory between images where the fading spaces and black time lines ask the film viewer to become a thinker. After all, as Marker notes in Koreans, the twentieth century "may have been nothing but an immense, interminable fade" (23).

2

Of the History of the Essay Film: Vertov to Varda

MARKER'S *LETTER FROM Siberia* and André Bazin's prescient characterization of that film the same year as an "essay film" are key historical markers in the emergence of the essay film from the literary and photographic heritage that preceded it and the postwar culture in which it developed. Despite the historical and mythic importance of this 1958/1959 moment, however, there is a specifically cinematic history that precedes it, embedded in the evolution of documentary and avant-garde cinemas during the first half of the twentieth century. Both the subject matter and the formal innovations of those earlier traditions, set against the dominance of narrative film, partially anticipate the more pronounced innovations of essay films. Equally important, though, are social and institutional forces that create new cinematic frameworks for a critical reception that would distinguish the essay film and its address in the second half of the twentieth century. By the 1940s, dynamics of an interactive reception of ideas, associated with the documentary and avant-garde films of the preceding decades, would dovetail with numerous other sea changes in film aesthetics and technology, as well as with larger shifts in post–World War II culture and epistemology, to introduce, most visibly and pervasively in France, the practice of the essay film. That practice has continued to evolve and now assumes a critical place in global film culture.

As it develops in and out of those documentary and avant-garde traditions, the history of the essay film underlines a central critical point: The essayistic should not necessarily be seen simply as an alternative to either of these practices (or to narrative cinema); rather, it rhymes with and retimes them as counterpoints within and to them. Situated between the categories of realism and formal experimentation and geared to the possibilities of "public expression," the essay film suggests an appropriation of certain avant-garde and documentary practices in a way different from the early historical practices of both, just as it tends to invert and restructure the relations between the essayistic and narrative to subsume narrative within that public expression. In the essayistic play between fact and fiction, between the documentary and the experimental, or between nonnarrative and narrative, the essay film *inhabits* other forms and practices, in the way Trinh T. Minh-ha suggests when she notes that the facts contained in her essay film *Surname Viet Given Name Nam* (1989) are the fictions of its stories. Or, to adopt Barthes's phrasing about his essayistic writing, the essay film *stages* film forms, from narrative to documentary, as a way of feeding knowledge "into the machinery of infinite reflexivity" ("Inaugural Lecture" 463–464). The essay and essay film do not create new forms of experimentation, realism, or narrative; they rethink existing ones as a dialogue of ideas.

Two well-known films that might be considered a rhyming frame within the history of the essay film are Dziga Vertov's Man with the Movie Camera *(1929) and Jean-Luc Godard's* 2 or 3 Things I Know about Her *(1967). Together, they represent two different versions of "city symphony" films, one a celebrated epitome of that type of early documentary and the other an adaptation of it that confirms the historical centrality of the essay film. For many, the preliminary signs of the essayistic in Vertov's film are evident in the opening announcement of the film that it is "an excerpt from the diary of a cameraman" and in Vertov's description of his role in the film as a "supervisor of the experiment," creating a cinematic language that would express the energy and social dynamics of the modern city. In part, the film is a documentary of a composite city in Russia (with footage from Moscow, Kiev, Odessa), and in part, it is a reflexive celebration of the power of cinematic vision.*[1]

Integrating these two movements, Man with the Movie Camera *begins with the awakening of a cinema theater as seats magically open to welcome spectators and the awakening of the city as a woman's eyes open and the cameraman begins his dawn-to-dusk drive around town filming immense activity, filled with the movement of automobiles and trams, workers and athletes, factories and shops. The reflexivity that links the mechanistic energy of the cameraman and the documentary reality of the city of course is what associates the film, for many viewers, with essay films. This is the activity of a constructivist vision, made especially apparent in the celebrated sequence that links shots of a seamstress at work and Elizaveta Svilova, the editor of the film, at her editing table, where she examines several images of faces and selects certain ones to insert into a crowd sequence: Here, film mimics daily life, and both film and human activity have the capacity to have an active impact on life through their work. Through this shared activity, the aim and power of* Man with the Movie Camera *is to transform the multiplicity of different individuals and social functions into a harmonized whole that transcends those vibrant differences. Graphically dramatized by the different shots that superimpose a human eye and the camera lens, Vertov's "cinema eye" (kino-glaz) overcomes the limitation of subjective human visions by integrating them within the larger objective truths of life (kino-pravda). [fig. 2.1]*

Between 1968 and 1972 Godard, with Jean-Pierre Gorin, would reestablish the historical connection with Vertov when they formed the Dziga Vertov Group, a collective aiming to reanimate some of Vertov's political and aesthetic goals. This occurs, appropriately, just after the period when Godard begins consistently to describe himself as a film essayist.[2] Thus, 2 or 3 Things I Know about Her *suggests connections and differences across the large historical divide between the 1920s and 1960s, specifically as this film inherits, inhabits, and adjusts the experimental and documentary strategies of* Man with the Movie Camera *into more contemporary essayistic perspectives.*

In Godard's fictional documentary as city symphony, the Paris of 2 or 3 Things I Know about Her *becomes the doubled "her" of the city and the character Juliette Janson and then doubled again when Janson is also identified as the actress Marina Vlady. Superimposed public and personal realms, Paris and Juliette intermingle and continually define and redefine each other as subject and object, while the character Juliette and the actress Vlady open a pronounced gap within the*

FIGURE 2.1   Harmonizing the city through the power of the eye of the camera (*Man with the Movie Camera*)

primary subjective identity within the film. In this Paris, commercialism, imperialism, and materialism are the cultural dominants that twist relationships to the point that prostitution becomes a viable employment option for Juliette, whose other self works as a conventional high-rise housewife. Just as Juliette's private and public experiences are stunningly divided, the private and public spaces of Paris (bedrooms, cafes, streets) likewise become separate zones, which unlike Vertov's city spaces, never geometrically fit together, visualized by the film not as a musical montage but as graphically demarcated mise-en-scènes.

As the title indicates, the film is an epistemological project about ideas and knowing, but embedded within that suggestion is the somewhat ironic awareness that modern knowledge is shaped and frustrated by fragmented and reified subjects within a landscape of acquisition, enumeration, and accumulation. While Vertov's film could be described as a mesmerizing and harmonizing integration of social subjects and public life, Godard's film becomes explicitly about the difficulty of trying to express oneself and to think through this modern, always mediated, world. As one character remarks: "We often try to analyze the meaning of words but are led astray. One must admit that there's nothing simpler than taking things for granted." As a project that attempts to think and know modern life through a exaggeratedly subjectivized whispering voice-over, a politics of semiotics pervades the film, mapping the world of the city and the self of Juliette as products of signs and symbols that need constant interpretation if language has any promise of mediating and humanizing the divide. Yet, ubiquitous ads and slogans abound as the pervasive filter that continually short-circuit or detour this possibility of a humanizing bond or link with the city and other people, so that expression itself, like Godard's whispering voice, becomes absorbed by the public places that surround it. [fig. 2.2] Toward the conclusion of the film, over a 360-degree pan of the

FIGURE 2.2   Juliette mapping the city (*2 or 3 Things I Know about Her*)

exterior walls of her apartment complex, Juliette reflects on her frustrated efforts to know the visibility of her world through the signs and symbols of self-expression that recalls the blur between verbal and visual expression that distinguishes the essay film from its literary precedents: "You could say it can't be expressed in words, but I feel that my facial expression has meaning." Indeed, just as Juliette continually engages in a semiotics of naming objects around her, the voice-over names and describes Juliette in terms of the framing ("she moves left") that addresses the viewer and her conscious and unconscious entrapment in a semiotic field of space and language. Juliette famously observes to her son that "language is the house where man lives," and in an often-cited sequence, a close-up focuses and refocuses on a cup of coffee, swirling with foam, while Godard's voice-over commentary reflects: "Maybe an object is what permits us to relink, to pass from one subject to the other, therefore to live in society." [fig. 2.3] Or, in the context of essayistic skepticism, maybe not.

While the use of montage in 2 or 3 Things I Know about Her recalls Vertov's film, Godard's film sharply juxtaposes urban scenes of construction and deconstruction with interior shots and close-ups of private lives to create multiple levels of interaction in a city permeated by too many sounds and images and without the overarching experiential harmony of Man with the Movie Camera. *Self and other become reduced in their mutual isolation and objectification, while this postwar man with the movie camera constantly signals his awareness of his own isolated position within the industrial language he exposes. Wryly articulated with essayistic intertitles such as "Eighteen Lessons on Industrial Society" (taken from titles of actual essays published by Gallimard in a collection called* Ideas), *Godard's encounter with this new city can only claim a tentative and temporary position:*

FIGURE 2.3   A coffee cup and the struggle to relink with the everyday (*2 or 3 Things I Know about Her*)

*"Since I cannot tear myself from the objectivity that crushes me nor from the sub-
jectivity that exiles me, since I am permitted neither to lift myself to being nor fall
into nothingness, I must listen, I must look around me more than ever at the world,
my likeness, my brother." While Vertov celebrates the possibility of a new documentary truth through the cinema, Godard's film inhabits that utopia as a significantly more essayistic, "improvised" truth: skeptical, provisional, self-critical, a
cinema that accepts its continually frustrated struggle to think the world through
language. It becomes a self-described "experiment" in which the viewer, along with
Godard himself, watch his "thinking aloud," not within the narrative or documentary
coherence of a film but as "an attempt at a film" (Milne 238–239).*

Essays describe and provoke an activity of public thought, and the public nature
of that subjective experience highlights and even exaggerates the participations of
their audience, readers, and viewers in a dialogue of ideas. Even the most personal
essays speak to a listener who will validate or trouble that personal essayistic voice,
and the more immersed that voice is in its exterior world, the more urgent the
essay becomes in embedding and dispersing itself within the public experience
and dialogue it desires. From Montaigne's implied epistolary address to his lost
friend and interlocutor Étienne de La Boétie to Jacob Riis's hortatory public lectures and photographs of the New York tenements for philanthropic audiences,
the essay presses itself as a dialogic and reflective communal experience, stretched
between the intimate other of self and the public Other that surrounds a self. In
this sense, one of the chief defining features of the essay film and its history
becomes eliciting an active intellectual response to the questions and provoca-
tions that an unsettled subjectivity directs at its public.

From the beginning of film history, films sketch these essayistic predilections as
the transformation of personal expression into a public debate and ideational dialogue. These terms become isolated and explored especially in certain documentary and avant-garde movements of the 1920s and then dramatically rearticulated
with the advances of sound as a destabilized voice in the 1930s and early 1940s.
With post–World War II cinema, these tendencies would grow into a distinctive
dialectic that both underpins and parallels the more prominent tradition of the
narrative art cinema, subsumed within a more dominant play of ideas.

As part of what I call a precursive history of the essay film, early film reception
regularly elicits not only a dynamic audience interactivity but one frequently based
in the kind of pedagogical response associated with essays, reformulated cinematically as the scientific lectures or travelogues.[3] Even after narrative cinema begins
to take shape and dominate film culture in the first decade of the twentieth century, many films continue to insist on the capacity of movies to address audiences

with the intellectual and social imperatives associated with lectures, social pamphlets, and other essayistic formats. A 1909 review of D. W. Griffith's *A Corner in Wheat*, about the capitalist exploitation of the wheat trade, aligns it explicitly, for instance, with an intervention in the public domain associated with editorials and essays: "The picture . . . is an argument, an editorial, an essay on a vital subject of deep interest to all. . . . [Yet] no orator, no editorial writer, no essayist, could so strongly and effectively present the thoughts that are conveyed in this picture. It is another demonstration of the force and power of motion pictures as a means of conveying ideas" (quoted in Gunning 135).[4]

By the 1920s, the work of Sergei Eisenstein and other filmmakers in the Soviet cinema most clearly articulate the possibilities of an essayistic cinema, while certain avant-garde films also experiment with the blending of formalist and documentary aesthetics in ways that foreshadow the essay film. Film historian Roman Gubern claims that in 1922 Benjamin Christiansen "inaugurated the formula for the essay film with his admirable *Haxan: Witchcraft through the Ages*" (278) in its combination of documentary and fiction, realism and fantasy. More often noted are Eisenstein's early references to the essay film and his desire to make Marx's *Capital* into a political and social science argument on film. In April 1928, he writes: "The content of CAPITAL (its aim) is now formulated: to teach the worker to think dialectically" (10). By the late 1920s and early 1930s, documentary films, often intersecting with avant-garde traditions in films such as Alberto Cavalcanti's *Rien que les heures* (1926), Vertov's *Man with the Movie Camera*, and Vigo's *A propos de Nice* (1930), likewise anticipate and adumbrate the structures and terms of the essay film that would make its decisive appearance in the 1950s.[5]

The advent of synchronized film sound in the late 1920s and early 1930s has, as many historians point out, a massive impact on documentary film and, less obviously, on the critical formation of a contrapuntal voice, a voice that would inform the gradual formation of a particular essayistic address in the cinema as a modulating inquiry into the reality of images. From Paul Rotha's multiple, heteroglossic voice-over presentations to the different uses of voice-over as a lyrical, ironic, or polemical commentary, the voice of the subject often becomes in these early years increasingly a dramatic engagement with documentary facts rather than a description of those facts. Writing about Rotha in the early 1930s, John Grierson calls for the orchestration and integration of three different audio methods within documentary films, the last especially anticipating the mobile essayistic voice: either in different films or in a single film, documentaries can now employ, according to Grierson, "a musical or non-literary method," a dramatic method, or "a poetic, contemplative method" (155). Recognizing this mobility in the documentary voice across numerous films during this transitional period, Stella Bruzzi accordingly counters tendencies to homogenize and standardize the range and movement of these documentary voices and expressions by examining the vocal flux of *Land without Bread* (1933), *The Battle of San Pietro* (1945), and other documentaries. As she points out, "the reductionism that has plagued discussions of documentary's implementation of voice-over lies in the persistent refusal to either acknowledge any differences between *actual* voices or to distinguish between very different uses of the voice within the documentary context" (51).[6]

Looking forward to the postwar essay films, this mobilizing of the documentary voice foreshadows the more definite play of even more mobile and self-reflexive linguistics and voices as a drama of subjectivity enmeshed in the world. As the essay film comes more clearly into historical view, one of its most distinguishing features becomes, as Humphrey Jennings's films would demonstrate, its foregrounding of its literary heritage in the material performance of language as part of its encounter with the dominance of a public culture of visual technology, significantly replacing the organizing voice of the narrator with the essayistic voice of the commentator.[7]

Besides the formal experimentations with image and sound that overlap documentary and experimental practices in these precursive years, as important are the institutional and social contexts that begin to locate a place for film that draws out the public and dialogic potential of these films, most prominently seen in the cine clubs that begin to spring up around the world, especially in France in the 1920s and 1930s. Throughout its literary history and thereafter, the dynamics of reception have been a distinctive dimension of the essay and its dialogic intervention in a public sphere, and the historical evolution of a specific kind of audience is crucial to its filmic practice, anticipating what Rascaroli notes as central to a definition of the essay film: a "constant interpellation" whereby "each spectator, as an individual and not a member of an anonymous, collective audience, is called upon to engage in a dialogic relationship with the enunciator, to become active, intellectually and emotionally, and interact with the text" (36). In the 1920s, the cine clubs emerge as central vehicles in the formation of this dynamic and of an audience for whom film was less about entertainment than a forum for debating aesthetic and social issues and experiences. Louis Delluc, along with Leo Moussinac, Germaine Dulac, and Ricciotto Canuda, is commonly credited with establishing the cine club movement in Paris, beginning with Club des Amis du Septieme Art (CASA), and the equally important arm of those clubs and their debates, magazines such as *Cine Club* and *Cinéa*.[8] Primarily associated with the evolution of the *film d'art* movement in France, these specialized clubs became a gathering place for artists and intellectuals and forums for movies about ideas, ideas about film, ideas about the social and expressive powers of the movies.[9] In the beginning of this cultural and institutional shift, Jean Epstein's 1921 commentary "Bonjour Cinema" rather excessively insists on the distinguishing possibility of a cinematic "photogénie" to create and think ideas in a new way. The cinema, he says, is "a product twice distilled. My eye presents me with an idea of a form; the film stock also contains an idea of a form, an idea established independently of my awareness, a latent, secret but marvelous idea; and from the screen I get an idea of an idea, my eye's idea extracted from the camera's; in other words, so flexible is this algebra, an idea that is the square root of an idea" (Abel, *French Film Theory* 244).[10] Paralleling the cultural, social, and intellectual activity of the French cine clubs, British writers and filmmakers embrace similar refashioning of film reception. The founding editor of *Close Up*, known as Bryher, claims in "How I Would Start a Film Club" that the primary goal of these clubs is "to build up an audience of intelligent spectators" (Donald et al. 292). Or, as Harry Potamkin puts it in 1933, "The film club is to the audience generally what the critic is to the spectator; that is, the film club provides the critical audience" (220), which for Potamkin has both an aesthetic and social dimension, with the latter the most important, as vehicles for the kind of intellectual and educative dialogue that the essay film would soon make its priority.

By the 1950s, the Cinématheque Francais, founded by Henri Langlois in 1936 with filmmaker Georges Franju, becomes the most important product of the cine club tradition (specifically, the Cercle du Cinema) and ushers in changes and new directions in the spectatorial dynamics of these clubs, changes that would provide the defining structure of essayistic cinema. In 1947, the International Federation of Ciné-Clubs was established, and by 1955 a European confederation of Cinéma d'Art et d'Essai helps to shape what is sometimes called "advanced European art cinema"—theaters that programmed more innovative and experimental films, often aided by tax rebates. Kelley Conway sums up how these reshaped cine clubs in the 1950s promote their own specific form of essayistic dialogue: "The ciné-club attempted to form spectators in very specific ways: through its diverse programming, through film education internships, and, above all, through the *débat*, the post-screening discussion. . . . The ciné-club did not aspire to replace the commercial cinema in its members' lives or to promote a renaissance in experimental filmmaking, as had the 1920s ciné-clubs. Instead, the postwar ciné-club invested in the formation of an active, educated viewer" (38, 41). That is, as signs of larger institutional and aesthetic changes, the cine clubs would stage and inhabit the possibility to rethink any film practice according in the formation of spectatorial formation that would come to define the essay film then and in the future.[11]

As part of a broader historical trend, the films of Humphrey Jennings stand as creative summaries of early moves toward essayistic structures and anticipations of the more definite essay films that would follow the war, balancing documentary representation with a pronounced subjective chord that consistently calls out for dialogic and ideational reflection. Associated both with the surrealist tradition that defined the interior explorations of his early work and with John Grierson's documentaries for the General Post Office and the Mass-Observation project, initiated with Tom Harrison and Charles Madge, Jennings made a series of films through the 1940s that bear the marks of both movements and concomitantly lean conspicuously into the essayistic forms that are about to enter definitively into film history. Organized in 1937, the Mass-Observation project, for example, turned some of the principles of ethnographic observations of other cultures to filming everyday experiences in England, whose traces appear in Jennings's Listen to Britain *(1942) and, as John Caughie notes in his discussion of Jennings (provocatively and correctly compared with Derek Jarman), "whose observations of the everyday were not so far removed from surrealism as one might suppose" (231).*

Listen to Britain *is a montage of daily experiences in England during the war: a man on his way to work, schoolchildren playing, soldiers waiting for a train, and so on. References to the war are unmistakable but muted signs of crisis within everyday life: The businessman carries an air-raid helmet, a sign points to an air-raid shelter, and many concert-goers wear military uniforms. With its power to permeate spatial divides, sound, notably the signature radio announcement "This is London calling," becomes an audial call for community throughout the film (and possibly U.S. participation in the European war), dramatized with scenes of entertainers performing, an afternoon concert by a Royal Air Force band, and a performance of Mozart's 17th Piano Concerto by Myra Hess in the National Gallery.*

In each case, the film draws attention to the power of sound and music to unite the audience through its expressive qualities. In the extended second sequence especially, the concentration of the interplay among the music, the audience's enraptured attention, and the cutaway to windows being bricked up (presumably in the concert hall) suggests Jenning's slightly surrealistic twist on a war documentary. [fig. 2.4] Here, actual images of war in process give way to the more important identification and solicitation of the responsive undercurrents of community and camaraderie that those events require, prominent undercurrents that follow the soundtrack of the concert into the streets of London, armament factories, and then the countryside. This play between expressive sound and a collage of public images anticipates the essayistic in both its restraint and its dispersion of a communal expressivity into the crisis of public life. [fig. 2.5] For Jennings, music and voice initiate the public dialogue that redeems individual hardship. More important, sound as expression here does not so much support or illuminate the pressures of the war experience but rather remains tautly in tension with them.

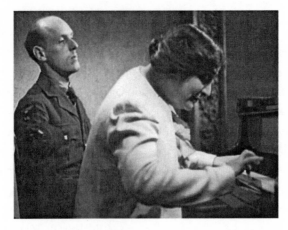

FIGURE 2.4   The music of war (*Listen to Britain*)

FIGURE 2.5   London calling a community to action (*Listen to Britain*)

Far from registering faith in a reality under siege, the fragile sound and music become an expressive measure of longing, recollection, irony, and hope.

In his analysis of Listen to Britain, *Jim Leach identifies the particular "unsettling" effect of this film as it wavers between propaganda and poetry, between a public gaze and a private eye, between impersonal and personal styles that results in a distinctive "ambiguity" whose "refusal to impose meanings implies both a respect for the personal freedom of the spectator and an awareness that meanings are always complex and plural" (157). Enacting a form of what Nichols calls "social subjectivity," the film creates a montage of fragile connections with individuals, classes, peace and war, and various cultural practices that, while tentatively destabilizing the public myth of "a people's war," also celebrate it. As the* film asks the audience "to listen," "the pull between sight and sounds adds to the fragility of the film's discourse" (164) and so elicits an "alertness in the spectator, who is asked to reflect on the experience of unity within difference" (159).

Another Jennings film made during World War II, A Diary for Timothy (1945) continues this early exploration of the essayistic but with considerably more emphasis on subjectivity, the temporality of a public history, and a resulting skepticism about the voice and mind of the public individual that will emerge in the coming years. With commentary written by novelist and essayist E. M. Forster, the story of Timothy Jenkins, born five years after the British entry into World War II, opens with a BBC broadcast reporting Allied advances in Europe. The film cuts to a row of bassinets and the cries of a newborn baby: "It was on the third of September, 1944, you were born. . . . You're in danger, Tim, for all around you is being fought the worst war ever known." Intercut with shots of mother and newborn and shots of urban rubble and planes flying overhead, this is "total war," involving all England but here focused on the child as subject. Through this child subject, the film becomes less about wartime crisis than an impending postwar world in which, as the commentator later remarks, it will be "back to everyday life . . . and everyday danger."

With a familiar voice replacing the traditional voice of God of earlier documentary commentary, the film orchestrates movements between the past, the present, and the future, spread across the four different social and subject positions of a miner, farmer, a railway engineer, and a wounded Royal Air Force pilot, all addressing the just-born child. ("All these people were fighting for you, although they didn't exactly know it.") The fissures between time periods (as when the farmer shows his family a film of five years ago when they were clearing the fields) and the anxious relation between experience and knowledge becomes an open question: Over the image of a baby buggy, the commentator remarks about these temporal intensities of the present, "you didn't know, couldn't know, and didn't care."

Here, also, sound in the form of the voice-over, radio broadcasts, and musical concerts figure in bridging public events and the individual of the community. Hess's Beethoven's Apassionata Sonata is interwoven with a radio account of soldiers' hardships in Europe and images of a London with bombed buildings being repaired by roofers. Drifting through these sounds and music, the commentator (Michael Redgrave) has little of the clarity or certainty that mark earlier documentaries, as he notes the newly lit streets had become more cheerful, "unless there were bombers around" or, over an air-raid siren, he hopes "you'll never have to hear that sound, Tim." As a central signal of the essayistic, the combination of the ironic and the future conditional characterizes even Christmas as it reminds the viewer/listener of "death and darkness, death and fog, death across those few miles of water" on "the day all children ought to be happy." A conversation about the sound of a V-2 rocket becomes a prophetic encounter in which the massive anonymity of death confronts the shaky possibilities of knowledge after World War II: Questions about where and when the rocket will hit elicits only "I know not" and "Do you know?" murmured over a surrealist pan of mannequin faces topped with hats.

Most significant, the second-person address of the film stands out here as a distinguishing redirection that would inform, explicitly or implicitly, the address of many later essay films. That address becomes a combination of warning and hope directed at both the child Timothy and the spectator inhabiting that newborn position, proleptic subjects still to be formed and so, with a critical irony, implored to think about the future. The wavering voice-over observes that "it's a chancy world" in which a miner's accident becomes one small indication that a postwar climate will bring new dangers and demands. [fig. 2.6] Yet, these new repercussive demands of postwar life in England, with the unemployment, broken homes, scattered families, will also be an ironically positive sign of the concomitant demands of a new public subjectivity: It will be "even more dangerous than before because now we have the power to choose, the right to criticize and even to grumble." For the new child and spectator, this is indeed "something else for you to think over," and only through a strenuous reflection on the past and present as they are documented in the film and as they reshape the future can the presiding questions of the film be answered by the spectator child: "What are you going to say about it, and what are you going to do? . . . Are you going to make the world a different place?"

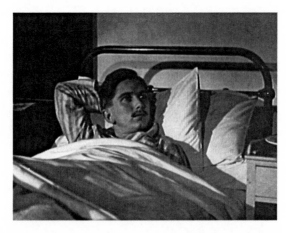

FIGURE 2.6   Reflecting on the warnings of the past and the hope of the future (*A Diary for Timothy*)

While many films before 1940 belong to the heritage of the essay film, my contention is that important historical distinctions must be made to demonstrate the significant achievements of this practice as it comes into its own. In this regard, the 1940s are the watershed years for the essay film, a period when many of its defining structures and trends begin to coalesce and the term *essay* becomes distinctly and more commonly associated with certain films. During this period, these films also begin more clearly to define themselves and their address according to my tripartite structure of subjectivity, public experience, and thinking. From 1940 to 1945, the essay film reconfigures notions of realism (and documentary representation) outside both narrative and earlier documentary traditions and asserts the intellectual and conceptual mobility central to an essayistic tradition. Just as a confluence of historical forces begins to appear, the French "filmology" movement associated with Gilbert Cohen-Seat takes shape in the 1940s, claiming the cinema as the singularly most prominent social force in postwar society and thus requiring serious academic study of, especially, how spectators understand and think through movies.[12] Also in the early 1940s, André Malraux delivers his lecture "Esquisse d'une psychologie du cinéma," arguing "the possibility of expression in the cinema" (14). And, in 1940, artist and filmmaker Hans Richter writes a prophetic essay, "The Film Essay," attempting to describe a new practice evolving from the documentary tradition that, instead of presenting what he calls "beautiful vistas," would aim "to find a representation for intellectual content," "to find images for mental concepts," "striving to make visible the invisible world of concepts, thoughts, and ideas, so that viewers would become "involved intellectually and emotionally" (195).[13] Together, these three moments announce and identify an increasingly consistent new direction in film practice that embraces and transforms the literary and photographic heritage of the essay as a way to create films that rethink the self as a function of a destabilized public sphere.

Most pervasively, the 1940s represent an epistemological foundation of the essay film for reasons that reach beyond the cinematic. As Paul Arthur notes, it was only "after the Holocaust—our era's litmus test for the role of individual testimony in collective trauma—that essay films acquire a distinct aesthetic outline and moral purpose" ("Essay Questions" 61). The crisis of World War II, the Holocaust, the trauma that traveled from Hiroshima around the world, and the impending cold war inform, in short, a social, existential, and representational crisis that would galvanize an essayistic imperative to question and debate not only a new world but also the very terms by which we subjectively inhabit, publicly stage, and experientially think that world.

No wonder that Alain Rensais's 1955 *Night and Fog* and its eerie encounter with the concentration camps becomes an early and widely recognized example of the essay film. As a documentary unable to adequately document the reality it seeks, it drifts through horizontal tracks, punctuated by archival stills, across the "peaceful landscapes" and "ordinary roads" that surrounded Auschwitz and Bergen-Belsen. Despite the "semblance of a real city" constructed as concentration camps, this is "a society developed, shaped by terror." In this encounter with the trauma of history, the commentator fumbles and stumbles through a kind of inadequacy structured as a type of dialogue between the images of Resnais and the literary voice-over script of Jean Cayrol, a survivor of the camps: "It is impossible for us to capture what remains. . . . The daily activities and signs no description, no shot can retrieve. . . . We can only show you the outside, the husk." As Sandy Flitterman-Lewis so perceptively notes, this film is a "constructive forgetting," a struggle to express the inexpressible that culminates in a coda that crystallizes what I would call the essayistic address: Here, the interlocutory direct address of the I-You voice-over changes dramatically to We and so demands an "active engage-ment" bonding the filmmaker and viewer in the responsibility to rethink his-tory (215). A landmark film in the early history of the essay film, *Night and Fog* reminds us that, as Resnais observes in 1962, postwar new wave cinema "is less a new wave of directors . . . and more a new wave of spectators." (quoted in Conway 38).[fig. 2.7]

In postwar France, perhaps the best-known pronouncement on the cinematic possibilities that would lay the groundwork for the essay film is Alexandre Astruc's 1948 "The Birth of the New Avant-Garde: The Caméra-Stylo." Here, the key terms of the essay film move from the background of earlier film practices to the fore-ground in a way that definitely emphasizes a new direction that would dramatize cinematic subjectivity as an intellectual enterprise moving beyond narrative and

FIGURE 2.7   Unseeable images (*Night and Fog*)

traditional documentary models but, unlike the so-called first avant-garde, capable of incorporating those models:

> To come to the point: the cinema is quite simply becoming a means of expression, just as all the other arts have been before it. . . . After having been successively a fairground attraction, an amusement analogous to boulevard theatre, or the means of preserving the images of an era, it is gradually becoming a language. By language, I mean a form in which and by which an artist can express his thoughts, however abstract they may be, or translate his obsessions exactly as he does in the contemporary essay or novel. This is why I would like to call this new age of cinema the age of the camera-stylo (camera pen). This metaphor has a very precise sense. By it I mean that the cinema will gradually break free from the tyranny of what is visual, from the image for its own sake, from the immediate and concrete demands of the narrative, to become a means of writing just as flexible and subtle as written language. . . . It can tackle any subject, any genre. The most philosophical meditations on human production, psychology, ideas, and passions lie within its province. I will even go so far as to say that contemporary ideas and philosophies of life are such that only the cinema can do justice to them. Maurice Nadeau wrote in an article in the newspaper Combat: "If Descartes lived today, he would write novels." With all due respect to Nadeau, a Descartes of today would already have shut himself up in his bedroom with a 16mm camera and some film, and would be writing his philosophy on film: for his Discours de la Méthode [sic] would today be of such a kind that only the cinema could express it satisfactorily. (159)[14]

These claims for personal expression on film would immediately be made technologically viable with the arrival of portable lightweight camera technology, introduced as the Arriflex system in Germany in 1936 and as the Éclair 35-mm Cameflex in France in 1947. Appropriately, these different "caméra-stylos" would also feature reflex viewing systems linking the pragmatics of filmmaking with the conceptual reflexivity of the emerging essay film, its exploration of subjectivity, and its "idea of the cinema expressing ideas" ("La Caméra-Stylo" 159). Especially attuned to the technological terms of this new cinema, Astruc, in his less-well-known "L'avenir du cinéma," even foresees its electronic future: "Nothing allows us to foresee what television will be become, but there is a good chance that it will contribute to the creation of a new cinema that will be able to be address more to the intelligence" (153), for like the development of lightweight 16-mm cameras in the 1940s, "tomorrow television is going to increase exponentially the possibilities of expression in the cinema" (154).

This relation among mobile technology, economics, and the essayistic under-lines the distinct historical forces that come into play during these formative years and suggests a larger point that remains a critical undercurrent throughout the longer future of the essay film: The power of essay may be significantly tied to a representational agency that emphasizes its ephemerality rather than perma-nency, which in turn may illuminate its notable prominence and success today. As with the early history of the literary essay and its connection with new forms of production and distribution, lightweight camera technologies of the postwar years through the 1960s and the Portapak and videotape revolution after 1967 (and later the Internet and digital convergences of today) significantly encourage and underpin the active subjectivity and public mobility of the essay film that begin with the claims and practices of the essayistic in the 1940s. Based in technological, industrial, and commercial shifts, a paradoxically public intimacy of address and reception has followed the essay through eighteenth-century coffeehouses and pamphlets and nineteenth-century lecture halls and journals to the film festivals and college art cinemas that define the essay film in the postwar years to the specialized television distribution of Germany's ZDF, central Europe's Canal+, Britain's Channel Four, and other cable and television venues that have often been the commercial vehicles for contemporary essay films. (As part of this evolving context, the changing economic demands of documentary filmmaking in recent years, including the rising costs of archival footage, music, and other copyrighted materials, might also be seen as part of this history of industrial and commercial encouragement for the less-costly personal perspectives and source materials of the essay film.)

That those cinematic foundations in the 1940s and 1950s are originally so largely French (just as the theoretical foundations of Benjamin, Adorno, and others are largely German) should help explain the prominent place of the French New Wave (and later the New German Cinema) in exploring the essay film from 1950 to the end of the 1970s. Within the historical context of postwar French cinema, moreover, several prominent historical and critical touchstones—regarding auteurism, cinema vérité, and the literary heritage of the French New Wave—emerge that not only inform French films of this period but also carry over into the extended global and contemporary practices of the essay film. In addition to Astruc's writ-ings, several specific films, documents, and trends signal and support this rela-tionship and highlight broader practical and conceptual shifts as this practice evolves through the 1950s into the 1960s, creating a historical and cultural context in which, by the mid-1950s, the term *essai cinématographique* is in frequent use in France.[15] In these defining years, these possibilities become articulated specifically through the potential of the "short film" to provide a freedom from the restriction of the authority of an emerging auteurism and from the documentary truth of cinema vérité, as well as the organizational principles of film narrative, all remade as a conceptual "sketch" capable of releasing a distinctive subjectivity as a public thinking. More exactly, a specific group of films and the contemporaneous or subsequent critical reception of them become flashpoints in the formation and recognition of essayistic practice during this period: Alain Resnais's 1948 short film *Van Gogh*; Jacques Rivette's 1955 essay for the *Cahiers du cinéma*, "Letter on Rossellini," with its characterization of *Paisa, Europa '51* and *Germany, Year Zero* and especially the 1953 *Viaggio in Italia* as seminal essay films; and, finally, Georges Franju's 1948 *Le Sang des bêtes*, and especially his 1951 *Hotel des Invalides*, as seen by Noël Burch as prototypes for an essayistic cinema of ideas.

Appearing the same year as Astruc's proclamation of a new kind of cinema that can express ideas, Resnais's *Van Gogh* is serendipitously emblematic of a short essay film that works as both a portrait and a critical commentary, a film less about painting than about the grounds for a cinematic expression that engages, questions, and reflects on a painterly style while evading narrative formulas and conventional documentary strategies. Bazin would rightfully insist that this film has little to do with popularizing a painting and a painter, but rather it announces a particular "aesthetic biology" that adapts the painting as a cinematic textuality, re-creating "not the subject of the painting but the painting itself" as a textual "refraction" ("Stylistics" 142). Godard would go even farther to claim for it an inventiveness and historical importance that points to a new filmic practice: "If the short film did not already exist, Alan Resnais would surely have invented it. He alone gives the impression that it is in his eyes something other than a short film. From the unseeing and trembling pans of *Van Gogh* to the majestic tracking shots of *Styrene* what is it, in effect, that we see?" It is, he continues, an "exploration of the possibilities of cinematographic technique, but one so rigorous that it outstrips its own purpose, and without which the young French cinema of today would simply not exist. From *Van Gogh* onwards, a movement of the camera gave the impression that it was not simply a movement of the camera but an exploration of the secret of this movement. A secret which André Bazin, another solitary explorer, also starting from scratch, by a moving coincidence discovered at the same time but by different means" (*Godard* 115).

By 1953, this filming degree zero produces the "Group of Thirty," a body of filmmakers that includes Resnais, Marker, Varda, and Astruc and revitalizes the short film as the grounds that would encourage essayistic practices. As Francois Porcile notes, the short film in this postwar context describes an incipient practice that, instead of suggesting juvenilia, describes an exploratory energy that liberates it as a kind of testing of both expression and address: "Next to the novel and other extensive works, there is the poem, the short story or the essay, which often plays the role of the hothouse; it has the function of revitalizing a field with fresh blood. The short film has the same role. Its death will also be the death of film, since an art that ceases to change is a dead art" (19).[16] At this point in history, the short film offers especially a form of expression whose concision necessarily puts that expression under material pressure as a fragmentary testing and provisional engagement with a subject whose incompleteness insists it is an artistic and intellectual activity in process. The significance of the short film also draws attention to what Guy Fihman, in exploring a philosophical and scientific background of the essay that begins with René Descartes, argues is one of the seminal features of the essay and essay film: innovation and experimentation (44–45),[17] possibilities that would attract both young and established filmmakers to return to the short film as a liberating break from narrative cinema.

Reconfiguring the implications of the short film in April 1955, Jacques Rivette's essay "Letter on Rossellini" identifies a trend that also can define longer films as cinematic drafts or sketches. In these films, he argues, "the indefatigable eye of the camera invariably assumes the role of the pencil, a temporal sketch is perpetuated before our eyes" (194),[18] and specifically in Rossellini's *Paisa, Europa '51* and *Germany, Year Zero*, there is "the common sense of the draft. . . . For there is no doubt that these hurried films, improvised out of very slender means and filmed in a turmoil that is often apparent from the images, contain the only real portrait of our times; and these times are a draft too. How could one fail suddenly to recognize, quintessentially sketched, ill-composed, incomplete, the semblance of our daily existence?" (195). For these films, and most recognizably for Rivette's *Viaggio in Italia* (1953), the model "is the essays of Montaigne," and "*Viaggio in Italia . . .*, with absolute lucidity, at least offers the cinema, hitherto condemned to narrative the possibility of the essay" (199). "For over fifty years now," he continues, "the essay has been the very language of modern art; it is freedom, concern, exploration, spontaneity; it has gradually—Gide, Proust, Valery, Chardonne, Audiberti—buried the novel beneath it; since Manet and Degas it has reigned over painting, and gives it its impassioned manner, the sense of pursuit and proximity." For Rivette, in these films "a film-maker dares to talk about himself without restraint; it is true that Rossellini's films have more and more obviously become *amateur* films; home movies" (196). Here "home movie," "amateur," "pursuit," and "proximity" assume, I would argue, those particularly positive values associated with an essayistic foregrounding and dramatization of the personal, a transitional, barely authorized, and relatively formless shape of personal subjectivity, the replacement of a teleological organization with an activity defined by the object itself, and a productively distorting overlapping of subject and object.[19]

The sketch as a historical prototype and marker of the essayistic thus becomes the vehicle for what Burch would later describe as the intelligent mediation of conflicting ideas. In his *Theory of Film Practice* and its concluding discussion of nonfictional filmmaking, Burch describes two contemporary models as the film essay and the ritual film. For the former, he identifies Georges Franju's 1948 *Le Sang des bêtes* and especially his 1951 *Hôtel des Invalides* as breakthrough films. These "active" documentaries "are no longer documentaries in [an] objective sense, their entire purpose being to set forth thesis and antithesis through the very texture of the film. These two films of Franju are *meditations*, and their subjects a *conflict of ideas*. . . . Therein lies the tremendous originality of these two films, which were to cause nonfiction film production to take an entirely new direction" (159). For Burch in the late 1960s, Franju becomes "the only cinematographer to have successfully created from pre-existing material films that are truly essays," and his heritage becomes especially visible in Godard's essay films of that period, such as *My Life to Live* (1962) and *Masculine, Feminine* (1966), in which an "element of intellectual spectacle" announces this distinctive "cinema of ideas," long ago dreamt of by such dissimilar filmmakers as Jacques Feyder and Eisenstein (162).[20]

In December 1962, referring to his beginnings as a writer for *Cahiers*, Godard, perhaps the most renowned and self-professed film essayist, would extend and to a certain extent canonize this alternative history of the art cinema by noting the bond between the critical essayists writing for *Cahiers du cinéma*, *Positif*, and other French film journals in the postwar years:

All of us at *Cahier* [*du cinéma*] thought of ourselves as future directors. Frequenting cine-clubs and the Cinematheque was already a way of thinking cinema and thinking about cinema. Writing was already a way of making films, for the difference between writing and directing is quantitative not qualitative. . . . As a critic, I thought of myself as a film-maker. Today I still think of myself as a critic, and in a sense I am, more than ever before. Instead of writing criticism, I make a film, but the critical dimension is subsumed. I think of myself as an essayist, producing essays in novel form or novels in essay form: only instead of writing, I film them. (*Godard* 171).

Explicitly drawing on the tradition of Montaigne and implicitly dramatizing with each film that central problem of thinking through our daily and public experience of signs, sounds, and images, Godard characterizes his work during this period as that of an experiential improviser and a thinking critic, working to transport the logic of essayism from short films to longer films such as *2 or 3 Things I Know about Her* (1967) and *La Chinoise* (1967).

While these prominent French currents leading from Montaigne through Marker, Bazin, and Godard describe the central path in the history of the essay film, the international foundations of that history, evolving from Griffith and Eisenstein through Richter and Jennings, has extended itself since the 1970s. Now a transnational practice, the essay film has proliferated through many new wave cinemas and various film cultures around the world, producing essayists like Glauber Rocha, Wim Wenders, Johannes van der Keuken, Patrick Keiller, Su Friedrich, Apichatpong Weerasethakul, and many others. If these filmmakers and their films have commonly been associated with auteurist notions of expressivity and narrative art cinema, they and others have consistently returned to short films (well after the essayistic testings of early films), while often describing their longer work as essayistic. In this alternative culture of the essayistic, expressive authority of the auteur gives way to a public dialogue that instead tests and explores the fissures within auteurist subjectivity by subjugating narration, experimentation, and documentation to thought.

The films of Agnès Varda provide an almost unique map of the historical movement of the essay film from its association with French cinema of the 1950s through its continued growth and expansion into the digital present. Since her 1958 L'Opera mouffe, *a sketch of Rue Mouffetard seen through the eyes of a pregnant woman, and the 1962* Cléo from 5 to 7, *her fictional sketch of a singer wandering Paris for roughly two hours of real time and film time, Varda has worked the terrain of the essay film across numerous projects, including* Jacquot de Nantes *(1991),* The Gleaners and I *(2000), and* The Beaches of Agnès *(2008). As a most appropriate recollection of the heritage and investment of the essay film in the cine club tradition, Varda follows* The Gleaners and I *with another film,* Two Years Later *(2002), a film that solicits and incorporates viewers and participants in the first film as part of a dialogic rethinking of that first essay film.*

The Gleaners and I is a series of sketches, a collage of short films constructed, first, as a meditation on gleaning. Describing the activity of collecting the surplus left after fields have been harvested, the idea of gleaning expands and contracts through the film as it triggers other associations, concepts, and debates. In the heritage of its literary and cinematic predecessors, the film proceeds digressively, spinning and turning the experience of gleaning as an idea that moves from the agricultural and the psychoanalytic to the aesthetic and political. Topics such as "The Origins of Gleaners" and "Gleaners Today" guide the course of the film as it wanders the fields and cities of France and its histories and moves according to the seemingly haphazard and associative ways of many essays, between specific experiences and general observations, between similarities and dramatic differences:

about the politics of waste and hunger in regulating the modern gleaners, about urban gleaners and supermarket garbage, about the gleaning of art objects and the art of gleaning. At one point, the film concentrates on a group of homeless young people in Prades prosecuted for picking through the garbage at a supermarket. Presenting the different points of view on the incident—those of the supermarket manager, the judge, and the young gleaners—Varda notes "each experiences it differently." Gleaning becomes in fact a crystallization of experience as a seemingly endless source of expression, such as that of "The Gleaning Chef," Edouard Loubet, "the youngest chef to have earned 2 stars in the Michelin Guide," in a kitchen where gourmet food is prepared and little is wasted. Later, an exposition of trash cans in Paris and an educational workshop on junk and recyclables together become a disquisition on "Art from Trash" and "Where Does Play End and Art Start?"

Ultimately, gleaning is defined here as a shifting identity dependent on and defined by the surplus and waste of the world, an identity that creates unique social bonds that drift through the flux of public life rather than inhabiting a position within that life, an identity built of fragments and transience. Abandoned furniture and other objects build "the Ideal Palace of Bodan Litnanski" inhabited by old broken dolls and other found objects, and lost souls (alcoholics, the jobless, and dispossessed who find food and friendship by drifting through streets and fields). Relationships, such as that between M. Plusquellecs and his homeless friend Salomon, are gleaned friendships (recalling perhaps Montaigne and La Boétie), a bond tentatively made like the gourmet meals they fashion from the chicken and rabbit they pick from the trash. Alain is a dietician of refuse, who in turn devotes himself to teaching the immigrant refuse of France. Quite appropriately in the midst of her travels, Varda stumbles unwittingly (or so the film claims) on the renowned Jean Laplanche, psychoanalytic theoretician and wine master of a vineyard, who suggests, in a reflection on reaping and death, time and age, fruition and meaning, that the connection between gleaning and subjectivity is an attempt "to integrate the Other above the ego . . . an anti-ego philosophy to show how man first originates in the Other." Here, gleaning, like the essayistic identity, is a parasitically productive activity, a subversion or rejection of the authority and primacy of subjectivity and selfhood, enunciated by a language that fails to offer any stable place or meaning—even for auteurist self-portraits.

If gleaning is an essayistic activity, essayistic art and filmmaking become kinds of representational gleanings. Throughout the film, numerous paintings and painters crystallize the art of gleaning, like Louis Pons, who appears flipping through a book of his paintings, whose compositional "junk" describes a "cluster of possibilities . . . each object gives a direction, each is a line." But the primary subject

of this metaphoric shift is Varda herself: Posed beside Jules Breton's painting The
Woman Gleaning, *Varda notes of this famous image of a woman in a field of
wheat that "there's another woman gleaning in this film, that's me," happy as she
says at another point, "to drop the wheat, and pick up my camera," a small digital
caméra-stylo that, for this contemporary woman, gathers subjective fragments as
digital recordings of a fleeting world. [fig. 2.8] For Varda and this essay film, representational gleaning moves across the cinematic image, specifically her digital
camera, allowing a continual sketching of the self as it dissolves in the world, especially as a mounting meditation on the drafting of self against the vanishings of
time. In one sequence, one of Varda's hands films the other hand as trucks pass in
the background, allowing her "to retain things passing." In another, Varda's reflection in the car mirror precedes a series of shots of that hand opening and closing like
a lens on images of different trucks speeding by on the road. "This is my project: to
film with one hand my other hand," she remarks. In this fragmentation of the self in
a passing world, the film sketches the passing and loss of self grasping at the world,
as a thing in the world: "To enter into the horror of it. I find it extraordinary. I feel as
if I am an animal. Worse yet, an animal I don't know."*

The Gleaners and I *is not, then, simply an essay film about a community of
individuals who live off the refuse and leavings of society; rather, it quickly becomes
also a subtle, sophisticated reflexive meditation on the terms of the essayistic and
its filmic practice. In this case, the essayistic becomes about the struggles to think
the self within a field of death and passing, where images of self are redeemed only
as a gleaned excess from the world. Over close-ups of garbage, Varda says, "I like
filming rot, leftovers, waste, mold, and trash," and appropriately, she visits a
museum in the vineyard consecrated to former owner Etienne-Jules Marey,
inventor of chronophotography, the "ancestor of all movie makers" and a pioneer in*

FIGURE 2.8   Varda as digital gleaner (*The Gleaners and I*)

the study of temporality and change in animal motion. Like the horror of seeing a self as an animalistic other in the world outside, Marey's imagistic time studies oddly anticipate Varda's own digital images, whose "effects are stroboscopic"; later, the film captures close-up fragments of Varda's eye while her hand holds a small mirror, creating a stroboscopic montage of pieces of herself within the image. [fig. 2.9] Scanning across the pages of technical handbook for her digital camera, the film returns to a medium close-up of Varda, who places her hand over the lens of the camera recording her. There follows a series of superimposed close-ups and then a decentered close-up of her combing her hair and then of her hand, as she comments, "For forgetful me, it's what I've gleaned that tells where I've been." As the concluding sequences make clear, The Gleaners and I *is ultimately a moving sketch that gathers souvenirs of a self, extended through a disembodied hand, fractured through rapidly passing and dying images, and left to drift into the world of others.*

A sequel to The Gleaners, Two Years Later *is an ingenious recollection and technological rehabilitation of the cine club tradition that fostered Varda's work in the 1950s and early 1960s, as it engages in a dialogue with individuals filmed in* The Gleaners *and other viewers responding to the first film.[21] In a sense,* The Gleaners *becomes a public souvenir that inspires and generates more souvenirs as expanding arguments, reflections, representations, and ideas, providing a cinematic forum for the dialogic debates, discussions, and differences that the essayistic invites and opens. Equipped again with her digital caméra-stylo, Varda re-creates the dialogic dynamic that the essay film inherited from the cine club format, now incorporating those responses in a way that rethinks and remakes the first film through the comments and criticism of its audiences. It begins with a screen of thumbnails of images from* The Gleaners and I *and propels itself through*

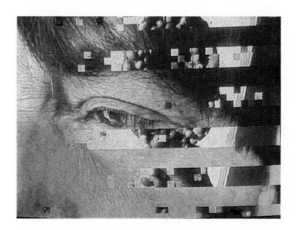

FIGURE 2.9   A stroboscopic self-image (*The Gleaners and I*)

the questions "What effect does a film have? What reaches the filmgoer?" [fig. 2.10]
*Responding to one curious fan letter (made from an airline ticket jacket), Varda
visits Delphine and Philippe in Trentemoult, who "transform everyday life" by sal-
vaging objects from the markets and streets. For them, "Seeing this film was like a
rebirth. . . . We had come from the death of a friend, and this film put us back in
touch with ourselves, with life. . . . That's what life's about, learning to adapt."*

*Particularly inventive in this second film is Varda's return to subjects and peo-
ple from earlier films. As an ironic reversal of that earlier historical path whereby
Cahiers du cinéma critics, like Truffaut and Godard, later become filmmakers,
now those filmed individuals become the critics of the film. Indeed, what may be
most essayistic about this second film is how it expands outward the questions and
issues of the first film to larger or different questions and issues. Gradually, the
film distinctly shifts from commentary about the first film to ideas about social
and political issues and relationships between people as it regenerates active subjects within the world through the centrifugal spin of the essay toward public life.
A painting seen in the first film has now been reborn for public exhibition; the
tumultuous relationship of "Claude M" and Gislaine's life has grown more stable
and secure; and thanks to the dialogue inspired by* The Gleaners, *Varda can "think*

FIGURE 2.10   Recollecting images as a public dialogue (*Two Years Later*)

of myself" differently. Typical of but more extensive than many of the returns in this film, Varda revisits "Alain F., market gleaner, newspaper seller, teacher," who has followed the impact of The Gleaners *and has become part of a public discussion of the film, one in which he is unabashedly critical (and conventionally mistaken, I would say) in his response to Varda's "self-portrait": "I think the film is well-done. It has reached a lot of people, but I think your self-portrait is not well-done . . . unnecessary." Just as a large concluding section of this film follows Alain into the streets of Paris to run a marathon, the movement of the film is decisively into the public arena, where Varda casually and quietly sketches the passing public, derouting the camera's point of view to capture fragmentary voices: "I walk slowly but often, sometimes with the camera pointing down to record the voices of people who don't want to be filmed."*

The response of the film and the responses in the film become variations on essayistic knowledge. Serendipitously perhaps for my purpose, the second film contains a card from Chris Marker with a drawing of his famous cat, Guillaume, and a memory of his CD-ROM Immemory, *in which there is a painting of gleaners following a tank and picking through blood. Images of gleaners then proliferate: Lubtchansky's "chromo-gleaners," embroidered gleaners, advertisement gleaners, stamp gleaners, "gleaners of stardust," and on and on through a representational catalogue of seekers after knowledge and meaning in the wake of the destruction, loss, and passing of the world. Even Laplanche returns to remind us that the subject of "psychoanalysis is gleaning": "We pay attention to things that no one else does—what falls from speech. . . . The analyst is also in a state of poverty . . . poor in knowledge." In the same spirit, a newspaper interviewer and later Varda's daughter suggest that the many fragmentary close-ups of hands and other body parts remind them of Varda's* Jacquot de Nantes, *a film about her dead film-maker-partner and an emotional connection that Varda claims had been visually recollected without thinking when she filmed* The Gleaners: "I refilmed on myself what I had filmed of Jacques Demy . . . how we work without knowing." In the end, it is precisely this essayistic work without knowing, whether it is addressed to La Boétie or Demy, that produces the desire to know and think through the best essays. As* Two Years Later *dramatizes so powerfully, essayistic ideas about self and others should return, remade, as a dialogic knowledge that comes back from other views and viewers.*

PART TWO

Essayistic Modes

3

About Portraying Expression: The Essay Film as Inter-view

<hr>

THE MOST COMMONLY highlighted feature of the essayistic is the personal or subjective point of view that organizes its observations and reflections, a structural position whose self-questioning activity is, I believe, one of the keys to understanding the distinctive power and complexity of the essay. The essayistic foregrounding of subjectivity as one of its primary topics has no doubt a heritage and historical path that includes, among other practices, biographical and autobiographical writings, from Augustine's *Confessions* through *Zen and the Art of Motorcycle Maintenance*, and modern visual portraiture and self-portraiture, from Hans Holbein's 1533 *The Ambassadors* through Frida Kahlo's 1940 *Self-Portrait*, in which the image of an individual is as much about subjectivity itself as it is about a particular person. After Montaigne and after more muted pre-Romantic essayists like Francis Bacon, essayistic subjectivity most visibly asserts itself in the so-called personal essays of writers such as Charles Lamb or William Hazlitt and has continued to develop, reshape, and retest that subjectivity in essays from George Bataille's in 1930s to those of Eula Bliss today. Essayistic subjectivity of course requires careful historical distinctions to evaluate and describe its positions and strategies, and distinctions must also be made about how these dramas of self-reflection become articulated in different material media, taking account, for instance, of how a print discourse describes and interpellates subjectivity differently from that of an imagistic discourse. Across these historical and representational differences, however, the essayistic concentration on images of self and self-expression has produced two of its most prominent and ubiquitous versions of the essay film: the portrait and the self-portrait essay.

Similar to the interdisciplinary heritage of other essay films, this particular kind of film extends the tradition of literary and visual portraits and self-portraits; reappears in the photos of August Sanders, Walker Evans, and others; and begins to assume its more definitive place and shape in postwar essay films since the 1940s. Of the many examples of the portrait and self-portrait essay film, a survey of its range and vitality would include Jim McBride's parodic *David Holtzman's Diary* (1967); Shirley Clarke's *Portrait of Jason* (1967), about a young black hustler; Wim Wender's homage to filmmaker Nicholas Ray, *Lightning over Water* (1980); Michelle Citron's autobiographical reflection on mother/daughter relationships in *Daughter Rite* (1980); Abbas Kiarostami's self-reflexive fiction *Life, and Nothing More . . .* (1991); and Errol Morris's stylized portrait of the mind behind the U.S. involvement in the Vietnam war, *The Fog of War: Eleven Lessons from the Life of Robert S. McNamara* (2003). Even as a very loose and limited sampling, this group of films suggests the different strategies and subjects of this kind of essay film: Using documentary found footage or home movies, displaying intimate images of self or analytical perspectives on public personas, creating fictional selves or revealing the many variations on a true self, portrait and self-portrait essays have become, arguably, the most prevalent of all essay films. No wonder, then, that early on Lukacs saw the "problem of likeness" in a portrait as emblematic of the essential truth of the essayistic, or more exactly "a struggle for truth, for the incarnation of a life which someone has seen in a man, an epoch or a form" (10–11).

All essay films of course are not biographical or autobiographical; all biographical and autobiographical films are not essay films since some films may represent an essayistic subject but not necessarily mobilize an essayistic way of seeing that subject. Still, the centrality of subjectivity to the essayistic makes the biographical and autobiographical tradition an absolutely primary site for essayistic grounding and intervention, not as a place to rehearse the coherencies often found in biographical and autobiographical films but instead as a place to challenge and confound subjectivity as it is played out in a public domain.[1] What distinguishes essayistic portrait and self-portrait films is the simultaneous enactment of and representation of a destabilized self as a central focus, topic, and, sometimes, crisis, a self whose place in a public history is at best on its margins or in some cases in an excluded or inverted position. That this fragmenting or opening of subjectivity forms the basis for other essayistic modes—the diary film, the travelogue, and so forth—is one indication of the fundamental position of this particular mode in considering the essay film. How those other variations on the essayistic overlap with it and differentiate themselves from it is then largely a matter of where they direct that subjectivity, the public arenas in which they discover or place it.

Foregrounding that image of self in especially emphatic ways, portrait and self-portrait essays tend to perform that self, implicitly or explicitly, as an inter-view that takes place between two or more views of that self, as a pronounced variation on "the forgotten image between two shots." Rather than representing subjectivity in the more conventional manner in which the self becomes the hero of a living history, a myth of that history, or a "strong enunciator" (in Rascaroli's view), these essayistic portraits often find their reflection in death masks, in which the struggle to see or be seen documents the fatal struggle to think about a self or oneself or, sometimes, the triumphant release of that self through the struggle with mortality.[2]

One of the most celebrated modern essayists and one of her most oblique essay films, Trinh T. Minh-ha and Surname Viet Given Name Nam *(1989), respectively, create a portrait of not a single individual but, as the title makes ironically clear, of numerous individuals who make up an entire nation and who collectively become one multiple subject. This cultural portrait of Vietnam is portrayed and performed in the film through the comments of numerous women, who represent that identity as doubly marginalized: as members of a country divided and fractured by decades of war and colonialism and as a gender removed and repressed by the dominant patriarchal forces within their nation. Less a documentary than a subversion of traditional documentary techniques and transparencies, the film is a portrait with the name and the face of a collective of women relentlessly subject to exile, displacement, and translation.*

Surname Viet Given Name Nam *is essentially about naming and representing identity or, more exactly, the impossible struggle to do so in a modern postcolonial age, questioning "authorized boundaries and subjectivities" across the shifting languages of English and Vietnamese (Trinh,* Cinema Interval *56). Interweaving poetry, dance, and proverbs, the film superimposes graphic subtitles and titles on the screen, sometimes in different parts of the frame and occasionally over characters' faces, to create what Hamid Naficy calls a "calligraphic accent" and what Trinh refers to as a "visualized speech." [fig. 3.1] Explored across a generational cycle of identities, language here measures the repressions and struggles of gendered enunciations bound within essayistic frames of experience, such as that "Of Marriage and Loyalty," where a circle of social imperatives vacate the female subject of identity itself: "Daughter, she obeys her father/Wife, she obeys her husband/Widow, she obeys her son." With broken English competing with folk songs translated into English subtitles, this drift of language through material experience becomes a continual slippage of expression struggling to name and rename lost or blurred identities.*

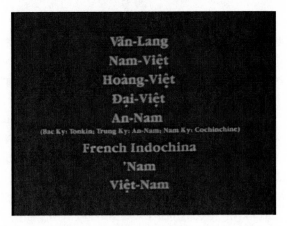

FIGURE 3.1   A calligraphic accent of titles (*Surname Viet Given Name Nam*)

Visually, the film decenters the framing and continuities of traditional por-traiture and portrait films as a way to dramatize this instability of identities, act-ing as a kind of debunking of those more conventional documentary formats and perspectives that assume a centralized subject. The close-ups of the five Vietnam-ese women in the film typically reveal only parts of their faces, which frequently remain obscured by dark shadows, cut off by the edges of the frame, or barely lumi-nous against the black or white backgrounds. [fig. 3.2] This imagistic fragmenta-tion and vanishing are further accented with freeze-frames that highlight their pictorial isolation rather than the expressivity of the faces of these women. At one point, for instance, the frame pans across a face, almost losing the image of the woman who speaks. Throughout the film, the repetition of these faces creates a montage effect—between frames and within a single frame—in which the fis-sures, slippages, overlaps, and shifts between the different close-ups produce a drama of differences from face to face. [fig. 3.3] In Trinh's words, "When handled creatively, repetition is a way of affirming difference. Rather than using it rou-tinely to reproduce the same, one can use it, to continue saying what one has said, to shift a center, to lighten the burden of representation, to displace a form from its settled location, and to create new passages through the coexistence of moments"
(Trinh, Cinema Interval *23).*

Central to this performance of naming and being named as a portrait is the interview process that structures the entire film, a process that foregrounds the connection between a performance of self and a naming of self through the eyes, questions, and presence of another. On the one hand, the film orchestrates this performance through community discourses and memories articulated through songs, proverbs, and other forms in which personal experience spreads itself

FIGURE 3.2   Off-center close-ups, cut off or fading into backgrounds (*Surname Viet Given Name Nam*)

FIGURE 3.3   An internal montage of differences from face to face (*Surname Viet Given Name Nam*)

though the many social voices and texts of a public culture. On the other, as one of the most innovative and notorious strategies of Surname Viet Given Name Nam, *the film uses Vietnamese American actresses to speak the previously recorded words of the Vietnamese women interviewed earlier (interviews first published in French in Mai Thu Van's 1983* Vietnam: un people, des voix*). [fig. 3.4] In this way, the film circulates the public experience of the war and its aftermath through fictive reenactments that undo the core of the conventional interview as a presumed expressive portrait. Layering memories of the experience of Vietnam during war, their transcriptions through different languages, and their performances by various actresses, the film thus, according to Trinh, "engages the politics of the*

FIGURE 3.4   A fractured face explaining her performance of another identity for the film (*Surname Viet Given Name Nam*)

*interview while entering Vietnam's history through collective and individual gaps.
That is, not in an easily recognizable way, through chronology, linear accumulation, and succession of facts on Vietnam . . . but rather through popular memory,
with its 'bold omissions and minute depictions'; through women's personal stories;
through songs, proverbs, and sayings"* (Trinh, Cinema Interval 23). *Public and
personal identity, expression, and portraiture thus dissipate "like ripples widening
on the surface of water. It's a reality that cannot be contained, that always escapes,
but that one cannot escape"* (22).

*Addressed through this kind of essayistic portrait, the listening viewer sees
and hears her own self within a conceptual play and along a conceptual periphery
that requires a continual interpretation and reinterpretation of those selves and
herself. Signaled by the "you" and "even you" in the responses of the interviewees,
the role of a witness-confidante-listener-insider in a traditional portrait interview
now constantly shuttles "across thresholds of insideness and outsideness"* (Trinh,
Cinema Interval 22) *where an expressive self is first and foremost the shifting
ground for rethinking the fluctuating face of that self.*

A large constellation of film genres and practices anticipate and surround the
essay portrait film, including early film sketches at the turn of the twentieth century depicting celebrated figures like President Woodrow Wilson or Mary Queen
of Scots. Biopics and heroic documentaries are, though, perhaps its most visible
mainstream counterparts. Especially after 1930, biopics proliferate and range from
the 1939 *Story of Alexander Graham Bell* and *Young Mr. Lincoln* to contemporary
films such as *Malcolm X* (1992) and *Capote* (2005); as George Custen points out in
his discussion of biopics from made between 1927 and 1960, these films, despite

their many differences, "constructed public history" through the narrative agencies of renowned individuals.[3] Indeed, despite clear differences in style and form, conventional documentaries from *Nanook of the North* (1922) to *The Times of Harvey Milk* (1984) frequently work in a similar way: narrating and constructing cultural and public histories through portraits of real individuals at the center of heroic chronologies.

The 2008 *Milk*, a Hollywood remake of the documentary *The Times of Harvey Milk*, is a good example of how, in the context of my argument here, clear distinctions between biopics and documentary portraits may often be less definitive than what they share as constructions or organizations of histories or counterhistories through the image of a coherent individual. Both the Epstein documentary and Gus Van Sant's recreation of it through the star-vehicle of Sean Penn depict the tragic rise and fall of Harvey Milk as he mobilizes the San Francisco gay community and achieves unprecedented political visibility and power for that community before he is assassinated by Dan White, a political associate who successfully mounted the infamous "Twinkie defense." The Van Sant film prominently appropriates documentary footage from the Epstein film (and other documentary sources) that provides a kind of concrete historical ballast and background against and through which the charismatic figure of Milk asserts himself as the agent of a new historical and political consciousness. While the narrative textures and points of view of the two films are certainly different, both films remain focused on the personality and determination of Milk, who despite his personal foibles and complexities becomes the agency for the transformative history of a new sexual politics. More important for my argument, however accomplished each of these films is, together they demonstrate that even an unconventional subject, like Milk, possessing the kinds of fragmentations and divisions associated with essayistic subjectivity, does not de facto produce an essay film. The essay film, rather, is a way of seeing that subject as much as it is about that subject.

Through the history of the biopic as the public history of a self, the representation of subjectivity has been shaped and defined by an image of the self—informed by psychological, sexual, and political structures—that work together to confirm a coherent image of subjectivity as the center of much cinematic practice and public history. As early as the 1920s, Béla Balázs locates the power of the close-up in which the human face describes an ontology of presence that anchors film narrative. As a "microphysiognomy" or "microdramatics" of expressivity, the close-up creates facial expression as "the most subjective manifestation of man, more subjective even than speech. . . . The most subjective and individual of human manifestations is rendered objective in the close-up" (60).[4] Much later, in larger, psychoanalytical terms, Lacan extends the power of Balazs's close-up to provide a model for the cinematic gaze that, for psychoanalytic film theory, is the primary visual support of the look of classical narrative cinema. Here, the gaze as "photographic image" defines a self through and in the "outside" of "life":

> In the scopic field, the gaze is outside, I am looked at, that is to say, I am a picture. . . . This is the function that is found at the heart of the institution of the subject in the visible. What determines me, at the most profound level, in the visible, is the gaze that is outside. It is through the gaze that I enter life and from the gaze that I receive its effects. Hence it comes about that the gaze is the instrument through which light is embodied and through which . . . I am *photographed*. (106)

As historical film portraits orchestrate that photographed self, the image of an individual typically becomes fixed within and through the gaze of history, either by absorbing the story of history into its agency or by mobilizing that image of self to secure history. Acting as an extended close-up of history, the cinematic self thus provides a stable and legible view of the past as present: as a communicative presence and expressiveness that articulates human presence in history and experience; as an agency that coordinates the exterior (historical) contingencies of the world around interior motives and meanings of the individual. Often dramatized in sight lines and eye-line matches that assert a communal and historical agency, the hero of history as a historical portrait appears as a duration and continuity in which the expression of a self harmonizes and organizes historical change and difference, even the change and difference of the death of that self.[5]

If this classical cinematic face is the image of the coherent expression of history, post–World War II culture and film history distinctly reconfigure its shape and formation. After the cultural and historical traumas of the 1940s, the place and value of subjectivity and its identity come under increased scrutiny and become increasingly problematic, not only because those traditional frameworks of human identity come into question but also because the fundamental authority of a humanistic subject is profoundly shaken by events of and surrounding World War II.[6] In an essay written around 1950 with significant import for essayistic portraiture, Bazin accordingly identifies and scrutinizes the troubling tendency in the classical tradition of biopics and documentary portraits as they insist on the status of the individual as myths of history. Commenting on three Soviet portrait films of Stalin, he describes the face of a subject in which the "biography is literally identical with History and shares the absoluteness of History" to the extent that "the contradictions of subjectivity don't apply." "You cannot reduce a man to nothing but History," Bazin concludes, "without in turn compromising that History by the subjective presence of the individual" ("The Stalin Myth in Soviet Cinema" 36, 37).[7] Especially in the wake of World War II, history and sub-jectivity necessarily and perhaps tragically divide. As a consequence of the increasingly fractured and contingent relation of the subject to public experi-ence, the authenticity of expression itself begins to waver against the backdrop of history.

Two films from different ends of the postwar period pinpoint and respond to this crisis of self-representation and expressivity in history. An essayistic narra-tive punctuated by intense and extreme close-ups, *Hiroshima Mon Amour* (1959), describes the encounter between a Japanese man and a French woman scarred by World War II and adrift in a painful crisis of identity and communication. Through-out the film, silences engulf the faces as shadowy and yearning surfaces of masks isolated as, in Deleuze's words, "sheets of the past" (*Cinema 2* 117–120). If this film offers a double portrait of the modern self in a postwar history, the faces of that self threaten to become disturbingly impenetrable and illegible expressions mask-ing the visibility of or even possibility of an interior self. Thirty years later, Johan van der Keuken's 1991 *Face Value* would continue this investigation of the faces of history by creating a European map as an imagined community of physiognomic surfaces, of prisoners, boxers, hair stylists, and priests. Spread from London to Prague, close-ups in this film describe a multitude of expressions that isolate, con-fess, and disguise themselves across a shared geography of differences; their self-descriptive words, on screen or off, repeatedly seem to almost express and yet fail to express the physical tactility of the faces on the screen. For this film, Deleuze's comments on Ingmar Bergman's cinema identify only a particular and extreme version of a larger postwar crisis in the fragile bond among expressions, faces, and identities: If the face once offered a place for individuation, mythology, and com-munication, the postwar cinematic face is, according to Deleuze, a "phantom" that "suspends individuation" and where the "facial close-up is both the face and its effacement" (*Cinema 1* 99–100).

Within this postwar context, essayistic subjectivity appears sharply differenti-ated from the more stable and coherent models of self shaped and sustained by traditional biopics, as well as other classical voices and narrational points of view. While these other enunciations of self tend to dramatize the central organiza-tional power of the subject (even when reflexively calling attention to its limits) to re-create the world and its history through that self, what best defines the postwar essayistic subject and its unique potentials—at least I believe in the strongest essays—becomes its capacity to unravel, deflect, and undermine, through the grid of an experiential reality, the surfaces of the selves it presents. As the essayistic works and explores these surfaces, the resulting portraits do not offer the spectator so much a view of expression but instead places that spectator in the interstices between the difficult and divided work of expression.

Against the myths of portraiture as the vehicle of expression, defined by spontaneity and depth, by direct expression/speech/language, and by signification of gesture and eye contact, the essay portrait develops, commonly and specifically, as an interview or inter-view in which the subject occupies what Trinh identifies as the interval within expression. Interviews usually suggest an exchange or dialogue in which the interviewer elicits or teases out the expression of the subject/ interviewee, a drawing out of the truth of that subject, but here Trinh offers a variation on the "frame" of the interview reshaped as an inter-view:

Questions and answers can sometimes force both interviewer and interviewee into awkward positions because we often feel compelled to bear the burden of representation. We know we are not simply speaking to each other or for ourselves; we are addressing a certain audience. . . . And since we are framed by this question-and-answer mechanism, we might as well act on the frame. If we put aside the fact that the popular use of the interview is largely bound to an ideology of authenticity and to a need for accessibility or facile consumption, I would say that the interview is, at its best, a device that interrupts the power of speaking, that creates gaps and detours, and that invites one to move in more than one direction at a time. (*Cinema Interval* 4)[8]

According to Trinh, the essayistic interview becomes a series of intervals as points of departure at which "the interstices of active re-inscription are to be kept alive" (*Cinema Interval* 25). Now, no longer the stable ontological core found in the traditional close-up, this image of the interviewed self fluctuates in the intervals between expressions, on the edges of the frames of history:

The process of self-constitution is also that in which the self vacillates and loses its assurance. The paradox of such a process lies in its fundamental instability; an instability that brings forth the disorder inherent in every order. The "core" of representation is the reflexive interval. It is the place in which the play within the textual frame is a play on this very frame, hence on the borderlines of the textual and extra-textual, where a positioning within constantly incurs the risk of de-positioning, and where the work, never freed from historical and socio-political contexts nor entirely subjected to them, can only be itself by constantly risking being no-thing. ("Documentary Is/ Not a Name" 96–97)

In this way, essayistic subjectivity becomes a dynamic inter-subjectivity determined by, rather than determining, the changing contingencies of an exterior world whose mortality principle now occupies the center, rather than the fringes, of the self.

Differently employed in films as various as Emile de Antonio's 1971 *Millhouse*, a searing portrait of Richard Nixon, and Marlon Riggs's 1989 *Tongues Untied*, an extraordinary self- and group portrait consisting of poetic "declarations" by gay black men "corned by identities" they "never wanted to claim," the essayistic interview as portrait tends to crack open, dissipate, or let drift the face and voice into the background of social and public space that the interview normally blurs. In the essayistic portrait, both the language of the voice and the image of the face/body tend to open up to an (historical, social, psychological, or physical) exteriority into which the individual is now subjected to a mode of thought. Or, in Michael Renov's rephrasing of Emmanuel Levinas, "The meeting—'face-to-face'—is an encounter of unique beings that respects both separation and proximity; it is a breach of totality in which 'thought finds itself *faced* with the other refractory to categories'" (*The Subject* 151).

From the biopic mythologizing of self in public events to avant-garde and cinema-vérité portraits that draw attention to the dynamic actuality of the subject, the portrait film has regularly represented modern subjectivity as celebrity subjects, as undiscovered subjects, and as subjects in crisis, in which psychoanalytic depth, coherence, complexity, and sometimes mystery anchor a sociohistorical world as background. Intervening in this tradition, the portrait essay film has in effect inverted that usual ratio of the interior self against the background of history while drawing expressivity into the conceptually open and fluctuating space of the interval, the inter-view, the interface. The portrait essay film offers the pathos and crisis of the self as moving image, in which subjectivity falters and drifts unsteadily—and sometimes blindly—between expression and presentation, struggling to think the face of a self that wavers and fractures within the foreground of history, nature, and society.

In Errol Morris's portrait essay Mr. Death: The Rise and Fall of Fred A. Leuchter, Jr. *(1999), the nominal subject is Fred Leuchter, an inventor/engineer/investigator who makes his reputation by refurbishing and modernizing electric chair equipment for the Massachusetts penal system. His success in modernizing that form of the death penalty leads, in a logic that puzzles even Leuchter, to his recruitment as an expert in other methods of capital punishment, including lethal injection systems and gas chambers. After this exposition in the first third of the film, the remainder of the film describes Leuchter's enlistment with a neo-Nazis group that draws him and his pseudoscientific expertise into a plan to prove that the Holocaust did not take place, specifically at Auschwitz. His concomitantly clownish and appalling scraping and chipping at the walls of an Auschwitz crematoria are followed by his uncomprehending alienation and professional unraveling back in the United States. The portrait here, similar to other Morris essay films, is a dreamscape of a body and mind whose radical isolation in historical and social space creates the figure of a "cocooned self" for whom, in Morris's words, "believing is seeing" ("Not Every Picture"). According to Morris, "Ultimately, it is a movie about denial. Denial about the obvious, denial of death, denial of self, denial of the Holocaust. But at its center, it is a failure to see the world, to see reality. Living in a cocoon of one's own devising" (Grundmann and Rockwell 6). The subject of this film is the overdetermined subject of history, a subject that tragically and comically collapses under the pressure of historical experiences and facts that this individual so insistently attempts to deny.*

*   As a twisted version of biopics and heroic documentaries,* Mr. Death *focuses on the individual as both the subject and the vehicle of history, an individual longing to become a myth of history. As with other essay films, however,* Mr. Death *distinguishes itself aggressively from its mythologizing counterparts by fracturing that traditionally coherent subjectivity, decentering it within social space, and detaching it from its historical ground. [fig. 3.5] If the mythologizing impulse of the traditional portrait film appears in the very subtitle of Morris's film,* The Rise and Fall of Fred A. Leuchter, Jr., *here it signals that drive only to differentiate its essayistic undermining of it. Even the details and biography of Leuchter's life begin*

FIGURE 3.5 Leuchter's decentered social space (*Mr. Death*)

to trouble his singularity: His name is pronounced and mispronounced by the numerous interviewees in the film, and through the course of the film he appears, like a frighteningly tragic version of Woody Allen's *Zelig* (1983), as, in different incarnations, a scientist, a spy, and anti-Semite, an American patriot, an engineer, and a clown. A mobile and multiplying portrait, Leuchter moves across a wide range of histories: personal histories, film histories, public histories, everyday histories, revisionist histories, marital histories, archival histories, none of which coordinate as Leuchter's attempted testimony to his life. [fig. 3.6] Even as he acknowledges the lack of logic and coherency in his odd career path and life, even as he progresses from an expert on the electric chair to a nationally sought-after expert on lethal injection, hanging, and gas chambers, he recognizes that these self-professions are completely "different concepts." As one commentator describes him toward the conclusion of the film, this is a biographical portrait of "criminal simplicity" in which Leuchter "came from nowhere and went back to nowhere."

The imagistic compositions of the film sustain and exaggerate this implosive isolation of Leuchter as subject. Against the myth of portraiture as the facial transparency, defined by spontaneity, development, and depth, *Mr. Death* creates a face, as a moving marker of the crisis of personal expression, that is both flattened and fractured. Rather than depicting the cinematic power of direct expression through speech and language and the revelations of gesture and eye contact, *Mr. Death* becomes an inter-view that portrays self-expression as fundamentally about denial and deferral, as a relentless effort to assert an overly determined self in a world that repeatedly rebuffs and fractures the image of that self. After the credits, there is, for

FIGURE 3.6 Overwhelmed by history (*Mr. Death*)

instance, an off-center close-up of his partial face in the rearview mirror of his car,
an image that is then doubled when the frame pulls back to a medium shot of his
head and face alongside the rearview mirror image of a portion of the same face.
[fig. 3.7] Anticipating the numerous canted frames that permeate the film, these
shots prefigure the multiplications of Leuchter's image throughout the film. Later,
for instance, while Leuchter sits meditating on a doctor's comment that his addic-
tion to coffee (forty cups each day) should have killed him already, the surface of his
face dissolves and distorts in its close-up reflection in a coffee cup.

Paralleling these distortions of the visual image of Leuchter, Mr. Death
dramatically torques the interview process itself in an unsettling realignment
of assumptions about cinematic portraiture as an expressive exchange. Typically,
an interview implies alternating perspectives as a dialogue that opens and deepens
the linguistic and visual space between question and answer through a performa-
tive activity that draws the subject out into history and social space. Or, as Morris
describes this usual social performance, the interview makes "use of many such
things—people's desire to get attention, people's desire to be important, people's
desire to tell their own story to someone else" (Grundmann and Rockwell 5–6). In
Mr. Death, however, the inter-view becomes better described as an interface that
highlights the limits and borders of the expressive and cognitive frames that
enclose and continually strain Leuchter's struggle to communicate himself coher-
ently with and through the world around him.

To dramatize and exaggerate this presentation, Morris expands something he
calls his Interrotron (a multiple-camera setup) into a Megatron (a twenty-camera

FIGURE 3.7 A canted and doubled self (*Mr. Death*)

setup), that places the subject before cameras and a monitor that links interviewer and the subject to create multiple technological distances, giving the impression of a kaleidoscopically first-person monologue that records how the subject performs himself rather than how an outside perspective sees him. In this way, the interviews of Leuchter describe stress fractures within his blindly insistent claims for himself as they draw increasing attention to the breaks and breakdowns in his almost comically desperate attempts to express himself "sincerely" in dialogue with a real world. His postures and speech—a peculiar smile as he recounts his theft of stones from Auschwitz, his incomprehension that he could be perceived as an anti-Semite, or his excessive theorizing about the science of mass extermination in front of his own camera—often seem like the extended and uncertain conversation of a man talking to himself, a broken mirror of an individual clinging to a coherent self-image rather than a dialogue within a three-dimensional world. [fig. 3.8]

As manipulations and stylizations of the portrait image, these formal and technological maneuvers of Leuchter's image create a technological distance that allows Morris "to scrutinize the interview process at the same time that I am scrutinizing the interviewee" (Grundmann and Rockwell 9). With Morris's presence and voice absent through virtually the entire film, Leuchter as interviewee becomes stylistically abstracted (most commonly through close-ups) as a performative self whose exaggerated expressive action becomes increasingly aware of its inevitable collapse. In Mr. Death, subjectivity is best described not, as with conventional portraits, as a realistic enunciation of self within depth and movement of a surrounding field but rather as a textured container—like a sealed cocoon, a locked

FIGURE 3.8   An extended and uncertain conversation with his own identity (Mr. Death)

cage, or an electric chair—in which the subject's failure to enter the exterior world acts out its own demise.

Oddly enough, Leuchter becomes a parodic essayist, testing, searching, and measuring history through the evasiveness of facts, but unlike Morris and other essayists who open subjectivity to thought, he learns nothing because he remains locked within the God-like authority of his singular self, unable to allow that self to experience the world. Robert Van Pelt, a historian of Auschwitz, bemoans Leuchter's attempt to find a truth in history as if he were Sherlock Holmes, while what blinds him so monstrously is his lack of real experience, his ability to think outside himself. How appropriate then that the film concludes with Leuchter's reflection on "The Legend" of the electric chair that warns that anyone who sits in an electric chair could be condemned to die in that chair. For Leuchter, that chair becomes his real and metaphoric myth of himself as the agent of history, a myth that he literally occupies and that, because he has not thought of himself outside that mythic chair, destroys him as a subject. As the opening flashing images of Leuchter caged in the Van de Graaf electrical generator suggest, his insistence on a determining subjectivity here makes Leuchter simultaneously the image of Dr. Frankenstein and the image of his monster. [fig. 3.9]

Morris's essay on Leuchter foregrounds the surfaces of a self-decaying and dying subject, an ironic reversal of Leuchter's own attempt to make history itself vanish and of Bazin's description of how certain cinematic portraits make history disappear into myth. Intermittent black leader regularly punctuates the film, and the resulting dramatic gaps not only accentuate the intervals where this inter-view takes place but also suggest the temporal disjunction and fragmentation

FIGURE 3.9 Leuchter in the electric chair: a monstrous myth of history (*Mr. Death*)

that refuse to allow Leuchter to interpellate a self smoothly into history, to reclaim history according to his disturbed myth of self. Like Morris's well-known use of reenactments here and in other films, the disruption of temporal and historical continuities works to create a fractured phantom within history, a version of what Nichols describes as the "specter that haunts the text" in reenactments ("Documentary Reenactment" 73), acting as "desubjectivization" of the subject in "the workings of the fantasmatic" (73, 77). For Morris specifically, a reenactment becomes consequently "expressionistic rather than realistic," working "in the service of ideas rather than facts" (Grundmann and Rockwell 8). As the hypnotic soundtrack, regular slow-motion movements, and eerie lighting suggest, the interview inhabits a space in which Leuchter becomes a surreal agent of a history in which ideas and thought must intervene in the shadowy intervals of self-expression. Perhaps this is what appears most clearly when, in the final minutes of Mr. Death, *the first sound of Morris's voice and words in the film insert themselves into the fissures in Leuchter's portrait: "Have you ever thought that you might be wrong, or that you could make a mistake?" he asks. In the silent gap that lingers after the question, Morris directly engages his subject in an essay whose efforts are "to lead . . . back to the world" (7).*

Because portraits and self-portraits focus on the presence of identity within the temporality of history, they have, perhaps throughout the modern history of the last 400 years, been entwined with death and mortality. When portrait films inherit that symbiosis of portraiture and dying, however, the image of a memento mori in Renaissance portraits materializes as a more fundamental formal figure located in the edited continuities and discontinuities that tend to subvert or trouble the stasis of the portrayed face/figure. As Paul Arthur notes:

The allegorization of death is a trope associated with the portraiture, especially self-portraiture, at least since the Renaissance. Since the portrait's temporal scope is inevitably fragmentary, a slice of contingent history rather than a sign of immutable identity, formal alternatives to duration—for instance, the staging of ellipsis through editing—can only partially subdue the uncanny collision of screen time with the temporal sphere of the spectator. For the viewer, a subject is always simultaneously present and estranged and in a manner distinct from that of painting or still photography. Caught in the hesitation between single still frame and the mechanically imposed illusion of continuity, the project of portraiture is sustained by a false promise of non-repetition as it is endlessly compromised by the fact of material disruption. ("No Longer Absolute" 114)

In this sense, cinematic portraiture normally strives to represent a subject as durable presence, embalmed and "mummified" as a continuity; yet, especially with essayistic portraits such as *Mr. Death*, the work of the essay film often intervenes to complicate and frustrate the achievement of that representation as presence in the "staging of ellipsis through editing." Bazin famously claims that "Death is surely one of those rare events that justifies the term . . . *cinematic specificity*," becoming in "the representation of a real death" a "violation" and "obscenity" ("Death Every Afternoon" 30).[9] For me, the task of many essay portraits is precisely to investigate and expose the obscenity of the self in death that cinema so commonly mythologizes, to expose the coherent mythologies of self on that ob-scene of public life by inhabiting that normally invisible ellipsis between film frames. As Marker's *Koreans* highlights at several points, the interstices at the center of the essayistic work specifically to draw the death of the subject into history. That "forgotten image between two shots" is the mortality of historical subjectivity itself, which essayistic portraiture so determinedly seeks to capture.

Little wonder, then, that portrait essay films have been especially engaged with different dimensions of mortality, frequently embedding the image of a self visibly in the ground of death and dying between the frames of imagistic continuity. Expressions always fade in time, and essayistic portraits typically aim to arrest that expression within time as a way to seize and conceptualize the authenticity of its passing. Wenders's essay film *Lightning over Water* (1980) is thus not simply a portrait of filmmaker Nicholas Ray or only about his impending death from cancer but, most important, about what Catherine Russell identifies as a "split subjectivity," various representational doublings, and struggles to conceive and articulate the death of the subject (*Narrative Mortality* 71–88). These are representational doublings and splits that, in this film, become a portrait of, in Bernardo Bertolucci's words, "the boundless frivolity of people about to die" (5).[10]

If essay portraits confront one subject with another as an inter-view and interval that is quintessentially a mortal space, self-portraits find that interval in the face-to-face portrait of a subject divided from his or her own self in a moment of mortality. Essayistic self-portraiture is consequently more than a variation on portraiture and is better described as an investigation of the essence of subjectivity itself as multiplication and loss. It becomes an intensification of the thinking through of self as a public discourse, experience, and history—and in that intensity appears the essential bond between self-expression and death. In *Poetics of the Literary Self-Portrait*, Michel Beaujour notes that, more so than the portraiture of another, self-portraits operate "through their topical dispersion, their restless metadiscourse, the splitting among the dislocated agencies of enunciation" (13) since self-portraits are composed "after the writer has already fallen into a formless and disoriented space, created by a loss of certainty," as, he observes, happens when Montaigne faces the death of his friend La Boétie (335). For Beaujour, "To ask oneself who one is, one must no longer be who one was: one must have lost certitude and penetrated into an anxiety that can also be called 'freedom of choice'" (337). More radically defined than the inter-view of the portrait of another, "the self-portraitist . . . is nothing but his text: he will survive through it or not at all. . . . What remains after self-portrayal is not the physician, the philosopher, or the semiotician, but rather the staging—each time different, displaced, and to some degree unforeseeable. But always recognizable—of some major places in an impersonal, transhistoric, and anonymous topic system" (343–344). For me, the essence of that topic system is history as mortality.

In this context, McElwee's *Sherman's March* (1986) is a critical parody of the dilemma of self-portrayal—a kind of an essayistic reflection on cinematic self-portraiture itself—as the self confronts its own displacement and potential formlessness and is left with the angst of choosing one of several possible selves within the vicissitudes of history, conquest, loss, and death, within, that is, an "anonymous topic system." His itinerary ostensibly follows the Civil War general's famous path through the U.S. South, following "shrines to the destruction," such as the ruins of Sheldon Church, which Sherman's marauders burned in November 1864, where the caskets superheated and exploded. Staged before and entwined with this public history, however, McElwee's historical travelogue quickly shifts perspectives. Beginning with the opening sequence in which he describes the sudden loss of the girlfriend and partner who was to accompany him in this travelogue, the film becomes a self-portrait about breakdowns and breakups in which the act of enunciation or portrayal of self ultimately stages the dispersal of that self. As he wanders through a graveyard at one point, his voice-over remarks, "It seems I'm filming my life in order to have a life to film—like some primitive organism that somehow nourishes itself by devouring itself, growing as it diminishes. . . . It's a little like looking into a mirror and trying to see what you look like when you're not really looking at your own reflection." Patricia Hampl neatly describes this flow of verbal commentary across the struggle of self-portraiture in *Sherman's March* as the "soundtrack of his thinking self" (71).

The challenge of the self-portrait essay film is thus to see oneself as what you look like when "you're not really looking at your own reflection," when the self becomes the same self as the most extreme Other, as the outside, as the world. In *Between Film and Screen*, Garrett Stewart investigates this "graven image as photogram" situated in various "traversed intervals" mainly on the edges of narrative cinema (152). He asks, however, questions that I consider at the center of the essayistic self-portrait, beginning with "Can the strictly *obscene* be made seeable?" (153):

How to see as the absentation of the subject's own sight? How to picture just this departure as the moment of the . . . conversion from subject to object? How, in certain cases, to link this as well to the related encorpsing of the scopic object—the visible thing rather than the ocular moment—in photographic arrest? And, in any case, after the scene of obliterated subjectivity has been played out, how to motivate the screen's continuing image as a survival of such death? If the moment is not fixated from without in a freeze frame, how to manage it as the eerily prolonged registration of an external world that—as the veritable proof of a self's absence from it—persists beyond human cognition? (154)

Variations on these questions haunt and test, I believe, the best essayistic self-portraits, yet few of these films dramatize that graven image between two shots so vibrantly or struggle with the resulting freedom of intellectual and aesthetic choice more visibly than does Derek Jarman's *Blue* (1993)

At the very beginning of Blue, *there is a verbal montage that puzzled me the first times I saw this film that is, in one sense, unseeable. After the opening invocation, the voice-over condenses a global angst into a surreally banal moment: "I am sitting with some friends in this café drinking coffee served by young refugees from Bosnia. . . . The war rages across newspapers and through the ruined streets of Sarajevo. Tania said 'Your clothes are on back to front and inside out.'" This conjunction of a world crisis and an odd incident of inside-out clothing now seems to me slyly to signal the fundamental project of* Blue: *to engage a global epidemic through the inside-out perspective of a blind body, an inter-view with one's own self that gradually disperses the self-portrait of that subject through the single blue that is the film.* Blue *is a version of that black leader of temporal disruption, found in essay films from Marker to Morris, transformed into a scintillating celebration of an ob-scene subjectivity within a blue prism of dying.*

    Jarman's film portrays a body ravaged by the AIDS virus, his own body. As part of the essayistic encounter, this "functional body" becomes defined by its activity and circulation within a particular public history, moving, interacting, evaluating, as well as layered by the particulars of everyday experience. In Jarman's ironic version of a "blue movie," the functional body becomes a body marked and scarred by sexual experience and for which the impossible expression of its own death becomes a meditation on and thinking about the macrocosms and microcosms of a dying world, where the "retina is a distant planet" and also "a pizza," encompassing and permeating that self.

Taking this angle on Jarman's film deemphasizes the poetic linguistics of the film and reframes it as an essayistic self-portrait in which an intensely personal self becomes its wordly Other. This perspective likewise moves at least this Jarman film away from the camp and baroque sensibilities of Andy Warhol, Kenneth Anger, and David Hockney found in his earlier films and looks closer at John Caughie's characterization of Jarman as "a traditionalist, consigned to the margins rather than choosing to work there," a traditionalist aligned significantly with the essayistic cinema of Humphrey Jennings and the Mass-Observation project with its "connection to surrealist observation" (229). As the self-observation of dying, Blue *becomes a self-portrait of the dying body turning from the inside of subjectivity to the outside of the world or, perhaps, infusing and restoring that dying inside with all that is outside.*

Throughout the tradition of the essayistic portrait, the outside has acted as the significant ground for depictions of a self, spreading and opening up subjectivity to an everyday historical world that infuses it. The geography of that everyday permeates Blue *not only as the spaces of hospital waiting rooms, cafes, and taxis but also as imaginings and thoughts that wander without borders through bucolic countrysides and wars in Bosnia. Across the body of* Blue, *simply crossing the street becomes an incident fraught with a catastrophic danger similar to that faced by refugees around the world. Early in the film the voice muses, "what needs so much news from abroad while all that concerns either life or death is all transacting and working within me" since "one can know the whole world without stirring abroad."[11] Here, the world stretches around the surface of the AIDS body, a doomed microcosm where viral and ethnic battles rage together. In a disturbingly prescient anticipation of a catastrophic world event, the voice of* Blue *dreams of an urban apocalypse whose cocooned victims never leave their bodies to see it: "As I slept a jet slammed into a tower block. The jet was almost empty but two hundred people were fried in their sleep. . . . The earth is dying and we do not notice it."*

Like the spaces of the world, history and time open up within the quotidian of the personal, spread thin through the lost moments of the everyday and approaching what Timothy Murray describes in Jarman's Caravaggio *as a "dead time" that doubles as "the eroticization of the moment" (125–128).[12] "There is a photo in the newspaper this morning of refugees leaving Bosnia,"* Blue *observes. "They look out of time. Peasant women with scarves and black dresses stepped from the pages of an older Europe." Within this history, the monotony of the everyday times the inevitability of death according to clinical procedures that keep the body barely functioning: "The drip ticks out the seconds, the source of a stream along which the minutes flow, to join the river of hours, the sea of years and the timeless ocean." This subject ticks slowly into a passivity and boredom in which both private and public history remain suspended in the interstice between then and later, a passivity and boredom that contain all the intellectual potential of just "waiting," that powerfully charged experience at the very center of this and many other essay films.*

All this work and movement of course multiplies and vibrates through and across the single image of blue.[13] *Temporally, nothing could better suggest potential passivity, boredom, and anticipation than the single blue image of the film, an image that transforms those memento mori of cinematic edits into a now-intransient and constant glow, waiting to be filled. Rejecting the use of celluloid that would stress its inevitable patina, Jarman chooses a blue "akin to the electronic video field, unadulterated by the human hand and sheer in the way only a pixel can attain" (O'Pray 206). Spatially, this "blue transcends the solemn geography of human limits" and provides, most famously, an inverted remedy for "the pandemonium of images" that, for Jarman, threatens thoughts of the world today. [fig. 3.10]*

Escaping the tyranny of the image and transforming the graven image of the freeze-frame, this blue space of subjectivity dissolves and disperses the self through a sort of pure potential and freedom associated with a single color field: "These facts, detached from cause, trapped the Blue Eye Boy in a system of unreality. For accustomed to believing in image, an absolute value, his world had forgotten the command of essence: Thou Shalt Not Create Unto Thyself Any Graven Image, although you know the task is to fill the empty page." "From the bottom of your heart, pray to be released from the image," he intones, so that he and "all these

FIGURE 3.10   Here presented in grayscale, an electronic field unadulterated by the human (*Blue*)

blurred facts that deceive dissolve in his last breath."[14] As Peter Wollen *remarks, this is an "after-image" of self that, as resonating potential demanding to be filled, "seeks . . . to restore monochrome to life, to history and meaning." Within the electronic field of blue, the film becomes "a critique of the very idea of purity," embracing "the clutter of life rather than the purity of monochrome." As such "it reaches far beyond minimalism or colour field, into the realms of poetry, symbolic discourse and, yes, politics" ("Blue" 130, 132, 133).*

Against this fixating and scintillating blue in which time and place are turned inside out, the drama and argument of the film plays out as an interweaving of voice, language, and sound. There are several registers of sound in the film: the musical compositions of Simon Fisher Turner, the environmental noises of daily events, and the many "voices-over" (of Jarman's own voice and those of Nigel Terry, John Quentin, and Tilda Swinton) that mingle and merge as mobile fragments of the texts of the film. While the audiolinguistic politics of Jarman's preceding film Wittgenstein *(1993) anticipates this emphasis on audio representations, here its radical use makes* Blue *one of the most unusual and powerful examples of essayistic self-portraiture in the cinema today, highlighting and abstracting the audio expressivity of the world as layered resonances that gradually dissipate into and replenish a space of blue potential.*

This uncentered mobility of sounds and voices exploits what exactly is most potentially radical in essayistic expression in cinema. According to Michel Chion, "the [cinematic] voice is there to be forgotten in its materiality" (1), and hearing that voice on the screen necessarily becomes "omnidirectional" (17). Associating that voice with a sexual stage that precedes visual differentiation, Chion argues for what he calls the "acousmatic presence" in the cinema (18–19) as a much more dynamic and powerful concept than the terms off-screen voice *or* voice-over *have usually allowed. This voice is an inside-out presence: "It's as if the voice were wandering along the surface,* at once outside and inside, *seeking a place to settle. Especially when a film hasn't shown what body this voice normally inhabits" (23). Defined by potential powers of ubiquity, panopticism, omniscience, and omnipotence, Chion's acousmetric voice "brings disequilibrium and tension." Inviting "the spectator to go see," the voice becomes an "invitation to the loss of the self, to desire and fascination" (24).*

For Chion, these powers of cinematic voice remain usually anchored, framed, or contained by the traditional conventions of spectacle and narrative. In Ophuls's Le Plaisir *(1952), Welles's* The Magnificent Ambersons *(1942), or Duras's* L'homme atlantique *(1981), the potential of the inside-out voice may be tapped, but, not incidentally I believe, it appears only through the black leader or ellipsis that places and carries that voice against the light of narrative spectacles.*

Through Jarman's expansive blue, however, the voice ascends to all its capacities to transform bodies and borders precisely by refusing to define itself in relation to a spectacle or narrative of bodies and borders, shifting through the numerous enunciating voices on the soundtrack and between the pronouns I and you of this moving subject.

In this blue body of a world turned inside out, where presence is spread like a vocal skin around the world, emerges a kind of thinking. A self-portrait of the geopolitics of a dying body, this radically blue image is far more than aesthetic bravura or a poetic analogue for a blindness brought on by AIDS, and the thought process here is more than an angry lament that echoes through the refrain of names of dead friends. At the center of Blue is, rather, an intensely calculated confrontation with the problem of representing AIDS in the world, a problem that haunts what Simon Watney has called those "spectacles of AIDS" like Jonathan Demme's Philadelphia (1993) and other grand cultural efforts to magnificently visualize this global tragedy of bodies. In Blue, says its voice, "we have to live with AIDS while they spread the quilt for the moths of Ithaca across the wine dark seas." What these spectacles often have in common is an attempt to dramatize the AIDS crisis as a grand worldly close-up and, in that image, to recuperate the crisis of the individual into a larger social, communal, or global family that would anchor, legitimize, and make meaningful that subjective loss.[15]

Blue, however, takes the opposite tack, and, like most ambitious essays, I believe, works not to valorize and redeem the politics of personal expression but to dissipate and release that expression as a politics of intellectual drifting and mobile reflection, in which subjectivity moves outside the functional body and a global crisis of loss is rescued in an extended moment of personal reflection and thought on the self as quintessentially Other, as dying.

So permeated by the flow of language, Blue creates the voice of blindness as a rescue and renewal of the geopolitics of the body. In Adorno's celebrated defense of the essay, there is a passage seemingly made for Blue: "The essay is concerned with what is blind in its objects," Adorno writes. "It wants to use concepts to pry open the aspects that cannot be accommodated by concepts, the aspect that reveals, through the contradictions in which concepts become entangled, that the net of their objectivity is merely subjective arrangement. It wants to polarize the opaque element and release the latent forces in it" (23). Grudgingly acknowledging that "awareness is heightened" by those global spectacles of AIDS, the voice of Blue still bemoans "a sense of reality drowned in [their] theatre" which it characterizes as "thinking blind, becoming blind." Instead, Jarman's essay works to pry open all that theatrical objectivity of a body dying of AIDS to release all the sounds and noises of its subjective arrangement, which is "thinking blue, seeing clear." If, for

Jarman, "Hell on Earth is a waiting room," full of dying, nameless identities, that waiting room is also an inexorably public place where one can do little but think, reflect, and recognize. Blue *becomes a cinematic waiting room and an endlessly blue leader where essayistic thinking becomes the recognition of continually expanding and echoing insight. Or, in bell hooks's words,* Blue *asks us to transgress bodily and all other geographies, to realize that implicit triumph when "death usurps the power of identity" and so to recognize that "we are always more than our pain."*

4

To Be Elsewhere: Cinematic Excursions as Essayistic Travel

SINCE THE ESSAYISTIC subject is a self continually in the process of investigating and transforming itself, one of the experiential encounters that most generally test and reshape that subject are, naturally and culturally, the spaces of the world. "Whatever I may be, I want to be elsewhere than on paper" Montaigne proclaims (596), and since then essayists have explored that elsewhere across new and familiar lands, traveling natural and unnatural geographies and temporarily inhabiting small and large places. Through this process of being elsewhere, that self becomes another and a different self, and the travel essay in particular has been a notable literary and cinematic practice that has discovered complex ideological and psychological significance through the journey, the walk, or the exploration. From Samuel Johnson's ramblings through London and Henry James's Italian journeys across art and culture, the travel essay has redefined self as a subject released and transformed through space. In his 1822 essay "On Going on a Journey," William Hazlitt announces his travels across the countryside as a way "to lose our importunate, tormenting, ever lasting personal identity in nature . . . and begin to be objects of curiosity and wonder even to ourselves" (77), and essayists from Montaigne to Bruce Chatwin have consistently explored different experiential spaces of the world where that self literally comes out of itself. Two centuries after Montaigne, Trinh asks: "Why travel, I would say, if not to be in touch with the ordinary in non-ordinary ways; to feel and think ordinarily while experiencing what can later become the extra-ordinary in an ordinary frame" (*Subtitles* 195).

Essayistic explorations of space have examined exotic lands and local neighborhoods, moved across distant jungles, wandered the crowded streets of cities, and traveled around small villages and countries across the globe. If Marker's *Letter from Siberia* can be considered one of the first cinematic travel essays and his *Sunless* one of the most ambitious and complex journeys around the world, a multitude of many other essay films have emphasized travel and space as a central motif around which complex ideas and reflections have been put in play. Bunuel's 1933 *Land without Bread* is one of the most remarkable precursors of this version of the essay, a bitingly satiric travelogue through a desperately impoverished remote region of Spain. Godard's essay films regularly incorporate this particular perspective and field, whether ruminating on neocolonialism in *Letter to Jane* (1972) or meditatively mapping the war-torn landscape of Sarajevo in *Notre Musique* (2004). The subject of Helke Sander's *The All Round Reduced Personality—Redupers* (1978) searches Berlin to find herself and to rediscover the then-divided city where she lives; Trinh's *Naked Spaces: Living Is Round* (1985) visits villages of Western Africa to undo and redo what she can and cannot know about herself and the villagers; and Anson Hoi Shan Mak's *One Way Street on a Turntable* (2006) works to locate a self in Hong Kong between movement and "rootedness" permeated by reflections on the work of Walter Benjamin. From Wenders's reflection on the city of filmmaker Yasujiro Ozu's eyes in *Tokyo-Ga* (1985) to Thom Andersen's observations on a city that disappears into its films in *Los Angeles Plays Itself* (2003), cinematic travel essays have experienced different sizes and kinds of space as the provinces of thought.[1]

If essay films continually overlap and merge their different registers and modes, variations like the travel essay highlight and emphasize their own particular experiential encounters. Whereas portrait essays turn images and sounds of self inside out and diary essays time that self according to different chronologies and daily rhythms, the travel essay discovers another self in the process of thinking through new or old environments and thinking of self as a different environment. They commonly represent subjective experience as epistolary, journalistic, and conversational and so allow subjectivity to play out its transformations in letters to home and elsewhere or in conversations with traveling companions or newly discovered strangers, who can be, in both cases, different and transformative interlocutors. If diaristic essays inhabit the changing time zones of the "everyday," travel essays move through different, new, or well-known environments to create essays in which the experience of space redefines a self within a constantly shifting "elsewhere." In the essayistic struggle to know, inhabit, and communicate spaces, the traditionally assured epistolary voice of a traveler becomes a drifting and dislocated voice—an absent subject in foreign lands, an alien at home, a mind exiled from nature—exploring interior and exterior geographies of everyday life through, for instance, the global anonymity of an urbanscape, the cultural flux of touristic mobility, or the ecstatic violence of the natural world.

Chantal Akerman's News from Home *(1977) is a strict, minimalist view of New York City enacted across the letters of a woman to her mother and read by the mother's voice-over in Belgium. More an essayistic travelogue than a diary, it is one of numerous essay films made by women directors that locate their voice and shifting identities in the dense public life of a city; in this case, it is a woman's visual encounter (and oblique verbal encounter) with New York City. What is so immediately striking and unsettling about* News from Home *is the insistent spatial displacement of the recipient of letters from home through a series of statically framed shots of the streets, while sounds of traffic, subways, and other ambient noises resonate through the intimate communications of the letters. Despite the unmistakably structural look of the imagistic repetitions and visual symmetries,* News from Home *is not, I believe, best understood within the confines of the avant-garde tradition of structural cinema but rather as an essay about the concomitant assertion and dispersal of a subjectivity through the public spaces of travel, places subjectively encountered as dramatically elsewhere.*

Giuliana Bruno rightly describes the wandering identity in Akerman's film as an "erotic nomadism" across a "transitional geography" that captures "the in-between spaces of everyday life" (103). An essential dynamic in the travel essay becomes distilled here, between home and elsewhere, but this elsewhere exists neither within the cultural signposts of a touristic landscape marked by famous places and architectural icons nor within the organic mysteries of a natural world of beautiful and sublime sights. In News from Home, *rather, the somewhat blank incidentals of an everyday place permeate the film as an inversion of a touristic gaze that tends to appropriate spaces and places as imagistic possessions like postcards. The opening shots of the film, for example, present an alleyway symmetrically framed by two buildings, while a car passes at the back end of the alleyway in the background of the stationary frame; a second car then turns, hesitates, and drives into the alley toward the camera before it passes out of frame, revealing three figures now appearing in the background of the shot and walking toward the camera. [fig. 4.1] Along with the relatively anonymous and empty geography of the scene, the rigidity of the frame and length of the shot seem to insist on a meaning or the potential revelation of a meaningful action that never arrives, the viewer almost taunted by the automobile whose hesitant decision to enter the alley ultimately provides no more significance than the three individuals who then occupy that space. Akerman and her cinematic point of view clearly do not appear in the*

FIGURE 4.1 An opening shot seems to insist on a meaning or the potential revelation of a meaningful action that never arrives (*News from Home*)

personae and embodiments created by other essayists. Instead, the rigorous com-positions become the strange but unmistakable articulations of that essayistic sub-ject as an absence within the insistence of the eye of the camera.

    Throughout the film, glimpses and signs of mobility suggest, then frustrate, the possibility of acting in this space, the experiential possibility to make some-thing happen, the possibility of inhabiting this foreign urban space as home away from home. Cars that move alternately left to right and right to left across the frame are a recurrent sign of a potential subjectivity encased in a machine, never however to reveal or humanize that agency. Crowds of people walk toward a cam-era in a subway tunnel, where the hum of noises makes the voice-over almost inau-dible, a thick audio texture that melds with the street noise. Pans often substitute for immobile frames, and in this particular subway sequence, a 360-degree pan occurs in the concourse, centering and then dispersing the singular point of view. At one point, a pan follows a car attendant crossing a lot and then loses him in a long shot as he vanishes down a street to the river. A traveling shot (from a car window) moves from downtown to uptown New York, along the west side of the city, stopping occasionally, while passing buildings, storefronts, cars, individuals, and small groups of people. The stop-and-starting movement of the image creates a city that appears only fragilely held together by a shot that has no destination in a city that, in this film, is no destination.

    This displaced subjectivity is also configured through the displaced maternal voice that Akerman performs as a voice-over reading of her mother's letters, a verbal performance that enacts an alternate point of view of herself. This alternative view of a self, dispersed through images of the city, attests not to a bond that could recover the daughter within a lost home but rather to the absolute elsewhere of that daughter displaced in a foreign place. Indeed, this displacement becomes even more pronounced in the almost desperate and urgent refrains asking the invisible daughter to "write more" and "when are you coming home?", the telling concern that "I wasn't sure of the address," and the observation about a party in Belgium where "everyone was there except you." Often nearly drowned out by the street noise in the image, the mother speaks of the family business at the shop, weddings, personal relationships, vacations, her boredom, an illness—in short, the "nothing special happening" of an everyday that is situated in the familiar. There may be news from home, but that news seems constantly to bemoan that a daughter is missing, and that there is little news returning: "My dearest little girl, I'm very surprised not to have had any news from you. . . . Don't leave me without news. . . . Don't forget us. Write." In this one-way dialogue between mother and daughter, between Belgium and New York, between spatial movement and stasis, the two figures tend to counterpoint each other. If "a sense of impaired communication subtends verbal exchange in all Akerman's work," that impairment creates, in Ivone Margulies precise reading, a "skewed self-presentation" in which what I would call the essayistic subject here "ventriloquizes her mother" to become mainly "a voided echo" (Nothing Happens 150–151).[2]

News from Home is a radical characterization of the outing of interior space of a subject, relayed through a maternal voice at home, as it aggressively troubles a spatial route through the exteriorized spaces of New York. To see, to read, to hear oneself in this space becomes a disappearing act. In the crowded interior of a subway car encased by the steady roar of its movement, there is no interaction or conversation with stationary passengers. At one point, a man seems pressured by the steady stare of the camera, moves down the car, and vanishes into the background of the next car. On a subway platform, an usually flat shot at a perpendicular angle to the platform shows planes of crowds on different platforms, crossing from one side of the image to the other, before trains arrive, between the camera and the platform, and visually "wipes out" the human figures. Through this long sequence, trains come and go like dense moving surfaces (sometimes covered with graffiti) that erase the illusion of a human depth. [fig. 4.2]

Essayistic experience in News from Home thus becomes synonymous with a kind of disembodiment: an absence within the materiality of the image and the maternity of the everyday. While radical contours of time and duration permeate the film, the geographies of space and distance become its center, not as a location but as a place of dissolution whose pull becomes both an emotional and an intellectual experience of that place. A series of stationary traveling shots conclude the film as ostensibly a return home but, rather more fundamentally, I believe, as a description of a self as a continually departing and disappearing subject: one, now

FIGURE 4.2   The illegible planes of subway platforms (*News from Home*)

looking west, from elevated subway car; another from the moving rear window of
a car; and finally a traveling shot from a ship leaving the harbor, gradually revealing
for the first time a New York skyline that is the familiar and knowable place that
the subject normally lives and moves through in guidebooks. [fig. 4.3] As that sky-
line disappears, within an increasingly extreme long shot, in a take that lasts more
than ten minutes, the subject of this essay may be going home, but only as a self
that has productively disappeared into that disappearing place of New York.

Traditionally, cinematic space has described a wide variety of representational
geographies ranging across narrative organizations, experimental explorations,
and documentary representations. With the "phantom rides" of the 1890s, film
spectators experienced virtual movements and scenic changes as if passengers on
trains, ships, and automobiles, early figures who would echo through the phantom
ride that concludes *News from Home*. As these first travelogues developed and
expanded their scope, cinematic travel aligned with both exploration and conquest, as images of the world unfolding across the moving gaze of the viewer,
whose proximity to new worlds remained comfortably virtual. With early cinema
and much of its legacy, these virtual voyages gravitated toward ethnographic or
explorative films and documentaries that valorized travel through and to real
lands where the subject experiences the geographically strange, mysterious,
threatening, and physically rattling, safely protected and distanced, however,
within an increasingly sophisticated ride. If Lyman Howe's *Hale's Tours and Scenes*
of the World (1904–1909) offered cinematic travelers spectacular and safe views of
Niagara Falls, China, and even urban centers, this heritage remained consistently
alive throughout the twentieth century. These early travelogues paved the way for

FIGURE 4.3 The disappearing subject of New York City (*News from Home*)

contemporary documentaries, such as *Winged Migration* (2001) or *March of the Penguins* (2005), to elaborate, technologically and visually, a similar experience of the world as a virtual ride through exotic and breathtaking territories, still capable of being visually and spatially orchestrated as the coherently omnipotent perspective of a cinematic traveler.[3]

Classical narrative cinema has, to some extent, simply codified these spatial experiences as temporal patterns determined by a protagonist guide who acts as the displaced surrogate for the spectator traveler. These films commonly organize a spatial play that evolves around interiors and exteriors in a narrative that begins as or soon occupies a kind of spatial exile (or "elsewhere") and then advances toward (or back toward) a domestic interior as home (or a lost but not forgotten image). Even in disparate film practices, classical narrative may be said to share or at least to travel similar paths between a real or metaphoric elsewhere and a longed-for home. For instance, Buster Keaton's *The General* (1927) follows Johnnie Gray (Keaton) into enemy territory, across a comically violent Civil War landscape, in his quest eventually to claim a domestic place and partner. The film *2001: A Space Odyssey* (1968) ironizes spatial and space travel across the history of humans and the universe only to return its voyager to an embryonic womb floating in outer space. *Into the Wild* (2007) follows the existential escape of a young man who flees a stuffy home for the wilderness; in the end, he dies in a rusting bus, the wrecked image of a return trip to a home tragically lost and nowhere to be found.

Through the course of the twentieth century, these cinematic travels have moved across the larger spaces of modernity as expanding global territories that, in turn, have more sharply demarcated local geographies. Shifting cultural and national boundaries and the continual crossings of those boundaries are some of the most common contemporary metaphors for how these changing spatial geographies have also created the ground for new subjectivities. Since the emergence of twentieth-century modernity and its climactic crisis in the 1940s, the disruption of traditional spatial organizations has occurred even on the more local levels of cityscapes and architectural arrangements. In the mid-1930s, Benjamin identifies the traditional segregation of locations and anticipates the potential explosion of it specifically and appropriately through the power of the movies: "Our bars and city streets, our offices and furnished rooms, our railroad stations and our factories seemed to close relentlessly around us. Then came film and exploded around this prison-world with the dynamite of the split second, so that now we can set off calmly on journeys of adventure among its far-flung debris" ("The Work of Art" 265). Only a few years after these remarks, social and cultural spaces would explode in far more literal and concrete ways through the concussions and repercussions of World War II, resulting in social and architectural fragmentations and mobilities of a new order. What I call the essayistic experience of modern space emerges from these prewar and postwar conditions as a self that must often travel directionless paths in search of homes that no longer exist and through landscapes strewn with colonial and other historical wreckage. Postwar road warriors, narcissistic taxi drivers, and gendered flaneurs consumed by material cultures now frequently become essayistic travelers through cities emptied of human interaction, through postmodern suburbs adrift in simulacra, and across natural worlds teeming with unrecognizable violence.

One way to describe and consider the various old and new ways that travel maps new spaces and subjects, as they become assimilated into film practices, is to distinguish between travelogues, journeys, and excursions. Providing a base line for this distinction, Bruzzi has fine-tuned the difference between travelogues and journey films this way: Travelogues tend not to be "structured around an argument or indeed around a desire to impose narrative cohesion" and so become "simply a chronicle of events linked by location, personality or theme" with "little sense that its participants have progressed in anything other than a physical way" (83, 84). On the other hand, journey films, at least those associated with cinema vérité and direct cinema (such as the 1969 *Salesman*), aim "to give coherence and logic to the potentially incoherent and illogical material" presented in these films (82). More recent journey films—which for Bruzzi include the documentaries *Hoop Dreams* (1994) and *Shoah* (1985), as well as films I would designate as essay films, Ross McElwee's *Sherman's March* and Patrick Keiller's *London* (1994)—"challenge these notions of certainty, predictability, and transparency" and in their shared distrust of "predetermine logic" "pursue narratives that are only superficially closed by their concluding images and words and are more preoccupied with charting moments of encounter and examining the act of journeying rather than of reaching a fixed destination" (82, 83). For my argument, I add a third category, excursion films, to designate more precisely the practices of essay films, defined by an organization less coherent than the serial form of travelogues and without even the shaky stability of the "narrators" and coherent travelers of recent journey films. With the excursive essay film, even the individual subject that motivates journey films is or becomes incomplete and unstructured, in a way suggested by the idea of the excursus as a rambling digression whose tour often appears more about the movement in space rather than a goal (which frequently becomes moot). An excursion as a form of travel implies an outing that returns to a starting point, and the essayistic excursion, like the structure of *News from Home* and like the excursive essay itself, maps that incomplete journey in a way that also describes or suggests how the excursion has fundamentally altered and destabilized the traveling subject.

Since the eighteenth-century itinerant conversations of Samuel Johnson and James Boswell through Scotland and the Hebrides, travels, journeys, and excursions have typically been recorded and documented as epistolary dialogues or simply as dialogues that imply an epistolary address, becoming, in Naficy's discussion of an "accented cinema," displacements of "the desire to be with an other and to re-imagine an elsewhere and other times" (101).[4] Throughout the twentieth century, travel films have re-created those epistolary expressions as voice-overs that document and counterpoint visual travels; today, these conversations regularly extend into the cyberspace of the Internet and electronic forums for travelogues. These various epistolary travels overcome the distances of space through a written script or the scripted voice as a way to make space habitable and knowable to a traveling subject—to bring other spaces home as a microcosmic verbalized social space harmonized through the implicit dialogue of interlocutors.

In the essayistic excursion, however, those conversations become disjointed and troubled through the spaces they aim to bridge and domesticate, creating gaps and ellipses in the implicit or explicit conversations of the epistolary and so tending to exclude its subjects from any habitation or subjective home. As in Marker's *Sunless* or Akerman's *News from Home*, the correspondents often appear to drift suspended in space within a continual dislocated and self-reflexive dialogue in which that epistolary conversation becomes a dramatically fragile form of social space. Perhaps the most renowned and important essay film of the twentieth century, *Sunless* is a global travelogue that is "not a search for contrasts but journey to the two extreme poles of survival," dramatically moving through Japan, Iceland, Guinea-Bissau, and the Cape Verde Islands; the voice-over that wanders these radically different cultures is the destabilized and unidentified voice of a woman who reads—and sometimes subtly comments on—letters sent home to Europe by a fictional Sandor Krasna, who may be a cameraperson, the filmmaker himself, or simply a traveler.[5] A more concise example of this excursively epistolary subject is the beginning of Helke Sander's *The All Round Reduced Personality*. After the sound-track broadcasts the voices of the American Armed Forces Network in Berlin, Sander as Edna Chiemnyjewski, another essayistic photographer enmeshed in the movement of the film, translates for the German postman a U.S. post office message on the envelope of a letter she receives: The message notes that (in 1977) Berlin does not exist in either East or West Germany. "Maybe we don't even exist," she remarks. Or, "maybe we're just being created," he retorts.

In Patrick Keiller's Robinson in Space *(1997), an anonymous companion accompanies the eponymous Robinson and acts as his epistolary spokesperson, describing and commenting on their conversations, experiences, and thoughts, as the two travelers depart London and embark on seven excursions to investigate the various sites, suburbs, and smaller cities throughout contemporary England. Especially alert to the odd and ironic contiguities revealed on their trip, they visit industrial parks, shipyards, and shopping malls as they assemble a running travelogue punctuated with literary quotations and philosophical observations. Before even leaving London, they see the Abbey School where Jane Austen was educated and which, as an early example of the disjunctive spaces of the film, happens to be next to the Reading Jail that imprisoned Oscar Wilde. Their journey then proceeds down the Thames Path to Cliveden House, toward Oxford and William Kent's Temple of British Worthies; two weeks later, they venture through the West Midlands to Derby and then onward to Birmingham and the Hiatt Works (an iron manufacturer). Their fifth excursion heads to Manchester, Halifax, and Yorkshire; later to the ports of Teeside; and finally to the Lake District and Blackpool—before the contract they received to record their journey is inexplicably terminated by the mysterious advertising agency that hired them. Less a travelogue or journey and more, to use a recurrent phrase in the film, a pilgrimage, the film is also what Keiller describes as a research project about external and internal mobility in England and the "arguably unattainable idea of dwelling" there ("The Future of Landscape"). The ultimate failure of the film to locate spatial homogeneities or even that idea of a dwelling, along with the gradual collapse and loss of Robinson himself, produces the triumph of an odd excursion that, in the end, is unable to return home and that eventually even loses sight of its primary traveler.*

Robinson in Space *is a sequel or companion piece to Keiller's earlier* London *(1994), in which the same two travelers wandered through different neighborhoods*

*in search of the identity of that urban center. Quickly signaling its literary heritage
early in this first film, there is a shot of a small billboard that reads "Welcome to the
Montaigne School of English." Noting that "it is now generally agreed that Montaigne lived for a time in London," Robinson and his companion observe that he
was "the first of a number of French writers who found themselves exiled here,"
and that even today London appears "full of interesting people most of whom, like
Robinson, would prefer to be elsewhere." [fig. 4.4] Indeed, Robinson himself
already recognizes that the essence of an essayistic life is in the ability "to get outside oneself, to see oneself as if outside." Like a later intertitle quotation from
Baudelaire, Robinson travels to be "anywhere out of the world," and in the London
of London, he decides he has discovered "the first metropolis to disappear."*[6]

In *Robinson in Space, the same two travelers embark on a trip to discover
the spaces of England as a way to explore ideas about production, reproduction,
and modernity. If* London *can be described as an obituary for urban life,* Robinson in Space *turns its explorations from the spaces of urban modernity to the
outlying regions and suburbs of London since, as Robinson wistfully recognizes in
that first film, "if we were to find modernity anywhere it would be in the suburbs."
That an ad agency commissions this excursion establishes the always metaphorically canted framework of this version of a journey as a comic satire about the
consumer packaging of space, as an excursion looking for saleable images of a
world that no longer exists.*

Inspired from the start by Daniel Defoe's Tour Through the Whole Island of
Great Britain *(1724–1726), these travelers continually discover signs of Defoe and
his novel* Robinson Crusoe *(homes where the novel was written, for example) as
wry markers of a longed-for geographical order and modern ideal. Yet, whereas
Defoe's journey aimed to be a comprehensive map of a preindustrialized England*

FIGURE 4.4   Montaigne in London, preferring to be elsewhere (*London*)

(also written, according to Robinson, as a way to gather political intelligence for Queen Anne's government), Robinson's excursion regularly drifts off course through a land that seems on the verge of vanishing into an undifferentiated space that reveals only "the record of sin" found in the beautiful countryside and the recognition that, since Defoe's time, the power of the regency has been replaced by a "particularly English kind of capitalism." This excursive essay accordingly appears occasionally like a twisted heritage film in which the cultural auras of places become replaced by technological and economic simulacra. Before a medium-long shot of a grand estate, the commentator observes early in the film: "We know of six Jane Austen film or television adaptations under way. All involving country houses mostly in the west of England." At the conclusion, a shot of a British Telecom phone card lying on the ground promotes "Welsh Heritage" with the image of Hadrian's Wall across an open landscape.

Here, the recurrent tension between a natural world and its reshaping by industrial technologies and economics spreads itself across a variety of regions as a collage of places and spaces that jar and collide with each other, a landscape of disjunctive regions and layers where everyday consumer culture surrounds grand markers of economic and cultural triumph. A dizzying variety of historical and social place markers are juxtaposed: the house where Mary Shelley edited her husband's "Revolt of Islam" and where she prepared Frankenstein *for publication; nearby, the British headquarters for Volvo and "Charter Institute for Marketing"; and a pub where Defoe "was supposed to have met the real Robinson Crusoe" by a factory manufacturing "Bendy Toys," itself near the Heathrow airport ("all the more unusual since most toys are made in China"). [fig. 4.5] The home where Defoe*

FIGURE 4.5 At a Bristol pub, where Defoe was supposed to have met the real Robinson Crusoe (*Robinson in Space*)

once lived becomes the gateway to the town of Ipswich, "still a considerable port probably even more so than in Defoe's time" but now most important as a container dock for a Hong Kong company that, in a typical global irony, owns the Orange telecommunication network. Indeed, transnational economics continually remake this world where "Britain's role as the fifth largest trading nation is essential for its economic well-being"; where cultural centers are found in places like "Merryhill," the site of the largest shopping center in Europe; and where the British Westland Group receives a 2.5-billion-pound contract to build American attack helicopters. Colliding and overlapping histories of literature, art, science, technology, popular culture, and especially economics thus remap this contemporary landscape not as teleological journey but as an excursion whose directions and geographies sequentially and simultaneously displace and dislocate each other— and ultimately seem to send Robinson himself into a state of total abjection and collapse.

Traveling this space looks, consequently, increasingly as if the travelers are moving through a concrete and visible (rather than virtual) Internet network of technological economies. Ships and ports, highways and bridges, communication companies, telephone booths, and Internet encounters describe pervasively possible connections and relays between the places and locations. [fig. 4.6] They lead the two travelers over and under layers of cultural and industrial pathways, emblematically and hilariously summarized at one point in a long shot of a Christopher Wren house cut with a medium shot of a small tunnel that allows toads to travel safely underneath the roadway.

An insistent politics and economics of global space spread and dissipate natural, cultural, and technological spaces of this England into a prehistoric outer space

FIGURE 4.6 Highways and other networks of technological economies (*Robinson in Space*)

that, for the two travelers, may represent, paradoxically, either a utopian or a dystopian geography. Early in the film, a pub named "The World's End" displays a sign showing a ship falling off the edge of the world into an apocalyptic other place, which later in the film blends into a technological and science fiction space. Toward Henley, they come "across a group of satellite dishes at a location we were asked not to name"; as their travel through England proceeds, the two men discover gigantic alien figures drawn on a hillside; later, they find the site of a Martian landing featured in an H. G. Wells novel. [fig. 4.7] At several stops, disciples of Buckminster Fuller ("Buckminsterfullerines," who, according to Robinson, arrived on earth in meteorites) remind the travelers that this technological future could be either the visionary new world of Fuller's spaceship earth or, more ominously, the dangerously dark tomorrow signaled by landmarks such as a U.S. military installation at Stowe, a U.S. Intelligence Center farther down their road, an Irish sea swimming with nuclear submarines, and stunning natural landscapes dotted with nuclear power plants. In an essay by the geographer Doreen Massey, the companions read that "amid the Ridley Scott visions of world cities, the writing about skyscraper fortresses, Baudrillard visions of hyper-space, most people still live in places like Harleston or West Bromich," everyday places on the edge of survival, visualized in a shot of a bland corrugated factory front across the road from "a chemical manufacturing plant called Robinson Brothers." Between the utopia of an imagined home and homeland and the dystopia at the end of this world, the travelers wander a middle earth described for them in an early intertitle from Henri Lefebreve's writing: "The space which contains the realized preconditions of another life is the same one that prohibits what those preconditions make possible."

FIGURE 4.7 Satellite dishes and alien drawings transform an English countryside into outer space (*Robinson in Space*)

If *Defoe's* Robinson Crusoe *narrates the discovery of the redemptive discourse of the personal, on an alien island made into a home, the travelers in* Robinson in Space *speak a language of quotations that seem only to make their home of England an increasingly alien and foreign industrial site. With an essayistic shuffling of expression similar to the displaced dialogue heard in* News from Home, *the voice-over monologue in* Robinson in Space *implies a running conversation between traveling companions meant to map distant spaces and places, but the linguistic locations of these selves become largely a rambling series of chatty comments and exchanges of one man quoting another man, who often relies on quite dissimilar texts through which to express himself. Essayistic expression here resembles a conversation in a foreign language in which the interlocutors patch together quotations as a form of descriptive communication, which becomes a kaleidoscope of inherited ideas, intellectual reflections, and personal thoughts that test and probe each new place as ways of understanding. If the consistently stationary camera of* News from Home *reoccurs here, it now creates images that appear like postcards of an alien world catalogued through a string of comments that make those images incrementally more jarring and unfamiliar, like advertisements of a futuristic world built on the edges of a disappearing past.*

Fittingly, the two companions are just two of the many nonconformist outsiders that populate their travels: from Adam Ant (once a student at an art school where Robinson taught) to Oscar Wilde (who apparently enjoyed Oxford despite an atmosphere of a "stifled sexuality") and Alan Turing (who cracked the Nazi "enigma codes" in 1942 only later to commit suicide after a public denouncement as a homosexual). Like these other outsiders, Robinson and his spokesman appear distantly removed from the places of their excursions as their conversations and commentaries enact a rhetoric of alienation from and perplexity about the very scenes they visit, a rather bewildered sense of the possibility of expressing ideas about those scenes, and finally, an understated but increasing desire to be elsewhere than where they are.

In the end, Robinson's travels lead him and his companion, almost as with conventional journeys, back to his hometown, Blackpool, a town that "stands between us and revolution." They return to a childhood town convinced it "holds the key to his utopia" but instead they find a rather unaccommodating and distant place, seen in long shots of the turbulent seacoast waves, large and visually dominant Ferris wheel, and the movement of faceless people and trolleys on streets of the town. About this time, "Robinson is beginning to act strangely," crashing a security gate and attempting to steal equipment from a fighter aircraft plant that makes the Saudi Arabian Tornadoes. In this final phase of his excursion, Robinson begins to fade away into the twilight zone that he has been traveling, into an oddly negative space in the future: "I cannot tell you where Robinson finally found his utopia," the companion remarks, for Robinson appears to have vanished into a waiting zone, waiting for change, for new ideas, for a true utopian discourse. In this unusually philosophical excursion, after all, the opportunity for ideas usually only takes place in places of waiting and departure. "Much of life for many people," Robinson reads earlier in the film, "even in the heart of the first world consists of waiting in a bus shelter with your shopping for a bus that never comes." Anticipating the conclusion of the film, Robinson disappears at that moment, when the bus finally arrives, for a sexual encounter with a stranger he contacted through the Internet.

Of the many philosophical or literary voices in *Robinson in Space*, Lefebvre's is one of the more prominent, providing a key sociological touchstone for the essayistic travels of the film. In *The Production of Space*, Lefebvre distinguishes "three moments of social space": "the perceived, the conceived, and the lived". The first is "spatial practice" (bedrooms, marketplaces, etc.); the second is "representations of space" (linear, geometric, etc.); and the third is "representational space (overlaying physical space and making symbolic use of its objects)" (39).[7] Together, these describe the spaces of experience as they are lived, conceptualized, and valued at the intersection of subjectivity and public life. If the first suggests the essayistic emphasis on the spatial practices of daily experience, the essayistic challenge to inhabit and actively understand that space according to the second and third arrangements indicates intellectual and subjective activities that map the drama of essayistic travel. *Robinson in Space* is an exceptionally mobile, ironic, and critical interlocking of these spaces as the travelers overlay lived experiences, their geographical representations, and the struggle to infuse them with shape, ideas, and value, a struggle that ultimately fails to cohere as a "dwelling" and leaves Robinson a drifting subject in both a figurative and a real outer space. Other essayistic excursions may arrange these moments of spatial practice in much different ratios of experience or, in some cases, dramatize the very incommensurability of certain travels and the ability to inhabit or coordinate their spatial dimensions.

In *The Practice of Everyday Life*, Michel de Certeau offers a parallel but alternative drama of subjectivity in space as a semantic and psychological model of "three distinct (but connected) functions of the relations between spatial and signifying practices." For him, subjectivity locates itself according to different ideas of space: Space can be experienced as different versions of "the *believable*, the *memorable*, and the *primitive*." These designate, respectively, "what 'authorizes' (or makes possible or credible) spatial appropriations, what is repeated in them (or is recalled in them) from a silent and withdrawn memory, and what is structured in them and continues to be signed by an in-fantile (*in-fans*) origin." As they work to organize "the topoi of a discourse" as a legend, a memory, or a dream, these mechanisms of emplacement ironically call attention to the fundamental resistance of space to be designated and inhabited and so "create in the place itself that erosion or nowhere that the law of the other carves out within it" (105).

Adapting de Certeau's model to travel as exploration and habitation to film, it is possible to see how narrative fiction films and conventional documentaries create and project, around the nowhere of that other place, the coherent spaces and journeys understood or colonized through a human agency or subjectivity that travels or inhabits them. Road movies, for instance, typically foreground the traveling subject as he or she flees memorial and legendary spaces to discover more primitive, "infantile," or dream landscapes, while documentaries often fold that determining subject into spaces and places they represent as the loci of legends and memories. Nature documentaries can thus stage space as the ground for the mysterious legends of nature itself, while city symphony films refigure the grids and alleyways of urban sites as the layered architectures of memories.

The excursive travels of the essayistic subject, however, significantly complicate those de Certeau's geographical orders precisely because of the individual's immediate or gradual inability to authorize, remember, or dream the spaces they travel. As a product of the spatial densities or excesses of their itineraries, essayistic travelers become, more often than not, transformed and undone as they struggle to stabilize themselves psychologically and linguistically in space, and this breakdown of agency is, as so graphically represented in the endless car wrecks of Godard's *Weekend* (1967), commonly signaled by the collapse of the vehicles that transport and move them as traveling subjects: Trains and subways run at speeds and in directions outside the traveler's control, automobiles veer off the road and frequently crash, boats disappear over horizons into hazy voids, and, most especially, bodies collapse as they walk themselves into the earth. If de Certeau associates the successful mapping of his experiential spaces with "walking in the city," the body of the walker in the excursive essay, as the vehicle of an intact subjectivity, tends to come undone or collapse and is no longer capable of mapping the world as a physical, semantic, or psychological dwelling. Under the physical, linguistic, and emotional stress of traveling through the experiential world, the walker as essayistic subject becomes a broken body overwhelmed by the space around him or her.

On these essayistic excursions, places and spaces then become empty and redundant streets, unsettled and unsettling frontiers, vacant and inhumane deserts, dense and impenetrable jungles, fragile and breakable surfaces, twisted and consuming mazes, and interstellar and alien voids. All of these create spatial puzzles that demand continual effort for the essayistic explorer to try to think through and out of these geographies, geographies that at the same time frustrate those efforts to map and locate a self in them. Essayistic excursions in space accordingly become subject to the mythical threat of the tower of Babel: a journey into the extremes of space, from the earth to the heavens, that, in its failed efforts to map itself as a human belief, a memory, or a dream, results in a cacophony of languages (or an impenetrable silence) unable to articulate the architecture of its own excursion. In this other place and lost body, however, the essayistic subject finds a spatial scaffolding on which to rethink itself.

The travels of Little Dieter Needs to Fly *(1997) is one of Werner Herzog's most complex excursive essays, following the journey of the child Dieter Dengler as he sets out from the ruins of Dresden overwhelmed and inspired by massive U.S. bombers that eventually launch him as a flyer into the space of the Vietnam war. In the end, his flight comes crashing to earth when, after being shot down in 1966, he escapes from a prison in Laos only to flee as a desperate walker through jungle mazes. In Herzog's film, Dieter theatrically reenacts his travel on foot, which he narrates and Herzog comments on in complimentary flat tones, so that the heroics and horror of this travelogue become a strangely pedestrian experience. He recounts how, during his escape, his and his companion Dwayne's bare feet were "cut to shreds" as they alternated the use of one sole of a tennis shoe. Eventually, these feet become barely recognizable "white stumps," covered with blood, mud, and leeches. In the final part of this recitation, Dieter sits stationary before the static and flat background of the landscape that had transformed him from a flyer into a walker. In an uncanny anticipation of* Grizzly Man *(2005), a meek bear becomes a mundane metaphor for the death that constantly stalks him and an "SOS" sign constructed from the debris of a parachute for the tattered speech that rescues him. Yet, even when rescued, his redemption becomes "just a mirage" compared to the visceral intensity of his escape, and the film concludes (before a funeral epilogue) with Dieter's visual ramble through a "heaven for pilots": a vast redundancy of grounded flights and planes, a recollection of the repeated airplane landings that open* Fata Morgana *(1971) and a stunning image of the inevitable grounding of vision and desire in its harsh encounters with the geography of the world.*[8] *Far from Keiller and Lefebvre's social spaces,* Little Dieter, *like Herzog's other essays, walks through geographies that recall and then fade like mirages of de Certeau's legendary places, memorial locations, and even the primitive wonderlands of nature.*

To associate Herzog's films with travelogues or, more specifically, excursive essays might seem reductive only if one does not recognize the experiential power of an essayistic encounter with the physical world and Herzog's distinctive and regular re-creation of its terms. Herzog toys even with the literary precedents of the essay in his 1978 Of Walking in Ice, *a somewhat off-center but still literary travel memoir, which transposes de Certeau's urban flaneur to a strangely natural world that increasingly seems a primitive dreamscape. Constructed from a journal kept from November 23 to December 14, 1974, this memoir describes Herzog's journey on foot, from Munich to Paris, as a quest to visit the dying Lotte Eisner in Paris, whom, according to Herzog's forward, "German cinema could not do without." In the quest to link the lost history of German cinema with its contemporary renaissance, this emphatically private literary account articulates many of the structures and terms that would be included in Herzog's most significant contributions to his essayistic travelogues within New German Cinema. Travel here occurs against a background of visual, audio, and physical surfaces that function more as spatial boundaries between self and world than do the borders of villages and countrysides he crosses as linear boundaries. Quickly, the putative directional quest gives way to a kind of excursive wandering through spaces that anticipate those future cinematic metaphors of an icy glacier, a dessert, a jungle, and most recently, a maze; and long before his anticlimactic meeting with Eisner in Paris, the intense loneliness of a spatial isolation begins to generate that central figure of the essayistic, "a dialogical rapport with myself" (66). From this rapport emerges a voice and language through which the world turns poetic, allegorical, other worldly—describing, for instance, "a forest turned into pillars of salt, a forest with its mouth open wide" (31)—and Herzog himself begins to wonder if he "is still looking human" (23). Rather than generating beliefs or memories, the experience of travel appears as an encounter with the world as a "Yawning Black Void" (44) that seems to eradicate self, consciousness, and most important, self-consciousness in a way that generates not knowledge of that world but a profoundly physical "knowledge coming from the soles" of his shoes (10). Here, the traveling subject begins to "possess the thoughts of animals" (15). Or, as he projects an image of himself on an acquaintance seen on the road, this road trip creates "thinking with such intensity that he metered his thoughts with vehement gestures, as if he were speaking" (26).*

Defining these experiences in Of Walking in Ice, *as well as Herzog's more cinematic travel essays, is one of the aphorisms from his 1999 "Minnesota Declaration": "Tourism is sin, and travel on foot [a] virtue," with tourism associated with cinema vérité filmmakers "who take pictures amid ancient ruins of facts." Following on its eighteenth-century beginnings, touristic travel becomes for Herzog travel through different versions of the picturesque where the traveler appropriates the world through images of it. Conversely, travel on foot means, literally, subjecting the traveler to the world as a way of losing oneself viscerally, emotionally, and intellectually in an experiential space and time that entrances, overtakes, disorients, and dissolves that traveler. Often approaching a state in which fatigue gives way to hallucinations, it implies a physical engagement with the world in which the movement of the body on the earth creates a kinetic movement of the mind, resulting in a consciousness not of the mind's appropriative powers but of its always physically diminutive place on the surfaces and edges of the world—as too small, too weak, too blind, too slow. Or, in Deleuze's words about Herzog's films, "The walker is defenceless because he is he who is beginning to be, and never finishes being small"* (Cinema 1 184–185).

For the most determined and conceptual travelers, "traveling on foot" thus generates that other defining principle of Herzog's essay films: the perception of an ecstatic truth ferociously differentiated especially from the "truth of accountants" practiced by cinema vérité. "There are deeper strata of truth in cinema," Herzog writes, "and there is such a thing as poetic, ecstatic truth. It is mysterious and elusive, and can be reached only through fabrication and imagination and stylization" ("Minnesota Manifesto"). If traveling on foot creates an extraordinary diminishing and dispersal of the traveler in and through the world, it ultimately releases perception from the conventional grounds of experience and invites perceptual "fabrication and imagination and stylization," often suggested in Herzog's films through the figure of flight. Here, one walks on the visceral boundary that defines a human experience of the world, on the edge of what Gertrud Koch describes much more critically as "the otherness of a sensual realm of experience" (79), and here the walker experiences the irrepressible and soaring desire to find or fantasize meaning there, even as a dream. At this essayistic crossroads of experience, subjectivity, and conceptualization, Herzog's travelogues become not reports of sights seen but transformative restagings and flights of self through extravagant testings of visceral ideas about human desire and possibility in the world.

Herzog's documentary films are then walks around the deserts, jungles, and mazes of the world in search of a truth found at the crossroads of fantasy and failure. From the desert plains of Fata Morgan to the remote bear mazes of Alaska in Grizzly Man and the struggles to understand the glaciers of Antarctica in Encounters at the End of the World (2007), what distinguishes these geographies is their sometimes fierce and sometimes comical confusion of boundaries and borders, insides and outsides, centers and peripheries. [fig. 4.8] Exploring these worlds becomes exploring the limits of experience as the experience of limits and thought, which invariably leads to a kind of failure or collapse: the bombastic collapse of human efforts and gestures before the massive indifference of a hostile world, efforts and gestures only able to call attention to the intense longing for significance.[9] Land of Silence and Darkness (1971) offers the controversial and extraordinary depiction of this dilemma as deaf/blind men and women grope and stumble

FIGURE 4.8   Walking the mazes of grizzly bear territory (*Grizzly Man*)

between dark surroundings and a fragile inner world; in The Great Ecstasy of
Woodcarver Steiner (1974), *the spectacular soarings of a ski jumper into a vibrant
outer space always end abruptly when he falls to earth. A heroic climb toward the
heavens and the mouth of an active volcano in* La Soufrière (1977) *concludes with
a comical whimper and descent as the expected natural disaster fails to respond to
the filmmaker's quest for an extravagant answer to the barren, deserted world
around him.*

*The fantastically primitive dreams of foot travel, the ecstatic truths of these
essay films describe consistently the radical diminution of a self within the experience
of a world so massively indifferent that it becomes, by default, a concomitantly
horrifying and casual dismissal of the human desire for sense and selfhood, a dismissal and a desire that in their collision leave behind only the material detritus,
artifacts, and scars of thought as physical testimonies to the mostly bathetic claims
of human intelligence and self-knowledge.*

*This is where I agree with Deleuze's claim that Herzog is "the most meta-
physical of cinema directors," at least if we understand metaphysics as that realm
where visions become ideas and experience generates thoughts. For Deleuze, "In
Herzog we witness an extraordinary effort to present to the view specifically tactile images which characterize the situation of 'defenceless' beings, and unite with
the grand visions of those suffering from hallucinations" (Cinema 2 12). The continual compositional showdown between the very large and the very small in Herzog's essay films concretizes the showdown between the physically opaque and the*

theatrics of desire as the figuration of limits. "As Ideas, the Small and the Large designate both two forms and two conceptions," according to Deleuze. "These are distinct but capable of passing into one another. They have yet a third sense and designate Visions which deserve even more to be called Ideas" (Cinema 1 184–185). For Herzog, in short, visions are hardly about transcendence but rather about that experiential convulsion in which the human engages inhuman geography and releases a sometimes sensual, sometimes comical, and sometimes ferocious idea. If in Herzog's essay films the visionary becomes an ordinary walk through extraordinary spaces, thinking becomes an active, gymnastic, athletic encounter with a world that refuses to accommodate it.

In both its literary and cinematic practices, the essayistic voice is, as we have said, frequently the central measure of a subjective movement through experience: authorial persona or audio voice-overs describe, comment on, question, reflect on, and often subject themselves to the visual and intellectual relation between an observing eye and the world and spaces it sees and experiences. Perhaps partly because of the visual eccentricities and splendor of Herzog's films, the essayistic voice in his films is, I think, generally underestimated. Yet, it is a precisely structured, epistolary voice of experience whose linguistic drama infuses Herzog's travelogues with the pressure of thinking so central to the essay film. If Herzog's subjects typically act out the strain between the theatrics of desire and the resistant surfaces of the world, his voice becomes the supportive, mediating, and interfering intellect that, in its wonderful reticence, does not and cannot resolve that tension. While there is certainly some irony in describing films so well known for their stunning images in terms of their audio track, it is Herzog's voice that foregrounds so importantly the energy of thought left along the road of a theatrically experienced world.[10]

Language and voice have been a preoccupation in virtually all of Herzog's films. From Last Words (1968) and How Much Wood Would a Woodchuck Chuck (1976) to Lessons in Darkness (1992) and Death for Five Voices (1995), the shape and texture of language emerges, in fact, as the central thematic, poetic, intellectual, and formal force in the films. In How Much Wood, for instance, the rapid and barely comprehensible stream of language from Lancaster County auctioneers becomes a frenetic stream of words attempting to keep pace with the collision of nature and capitalism. Lessons in Darkness, a science fiction about a collapsing "planet in our solar system" (which is of course our own planet), opens with "a creature [trying] to communicate something to us" and later we hear that those many individuals traumatized by war "don't ever want to learn how to talk."

In his essay films, Herzog's voice-over is a hovering counterpoint to the other voices and languages within these films, most obviously as a way to foreground his *presence as a reflexive intelligence surrounding and permeating the images on the screen. It is the linguistic shape of that voice in which one hears the urgency of essayistic thinking, which might be characterized in terms from* The Mystery of Kaspar Hauser *(1974) as calmly moving between silence and screaming. Fairly consistently through his travel films, Herzog's language employs mythic aphorisms, conceptual paradoxes, philosophical abstractions, wry wit, and quizzical reflections interjected into the films through a voice pacing itself along a vocal range of tones from the extraordinarily calm and rational to the insistent, bemused, and quizzical. Most striking and important for me is the grain of Herzog's voice in its overarticulated pronouncements and articulations that call attention to the material fragility of language itself. Above all, I would describe the distinctive qualities and power of this epistolary voice as reticent in a way similar to Thomas Elsaesser's description of Herzog's creationist language spoken by Lotte Eisener in* Fata Morgana *as "deliberately inadequate and highly ironic" to imply "other modes of understanding which are subverted by a commentary both ludicrous and solemn" (*New German Cinema *166). Reticence becomes in these films a way of calling attention to the necessity of another language, consciousness, and significance as the vehicle for mapping and engaging the world, while acknowledging the strain and difficulty of reconciling conceptual ideas with the fierce or blank inhospitality of that world.*

Herzog's Grizzly Man *is not only a superb example of my earlier points about the pedestrian ecstasies of Herzog's excursive essays but also one of his most pronounced deployments of essayistic voice and language as epistolary engagements with another person's video letters, a dialogue along the charged line between human efforts to authorize, remember, and dream a natural space and the absolute resistance of the space. The film is partly an excursion into the natural world of the grizzly bear colonies of Alaska, but more accurately an essay on the impossibility of that journey and a testimony to the inevitable destruction of the human subject in attempting to articulate that place. Indeed, Adorno's observation could be the motto of this film: The essay "honors nature by confirming that it no longer exists for human beings."*

Like other Herzog films, the center of this film can be characterized in terms of that tension between the theatrics of vision and the visceral, tactile surfaces of the world, between the enfeebled human and "the overwhelming indifference of nature," as ideational visions stretched between the small and large—all most specifically and concretely figured in the encounter between the gigantic grizzly bears and the alternately silly and paranoid Timothy Treadwell, who believes he so harmoniously bonds with those bears. In shot after shot, the large and lumbering figures of the bears and the vast landscapes of the Alaskan wilderness literally rake the figure of a fidgety blond surfer boy to create the intimate and electrifying edge along which the film travels. At one point, Treadwell films a ten-foot grizzly against a pine tree, and when the bear wanders away, Treadwell giddily positions himself in that absent body, a bizarre image of the small inhabiting the large and an eerie anticipation of Treadwell's death when consumed by a grizzly. At this stage, Treadwell act outs his physical proximity to the space of nature as an almost speechless excitement.

What I find most provocative and distinctive in this film, however, is how Herzog's visionary realm becomes largely a product of the artifact of Treadwell's videotapes of himself and his travels into the bear colony, so that Treadwell is a subject known and engaged by Herzog primarily as a videotaped object like a moving postcard, an artifact that, as Adorno notes, has always fascinated essayists more than origins or presences. For Herzog, Treadwell's self and world are inseparable from their fabrication through his ubiquitous video camera and his relentlessly theatrical self-portrait, and this alone signals the crucial distance Herzog maintains as an observer of cinematic theatrics attempting to transform the world into its stage.

More explicitly than perhaps any other Herzog subject, Treadwell constantly composes and carefully stages himself against the background of the world and the world within the frame of his camera: Often, he sets up and films several times various takes to polish his verbal delivery, try out different bandanas, or fix his hair or to perfect his entrances into the frame to simulate dramatic action. [fig. 4.9] The prominent lack of shot/countershot exchanges becomes a necessary

FIGURE 4.9 Treadwell as auteur filming "Wild Timmy Jungle Scenes" (*Grizzly Man*)

structural product of this imagistic narcissism, remarked, for instance, by Herzog
when he comments on the complete absence of eye-line shots of Treadwell's girl-
friend, Amy, and culminating in the concluding close-up of the "overwhelmingly
indifferent" eyes of the grizzly that may have killed Treadwell, eyes whose blank
stare speaks, for Herzog, "only of a half-bored interest in food." [fig. 4.10]

Despite Treadwell's relentlessly comic and bathetic insistence on his identification with grizzlies, wild foxes, and their natural world, this film, like much
of Herzog's cinema, refuses the logic and spatial bonds of classical naturalized
identification. Grizzly Man is, in short, not so much a portrait of a man's excursion into the extremes of the natural world but a meditative reflection on that
excursion in which a passionate subject acts out his longings and frustration on the
surface between self and world, here less the surface of the icy soles of one's feet
than the surface glass of a camera lens. Like other Herzog essays, although here
more grotesquely, the insistent and relentless interiority of the reflective subject,
Treadwell, ironically succeeds only when it becomes exteriorized and ingested by
the world he wishes to possess.

Especially in this odd excursion into the wilderness, voice and language are
the critical vehicle for mapping this journey between interior and exterior spaces.
Mary Ann Doane has theorized the peculiar and powerful movement of the film
voice, particularly as that voice aims to locate the "phantasmatic body" represented
by film but, especially through voice-off, voice-over, and asynchronous or "wild"
sound, as it threatens to "expose the material heterogeneity of the medium" (374).

FIGURE 4.10 The look of "the overwhelming indifference of nature" (*Grizzly Man*)

FIGURE 4.11 Listening to Treadwell's death: Herzog's reticence and the fate of language (*Grizzly Man*)

For Doane, the audio voices of film are capable of identifying, crossing, and mud-dling boundaries according to interior audio spaces, voice-off spaces, disembodied voices, and the capacity for voice "to lend itself to hallucination" (381). Indeed, a fortuitous beginning to this play with language and voice in Grizzly Man *is Tread-well's own high-pitched, childish tones, terms, and sentence structures: Calling out to grizzlies he has named "Sergeant Brown," "Rowdy," and "Mr. Chocolate," whis-pering conspiratorially about his secret hideaways from intruding tourists and park service personnel, and throwing tantrums like a boy refused his toys, Tread-well becomes a dreamy, primitive vocal mix of Kaspar Hauser and Aguirre. In one of the most remarkable cinematic demonstrations of self in the film, Treadwell launches, in repeated takes, into verbal attacks on the National Park Service, barely able to control his flood of words and expletives. Here, he addresses himself as his own imaginary audience as if he is a Travis Bickel in the wilderness and generates a rant that reminds Herzog of his own experience of a former actor, Klaus Kinski, who also would lose any sense of boundaries.*

Throughout the film, Herzog's intervention as the audio voice-over is in one sense a standard essayistic strategy, but here it forecloses all possible Romanticism in this excursive nature film. In the end, Herzog's voice-over remaps Treadwell's own cinematic travelogue to another world through his reframing of it as a revela-tion that these travels are not about the place of nature but about the space of an inner self and the collision of that psychosemantic space with the massive outer space that refuses it until death. That, as Herzog says at the conclusion of the film, "is what gives meaning" to Treadwell's life.

The central scene in the film is an audio scene when Herzog listens to Treadwell's death, recorded for six minutes by a video camera with a lens cap still in place. Herzog sits in the room with Jewel Palovak, Treadwell's friend who was given the tape, the only scene in the film in which Herzog is visible as the mediator and the commentator. [fig. 4.11] He emphatically insists that Palovak should "destroy it" and explains his decision in this scene not to replay this recording of Treadwell's last words since, as Herzog put it, he needs to respect the privacy of death and did not want to make Grizzly Man a "snuff film." If the unheard screams and grotesque sounds of Treadwell's death represent in many ways the fate of language and voice living on an edge that it refuses to recognize is a razor's edge, Herzog's dramatic reticence here announces an audio gap at the very heart of the film. It is a terrible audio hallucination without images, a screaming voice without sound, and an essayistic commentary that can only mutter in response. At this limit is where essayistic thinking hovers, where, in Seung-Hoon Jeong and Dudley Andrew's Bazinian reading of the film, Grizzly Man clears a space "to think about the unthinkable" (12).[11] In this space where the visible disappears in the horribly literal collapse of a subjective interior within an exterior world, the excursive essay pinpoints the limit of language and voice in the articulation of experiential space.

5

On Essayistic Diaries, or the Cinematic Velocities of Public Life

FROM ITS LITERARY origins to its more recent cinematic and electronic incarnations, the essay has inherited, approximated, and overlapped with, among its many precursors and relations, diary writing. At that mythical sixteenth-century beginning, even Montaigne's writings appear somewhere between the epistolary and the diaristic as self-proclaimed descriptions of and reflections on his daily activities, thoughts, and experiences, not simply recording events but often revising those daily records with the new perspectives provided months and years later. Following Samuel Pepys's detailed accounts of daily life in seventeenth-century England, essay writings of the late eighteenth and early nineteenth centuries flourish as more oblique, public versions of the essay as diary; they take the form of weekly commentaries and editorials suited for and produced by a rapidly expanding newspaper and journal industry modeled on the temporal pacing of daily life. Ranging historically from ninth-century Japanese pillow books through twenty-first-century blogs, diaries map the expressions of an individual according to different temporal chronologies and rhythms, perhaps as detailed sequential organizations, sometimes with dramatic ellipses, and invariably according to various rhythms usually associated with daily life and experience.

The essay film quickly and regularly appropriates this practice. In 1929, Vertov's *Man with a Movie Camera* begins with the prefatory title: "an excerpt from the diary of a cameraman," and from the early twentieth century to today, film documentaries give way to essayistic versions of diaries in movies such as Alberto

Cavalcanti's precursive 1926 *Rien que les heures*; Jennings's 1945 *A Diary for Timothy*; Jonas Mekas's 1969 *Walden: Diaries, Notes, and Sketches*; Nanni Moretti's 1994 *Dear Diary*; and Kim's 2002 *Gina Kim's Video Diary*, as well as less-obvious examples, such as Michael Apted's series from *7 Up* to *49 Up* (1964–2005).[1] While this diaristic tendency in essay films certainly recalls the autobiographical dimensions found in most essay films, particularly portrait and self-portrait films, my emphasis in this chapter lies elsewhere, namely, in how this recuperation of diary writing by essay films serves most notably to highlight the dramatic ways the essayistic in general reconfigures temporality as a form of public thinking, as a kind of public diary.[2]

Here, I want to introduce some ideas specifically about the temporalities of the essay film. I locate these thoughts in relation to the heritage of the diary films remade as essay films, exemplified in Jonas Mekas's *Lost, Lost, Lost* (1976) and Nanni Moretti's *Dear Diary* (1994), draw briefly on some ideas of Paul Virilio about speed and what he calls "non-place," and anchor my concluding points in Alan Clarke's televisual essay *Elephant* (1988), an extraordinary example of an engagement with the velocities of public life, a public life in an Ireland that remains a modern location continually reconfigured by time, a location often less about a place than about mistimings, nostalgias, displaced histories, terroristic alarms, daily emergencies, and most recently, the economic speeds of computer industries. Shaped by the kind of temporal dominant associated with the diary, *Elephant* opens up multiple cinematic velocities as experiences grounded in reflexive agency and thought, enacting those different temporal experiences as endurance, immediacy, duration, boredom, shock, speed, anticipation, and exhaustion. In their distinctive ways, each of these films enacts an essayistic temporality that is essentially about the timing of thought as an active figure of public subjectivity. Especially central to these and all essayistic temporalities, as they immerse themselves in the daily losses that diaries can merely record, is the violence of time and the timing of violence, a configuration of violence that is most fundamentally a dramatic confrontation with and reflection on the teleology of closure naturalized by film narratives.

The first volume of a project originally titled Diaries, Notebooks, and Sketches, *Jonas Mekas's* Lost, Lost, Lost *appears on the verge of the explosive expansion of essayistic film practices in the 1980s and 1990s. Shot over a fourteen-year period from 1949 to 1963 and edited twelve years later in 1975, it is Mekas's autobiographical reflection on arriving in New York in 1949 as a postwar Lithuanian refugee and is one of his earliest diary film projects, which also include his online site of daily digital films,* 365 Films *(2007–).* Lost, Lost, Lost *describes his isolation, "the pain of exile," his cultural wanderings through the streets of lower Manhattan, and his gradual emergence as one of the central figures in the New American Cinema as it evolved into the 1960s. At the heart of the film is a fraught and anxious struggle for personal expression in a foreign land, permeating Mekas's travels and displacements through different New York cityscapes and Lithuanian subcultures. Whereas Akerman's* News from Home *is an essay that vanishes into the streets and spaces of New York, Mekas's film explores New York as a variety of temporal configurations in which he makes and unmakes himself according to changing times.*

Over images of fellow expatriates, family gatherings, protests, and meetings of artists, Mekas's voice moves across film footage shot in the 1950s but viewed many years later across a historical gap that fractures and highlights the multiple temporalities of the encounter. One intertitle identifies the central refrain of this essay as "I'm trying to remember," and these tentative and layered remembrances continually struggle to engage the varieties of past experience as an intellectual effort to see and hear Mekas's variously "timed selves." [fig. 5.1] According to Renov's reading of Lost, Lost, Lost *as an essay film, the film becomes "a series of histories" (Subject 76), which I would rephrase as a series of temporal time takes ranging from those of the everyday experience of an expatriate to the public history*

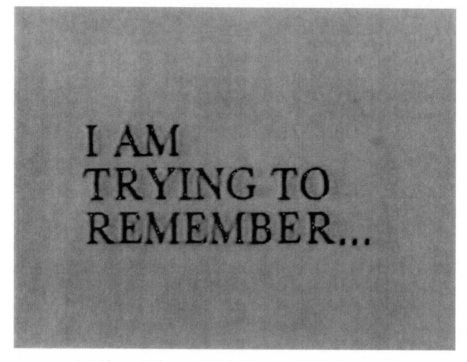

FIGURE 5.1   Intertitles pausing between Mekas's different timed selves (*Lost, Lost, Lost*)

*of the cold war, from bucolic memories of a lost past to a frenetic participation in
the daily pulse of modern New York, from painstaking chronicles to spontaneous
moments: "long lonely nights," "dreaming with no memories," the time when
"spring came very slowly," "long days in the waiting room," the ritualistic times of
baptisms and burials, leisure times dancing, seasonal times of transitions, political
times protesting, family times celebrating, and of course the time zones that
stretch between Lithuania and New York.*

*Prominently infusing all these temporalities are the reflective times that punc-
tuate the different temporal zones of the film. An early comment notes the challenge
of thinking about these various chronologies of self: "You'll never know what a displaced person thinks in the evening and in New York," he says, and throughout, the
crisis and imperative of the film is found in Mekas's wavering voice looking at old
film footage as a way of trying, from the present tense of the film in 1975, to remember different lost times from the 1950s and 1960s as modes of rethinking himself.
[fig. 5.2] Underlining the centrality of thought as the temporal movement of a diary,
Mekas writes about the connection between written and filmed diaries, in which
diaries elicit an intensely difficult activity of intellectual reflection on past, present,
and future selves. Like the process of writing a diary entry, he says, when filming a
diary "I am also reflecting. . . . I do not have much control over reality at all, and
everything is determined by my memory, my past. So that this 'direct' filming
becomes also a mode of reflection. . . . Your day, as it comes back to you during the
moment of writing, is measured, sorted out, accepted, refused, and reevaluated by
what and how one is at the moment when one writes it down" (191–192).*

*The diaristic effort to remember through reflective thinking thus becomes
subject to numerous starts and stops, pauses and accelerations, all of which
engender a self struggling with representing numerous scarred past selves, like the*

FIGURE 5.2 Displaced in the lost times and streets of New York (*Lost, Lost, Lost*)

graphically aged scratches of the 16-mm footage of the film. This becomes an essay-
istic subject made and unmade by the different temporal speeds of refound footage,
lost repeatedly through multiple timings, immediacies, repetitions, and deferrals
that always define who I am as when I am and when I was.

The different shapes of cinematic temporalities have been a central part of film
practice since the pioneer work of Étienne-Jules Marey and Eadweard Muybridge
in the nineteenth century, moving increasingly to the foreground of filmic structures and forms since then.[3] In *The Emergence of Cinematic Time*, Mary Ann Doane
explores the various figures and logics that characterize the complex temporalities
of early cinema, refining the representations of time in those years before the
dominance of narrative according to a variety of specific temporal categories: as
"afterimages" identified with futurist paintings and photography, as the "dead
time" depicted in films such as Edison's famous *Electrocuting an Elephant* (1903),
and as "archival time" anticipated by nineteenth-century chronophotographer
Marey. The varieties of early temporal figures such as these would, I believe,
predict the temporal flexibilities and experiences that inform essay films many
decades later, a point Doane suggests in her keen connection between the shapes
of early cinematic temporalities and Thom Anderson's 1974 essay film *Eadweard
Muybridge, Zoopraxcographer* (199–205).

As cinematic temporalities become more consistently encoded in terms of physical mobility in the first decade of the twentieth century, classical narrative cinema
begins to privilege spatial movement as the measure of a temporality aiming to
blur the gaps and intervals that mark alternative and contingent time schemes in
film. The emergence of a classical cinematic subject within these practices has
commonly been formulated according to a theatrics of vision that relates identity
to the conquest and possession of property,[4] and one indication of this penchant
is the rhetoric with which film scholars and critics have come to refer to various
subject "positions" in the cinema as the product of a "fixing" that locates, directs,
and often arrests temporal movement. Both the psychoanalytic and the semiotic
traditions informing these inquiries have usually developed the visual terms of
these positions as "emplacements" by which the subject follows and is defined by
movement within a theatrics of sight. Read within classical narratives, the action
of a central character mediates time through space, so that the time of those
actions ultimately becomes meaningful and legible in the progressive or continuous conquest or stabilization of the spatial field that absorbs temporality. Lost-
within space, the time of classical cinema as continuous duration or "enduration"
is thus, in one sense, no too far from Benjamin's notion of a"homogeneous, empty
time" ("On the Concept of History" 396).

John Ford's 1952 *The Quiet Man*, that most classic of Hollywood films, accordingly follows Sean Thornton (John Wayne) as an Irish American boxer who returns to the family village in western Ireland, where his attempt to forget a violent trauma in his past becomes entwined with his courtship and marriage to a local woman, Mary Kate Danaher (Maureen O'Hara). Typical of Ford's films, this quest for identity develops in terms of the reclamation of territory as property, and while the displaced status of Thornton's personality gives a postwar twist to this classical plot, the narrative maps the crisis of identity as a recuperation of a private, familial past within the bucolic mise-en-scènes of a mythical, public Ireland where the present and the past inhabit a seemingly static, homogeneous time zone—even to the extent of references to the timelessness of the IRA (Irish Republican Army). The two crucial temporal points in this movie are, as the voice-over narrator indicates, "to begin at the beginning" and, as the metaphoric horse race at the center of the film suggests, how time ends. From the inertia of the hero's "quiet" to the climactic action of the fight across the countryside, space and place—of family and home most obviously—gather, fulfill, anchor, and endure the time of action, which ultimately becomes naturalized as a violent conclusion of that temporality.

Within this field of vision, spatial arrangements and configurations determine the significance of temporality and blend temporal differences into a single field. As numerous scholars have pointed out, cinematic time has been mapped and theorized, fairly consistently, as a temporality of continuities, durations, and logical motivations subjected to what Erwin Panofsky calls (borrowing from Henri Bergson) "the spatialization of time" (218) or what Bazin has described as "embalmed time" ("Ontology" 14). In *The Quiet Man*, the classical narrative patterns of romance and suspense or the psychological figures of memory and desire might be said to be ultimately founded in what Christian Metz has described as the "inertia" of the cinematic viewing as, at best, a regressive nostalgia. In this past as always already present, temporality follows the well-rehearsed logic of linear continuity and character motivation by which a character pursues his or her desires, overcomes obstacles, and usually transforms that subjectivity into the terms of a social or public symbolic. As with the conventional use of the cinematic figure of "flashback," temporality becomes primarily a rediscovery of the individual's aesthetic *place* "where purposive action is replaced by inertia" and "channeled along the 'regressive path' that creates from unconscious and preconscious impulses the illusion of perceptual images" (Metz 114–118).[5] These formal considerations, moreover, reflect an organization of public experience. Within this framework, the temporality of classical cinema rests on a separation of a public time and leisure time according to which the multiple temporal actions of a public sphere and history might be reabsorbed and reshaped within the organized leisure space of the cinema. The geographical return of the Irish American Thornton to a lost country indexes, in an important sense I believe, a movement out of time and history, into the "leisure temporality" that classical cinema has so successful created, textually, socially and economically, as the territory of a virtual vacation.

While documentary films describe important variations on this spatialized temporality as the continuity and duration of a leisure time, they nonetheless tend commonly to create their own fairly coherent and homogenized time schemes. In *Documentary Time: Film and Phenomenology*, Malin Wahlberg has provided a sophisticated elaboration of many of the shapes of documentary time through patterns of "unfoldings," flux, intervals, and duration. Overarching these different phenomenological experiences of documentary time are, I would add, more fundamental organizations that reflect the temporalities of, for instance, eternal myths, diurnal cycles, progressive quests, or archival memory. Early documentaries such as Walter Ruttman's *Berlin, the Symphony of a City* (1927) or Robert Flaherty's *Man of Aran* (1934) create, in the first case, the temporal rhythms of the dense harmonies of a twentieth-century city and, in the second, the daily patterns of an isolated rural life. In each case, there is a coherent temporal paradigm that reflects, on the one hand, modern time and, on the other, natural time.[6] As significant swerves from these more classical documentary temporalities, even the films of cinema vérité and direct cinema, such as Jean Rouch and Edgar Morin's *Chronicle of a Summer* (1961), are less about subjecting the varieties of time to thought than about recasting documentary time as a relatively unified performative immediacy. Albert and David Maysle's *Gimme Shelter* (1970) stands out as it documents a string of self-absorbed performances by the Rolling Stones that culminate in an ambiguous freeze-frame of Mick Jagger, a subject either unable or refusing to understand or assume a distance on the historical myth he has created as a series of performative intensities in concerts across the United States.

Especially as they approach the 1940s and follow that watershed decade, different film practices and the larger cultures they inhabit demonstrate and reconfigure traditional temporal coherences and organizations as the multiple material temporalities of modern experience, as what Hansen, following Benjamin and Kracauer, calls the experience of a "matrix of conflicting temporalities" (*Babel & Babylon* 13). At the center of these conflicting temporalities is the strain of memory as the nexus between self and place, especially fraught, not surprisingly, in those postwar European cultures and cinemas of German and France. If human memory traditionally maps duration as a coherently located self, that coherence comes violently apart by midcentury for numerous reasons. In this period, the strain of memory across public and global space continually threatens the disappearance of memory and the concentration of time in an accelerating present tense. Public space and experience then take the form of contending temporalities that replace the tradition of temporal coherence with different experiential velocities, whose lack of clear motivation produces, in the cinema and elsewhere, the disjointed spaces of montage and the restless spaces of unresolved long takes.

At the center of these different temporal experiences has been the figure of speed, which, as both a cultural and filmic experience, denaturalizes the experience of time, undermines the power of human agency to control that experience, and consequently makes more viscerally and psychologically apparent the many temporal experiences that are *not* timed according to that base line of speed. In *The Speed Handbook: Velocity, Pleasure, Modernism*, Enda Duffy explores this temporal figure and its "adrenaline aesthetic" (9), identifying speed, following Aldous Huxley, as the heart of the new experience of modernity, as it appears repeatedly and centrally in the modernist literature of Fitzgerald and Joyce, the ubiquity of faster and faster automobiles, and both the content and editing pace of twentieth-century movies. Within this recent cultural history, speed not only occupies the center of modern experience but also denaturalizes, exaggerates, and abstracts time in a way that calls attention to the variety of other temporalities besides speed, varieties that have multiplied as the many temporal shapes of experience today.[7]

In contemporary film and media culture, cinematic speed has come to refer to both dimensions of Jacques Aumont's two cinematic times: the ocular time of the image and the pragmatic time of the viewing situation.[8] Following this scheme, not only is there the rapid pace and sensations that are part of the movies we watch, but also, at least as important, there is the rapid rate of consumption of the movies we circulate through our lives. Along with the shock values of increasingly elaborate special effects, Hollywood in particular has moved toward a velocity of effects, rapid bodily movements, and quick unmotivated actions and sensations, witnessed in so many contemporary blockbusters like *The Matrix* series (1999–2003) and *Avatar* (2009). Paralleling this textual dimension of cinematic speed, the emphatic velocities found in so many movie narratives today have become part of a larger public fabric based in a general acceleration of consumption and information, in which the rapid reception of movies dramatically participates and encourages. The not uncommon experience of a viewer renting or downloading four or five films for the weekend or the fast and aleatory remote control movements through single movies only anticipates the inevitable convergence of film viewing and computer activities, by which movies are watched on the same screen and with the same quick transformations where one does the shopping, chats with numerous friends, and engages in Web discussions, a convergence that serves to underline how the different speeds with which we watch movies today are part of a more general cultural acceleration in the search for or desire for information, experiences, and stimuli.

The possibilities and imperatives associated with temporal multiplicity, acceleration, and fracturing are, then, the heart of modern and contemporary screen cultures, with film now solidly part of televisual culture and gradually being overtaken by computer monitors, on which viewing images has evolved from a "total flow" to the "rapid, multidimensional flow" of overlapping temporal experiences. An early experiment with digital filmmaking and shot entirely with handheld cameras, Mike Figgis's *Timecode* (2000) is a suitably graphic approximation (and perhaps parody) of this condition. Entwining the daily routines of four central characters connected to an adult film company, the film restructures the single image of film as four quadrants within the projected frame to present four simultaneous and continuous takes that record the (mainly narcissistic and melodramatic) business of actors, directors, and producers. At times the same interaction of the characters is depicted from different angles in two different quadrants, while throughout film cell phones connect and disconnect the characters along another electronic register. Although a fiction film, it documents the overlapping time zones of different subjects locked within the temporalities of their separately screened subjectivities: delayed, bored, anxious, synchronic, and, above all else, urgent.

Where these cultural and technological shifts dovetail so decisively with the essayistic is that, as many filmmakers and media artists have recognized, the temporal pace and layered fabric through which private and public experiences intersect are often most accurately represented and reflected in television, the televisual, and the present and future incarnations of the many other digital monitors and technologies that do and will permeate daily life. More so than ever before perhaps, the experience of public life as an interaction with private life has, especially through the proliferation of these new and other media, become the different vectors and ways of "spending of time," with public life a function of the layers of temporal zones that inhabit it. Here, outside or on the margins of conventionally coherent temporal patterns, the cinematic essay offers unique access to those multiple and conflicting temporalities as a rethinking of public experience. Perhaps especially through the televisual and the ever-changing digital screens, the essayistic discovers multiple zones of rapid repetitions that refuse to repeat.

If speed pervades public and private life today, the essayistic therefore reframes and rethinks it specifically between two symbiotically related temporal figures that follow from—to borrow Patrice Petro's terminology for two essential experiences of modernity—the social and psychological shocks that pervade modern life

and the aftershocks that describe the fading away of those intensities (57–81).
Rapidly moving between shock and after shock, these two temporal experiences
describe alternately—and often simultaneously—the experience of emergency as
a response to the pressure of sensory and cultural overstimulation and the experience of boredom as a reaction to that overstimulation. Under the extreme pressure to respond to a climate of speed, *emergency* becomes the shocking anticipation
of the impending closure of a time that will, like a horse race, run out, a closure
that, in terms of a human telos, implies the end or death of the subject. As an
awareness of the extreme lack of speed, *boredom* becomes an experience of the
repetition or vacating of a temporality that refuses to progress and so describes a
potential subject, as in Jarman's *Blue*, in waiting, after shock, wandering in the
"unbearable experience of being in the everyday" (Petro 61).[9] As alternating reactions to the experience of speed, boredom and emergency thus produce the multiple and often-conflicting figures of the subject as various temporal configurations
and ideas, the subject as, for instance, "bad timing" or "time being," as the "what
of" of memory or the "what if" of speculation, as "past potential" or the "future
conditional." This is the essayistic self in repetition; the self as waiting; the self in
shock or surprise; the self in multiple memories; the self in anticipation.

The essayistic diary is then the record of the dispersed and reflective subject
across this temporally layered landscape. Under the dominant of speed, the essay
film, specifically in its diaristic attentions to time, offers the possibility to identify
and retime experience as a variety of temporal potentials and imperatives for the
subject, particularly as they are associated with rethinking the self in public life.
Inhabiting the classical address of "dear diary," the essayistic diarist/subject
becomes a subject divided and spread through temporal zones; typically, these
expressions describe the encounter between an individual and herself or between
that self and various social figures and experiences that continually retest that
individual as a new moment or as a new day, creating not only various temporal
chronologies of self but also gaps and tensions between the personal time of the
subject and the time of a public sphere that continually refuses, attracts, or incites
that shifting subject. If speed potentially offers the excitement and thrills of losing
control, the essayistic diary offers, in response, a series of temporal imperatives
and potentials, drawn between emergency and boredom, that offer the subject, in
the midst of losing control, the opportunity to know, to change, to remember, and
even to act through that rapidity of experience.

Nanni Moretti's 1994 autobiographical essay Dear Diary *is only ostensibly a conventional diary and is more exactly an essay that employs the diary format to
engage experiential temporality as ideas and action. Opening with a close-up of*

Moretti's hand writing while his voice-over announces the presiding address, "Dear Diary . . .," the first part of the three-part structure of the film that starts with the episode "On My Vespa." While Moretti rides through the virtually empty streets of Rome during the August vacation period, he and the camera survey the exteriors of homes and buildings, and he remarks how he would like to "make a film of houses" that has dates to mark the neighborhoods according to historical eras, to re-create a public space as time coded. As he weaves through the streets dating the different buildings he passes, he embodies a kind of unfettered movement that comically intrudes into this public space as unexpected interruptions: He joins a band on stage, accosts a driver to explain his interest in making only small groups of friends, and harangues a man on the street about the way new neighborhoods and habits are destroying the old Rome. Bruno has suggestively called the film "an architectural notebook" in which "a montage of the city's history takes shape" (35, 36). I would rather call the film an architectural diary since it works specifically to interrupt the public spaces in the film as a series of different temporal experiences in which the mobility and movement of the body are re-created as different temporal vectors continually embedded in and thinking through those experiences. [fig. 5.3]

Comically inspired by Jennifer Beales's performance in Flashdance, Moretti articulates all this movement as a longing to dance, a longing for a movement and mobility freed of fixed trajectories or static visual positions. When he coincidentally encounters an amused Beales on the road during his travels, he explains to her

FIGURE 5.3 An architectural diary of Rome on a Vespa (*Dear Diary*)

that "I could dance instead of watch," a somewhat cryptic claim that is acted out later in a café where he spontaneously dances before a musical performance on a television monitor. Beyond the verbal and physical humor of these scenes, they signal a key thematic regarding the essayistic address of the film: In this mode of experience, the tradition of voyeuristic looking and the boredom associated with it longs to give way to public performance defined by creatively unpredictable temporal rhythms.

This attention to alternative experiences of the world that I associate with the activity of the essay becomes here a consistent motif in the film, played out as a "restless thinking" that resists certain emplacements and deterministic temporalities, or what one study of the film describes as the distinctive power of the diary to articulate a "crisis of authority" and to refuse the "superfluity of authority" (Mazierska and Rascaroli 41). At the beginning of the film, during the slow months of that Roman summer when the film fare is limited, the cinephile Moretti bemoans the fact that the only films available for him to see are three equally boring types: repetitious pornographic films, static art films, and frenetically violent films like the pseudoportrait film Henry: Portrait of a Serial Killer (1986). After watching an Italian art film, he complains that the characters just sit around bemoaning their lost and "defeated" generation, while whining about how they have "all changed" for the worst. Later, an irritated and restless Moretti passionately writes in his diary a rebuke of that art film logic and its generational logic of loss and boredom within an empty time. He insists that he refuses to accept the boredom of his generation and its films and instead remains determined as the active and content agent of his own present and the temporal explorations of his own film. [fig. 5.4]

As the sequence suggests, Moretti's active confrontation with empty time extends especially to other forms of cinema and media. Disgusted with the monotonous and repetitious violence of Henry, he physically confronts a film critic who had positively reviewed the film and forces him to confess to a litany of stupid reviews. Later, he watches his traveling mate, Gerardo, a scholar of James Joyce, transform from a condescending and confirmed disciple of Hans Marcus Enzensberger, who says "television is nothing," into a passionate follower of and apologist for soap operas and American television. This shift to television redirects, albeit tongue in cheek, the earlier confrontation with cinematic violence and artsy vacuity to more sociologically open and varied time zones that might allow for more active intellectual and imaginative engagements, regardless perhaps of the quality and content of the images (where, for instance, even soap operas become a time "for children to daydream"). Later, on the top of a volcano, however, that obsession becomes simply another version of a subjection to another temporality, as

FIGURE 5.4 After seeing *Henry: A Portrait of a Serial Killer*, a diary entry that reviews and refuses violence and boredom (*Dear Diary*)

Gerardo shouts out desperate questions to American tourists about soap opera characters and episodes that he has not yet seen in Italy.

In the second episode of the film, "Islands," Moretti and Gerardo visit the islands of Lipari, Salina, Stromboli, and Alicudi, and with each new island, Moretti appears increasingly isolated amidst changing and multiple temporalities. On the first island, for instance, he encounters with annoyance a kind of frenzied hyperactivity in the streets, and on the second, he finds a kind of determined and regressive need to control time, where obsessed families have only one child and where, in the words of one mother, a young child will remember "nothing" of his first three years but immediately after toilet training begin "to act like an adult." On Alicudi, "everyone lives alone" in an isolated stasis, primitive timelessness and, as Moretti writes in his diary, "deadly calm."

The structure of this essayistic diary makes unexpected chronological leaps and detours, each of which might correspond to temporal experiences that in turn elicit extended moments of reflection or thinking, moments that are dramatized in several long meditative sequences featuring Moretti alone on the coast, alone playing soccer, alone writing in his diary. On Salina particularly, he finds himself immersed in numerous families comically tossed and turned by the different schedules and time lines their children impose on them or they on their children. Yet, amidst this often-hilarious chaos of expectations and demands, the film shifts to an extraordinarily quiet time when Moretti wanders through a long shot and long take along the waterfront, visibly in thought about, among other reflections, his fear of "wasting time." [fig. 5.5]

In an unexpected turn, the third and final section, "Doctors," crystallizes temporality as a graphic but quietly violent invasion, a sudden and mortal emergency. Moretti develops chronic itching and seeks to remedy it with endless medical ointments and prescriptions, bran baths, and acupunctures, ultimately discovering that it is a curable lymphomatic cancer. The disquieting emergency of this last section recalls the lyrical conclusion to Part I (a sequence without dialogue and only a melancholic piano track) in which, in a lengthy, meditative following shot, Moretti rides his Vespa along the coast to make a pilgrimage to the place of Pasolini's violent death. Faced in this concluding section of the film with his own illness and potential death, he experiences a slow epiphany about the temporal inevitabilities of life, and this new awareness leads him to two concluding lessons about time that he carefully inscribes in his diary: First, he dismisses the temporality of prognostications by doctors who "can talk but not listen," and second, he has learned to replace the boredom of waiting rooms with the concrete daily ritual of "a glass of water every morning." [fig. 5.6] Whereas essayistic travelogues might be said to disperse subjectivity into a destabilized spaces, in Moretti's Dear Diary, *subjectivity discovers, in short, how to continually reinvent itself between the extremes of boredom and emergency as a series of different, daily, and redemptive time zones.*

FIGURE 5.5   Thinking through the chaos of time (*Dear Diary*)

FIGURE 5.6   Recording the mortal lessons of time (*Dear Diary*)

The work of Paul Virilio is an especially useful touchstone here: in theorizing speed as the central velocity of contemporary experience, in describing the evacuation of its determining spatial logic, and in suggesting the central terms of an essayistic subject within those temporalities. Extending Virilio's own argument, I also find this work important as it suggests how the velocity and timing of experience may provide the registers in which the imperative *to act* can become both a temporal and an intellectual process.

In *The Vision Machine*, Virilio argues that, in the twentieth century "an aesthetic of disappearance had arisen from the unprecedented limits imposed on subjective vision by the splitting of modes of perception and representation." Bound up with "industrialization of vision" that increasingly suffuses visual experience through televisual images and across computer screens, this "splitting of viewpoint" has removed us from the place of direct observation and moved us toward the place where the "instrumental virtual images will be for us the equivalent of what a foreigner's mental pictures already represent: an enigma" (49, 59–60).[10] At the same time, the prominence of velocities of speed have effectively negated the classical logic of time and concomitantly effaced geographies of place as viewers rapidly execute sights rather than inhabit locations. Today, he notes, "the strategic value of speed's 'non-place' has definitely outstripped the value of place" (31), so that the modern subject becomes situated between the time of dis-placements (demonstrated perhaps in Moretti's wanderings through the present) and the time of non-placements (opened through the futuristic images of new technologies).

Located in that enigmatic non-place of an industrialized vision, subjectivity becomes a continually rapid reconstruction of self within an "intensive time." For Virilio, a key metaphor for and evidence of this intensive time is the altered "speed of exposure" that characterizes the technologies of the virtual image and the new subject that image inscribes, as the new speeds of exposure differentiate the virtual image from the traditional photographic or filmic image. Following this accelerated exposure time, surprise becomes the determining temporal rhythm of the subject of the vision machine: "If photo-cinematography is still inscribed in extensive time, promoting expectations and attention by means of *suspense*," contemporary vision machines are "inscribed in intensive time, promoting the unexpected and a short concentration span by means of *surprise*." Without the continuity of reflective memory and anticipatory vision needed for suspense and with a vision that develops unexpectedly through a logic of always surprising and shocking images, the subject experiences time but not sight, resulting in a type of blindness "very much at the heart of the 'coming' vision machine', . . . an intense blindness that will become the latest and last form of industrialization: *the industrialization of the non-gaze*" (*Vision Machine* 72–73). Almost a theoretical elaboration of the 2002 *Minority Report* (in which sightless "pre-cogs" constantly and rapidly monitor and foresee images of future crimes), images generated by blind and surprised subjects become future sights, and the experience of seeing becomes, by default, the unfettered act of foreseeing through the open field of non-place, in which the "act of seeing is an act that proceeds action, a kind of pre-action" (61).

Pushing the implications of Virilio's argument, vision machines can thus describe a time of potential and provisional future place, designating the possible move through the blindness of non-place to a foreseeable future place as a choice or even an temporal imperative. Unlike the closed places of an extensive leisure temporality that naturalizes a more or less-violent death of the subject as a narrative closure, this foreseen place continually violates that surprised self and its non-place by redefining both as an intensive temporal potential. Visionary speeds place the individual at the troubling crossroads of past and future images, suggesting at once the rapid disappearance of public realism and the individual's need to rethink identity in terms of the pressured timings of future experience and future realities. Seeing within a non-place is indeed a surprising blindness, but a blindness with the necessary potential for seeing renewed times, where non-place can become a temporally actionable place.

While Virilio's speed clarifies the increasingly temporal state of subjectivity, its significance is, more fundamentally I think, that it opens experience to many different potential velocities as the shape of contemporary subjectivity (inside and outside new visual technologies). Other temporal tenses abound as variations on this *praxis of speed* as remodulations or reformulations framed between boredom and emergency; these remodulations include time codes of the repeated, the delayed, the preparatory, the immediate, the simultaneous, the suspended, the late, the urgent, and the anticipatory. They all imply different notions of agency, motivation, causality, and transformation, and they all relate in turn to different positions for envisioning desire and rationality in relation to the efficacy of action as foreseeing: action as, for instance, measured, delayed, short termed, and even political.

In each case, the essayistic expression of the velocities of experience describes a crisis point at which the contemporary subject, in all her surprised blindness, must locate the action of thought as a participant in what I call a public diary. As the site of the formation of experience, those intensely temporal subjects of Virilio are still public figures whose blindness and shock necessarily inhabit a historical space permeated by a variety of tenses through which the imperatives of action involve constant and continual reinventing a self simultaneously as a past history and as a future conditional. The essayistic subject today is, in short, restlessly and relentlessly subject to "time takes" in which how she represents herself in time and how she spends time may be the most important experiential present and future as part of what Duffy has termed "a politics of speed" (7) that is always accelerating into the future.

For me, the films of British filmmaker Alan Clarke are particularly pertinent examples of expansive boundaries of the contemporary essay film—notably in their exploration of temporal potential of televisual cinema—to reshape the diary as a public diary. Only drawing international attention with the release of a DVD collection of some of his films, Clarke has been called a "genius of television" by David Thomson (161): for Thompson, Clarke's nearly sixty productions for film and television are comparable to the work of Ken Loach, Mike Leigh, and Stephen Frears, who has called Clarke "the best of all of us." As described in an interview in the film Director: Alan Clarke *(1991), the common misunderstandings of many of Clarke's films is a product of a paradox found in many essay films: The topics and situations tend to concentrate on "normal houses with normal people," and like his controversial* Scum, *a film about a juvenile detention center that was banned by the BBC in 1977, these films "look too much like documentaries."[11]*

A diary of public life in Northern Ireland, Clarke's 1988 Elephant *takes place in the "ordinary space" and time of the 1980s, not far from territorial conquests of Sean Thornton in* The Quiet Man *decades earlier. The film explores the spatially eviscerated public place of Belfast, where that space and the individuals who*

populate it threaten to disappear between the two vectors of history and inevitability, between emergency and boredom, between shock and after shock, where the
state of war at the center of Virilio's geopolitical world is a continual, rapid, and
violent attempt to erase the past, like a series of bloody diary entries tearing out
the previous day in anticipation of tomorrow's entries. Sometimes mistaken as a
kind of experimental cinema and certainly not to be confused with Virilio's digital-
ized virtual images, this film is too much about the public experience of time and
space, mapping an experience of space and time as non-place populated by blind
subjects and structured as a relentless series of violent timings.

Produced by Danny Boyle, Elephant is located in a Belfast torn apart by terrorist killings, a place of temporal emergency and exhaustion. Elephant describes
a location where memory has become a rapid cycle of indistinguishable deaths and
where all the visible subjects seem blind to the historical elephant in the room.
What we see of Belfast are eighteen parallel sequences of mostly interminable
walking and matter-of-fact murders with only a few words of dialogue in the entire
film. Set against a variety of empty and often impoverished streets and buildings,
eighteen sequences repeat the walk of the man on the streets as he approaches his
victim, shoots and kills that individual as a blunt, untheatrical gesture, and then
departs—eighteen times. Night and day alternate in no recognizable pattern, and
the differences between leisure time and work time become irrelevant in an atmosphere defined largely by dull but horrifying routines.

There is little ostensible variation in each sequence as one or two unidentified
males approach a public place (such as a neighborhood swimming pool, a ware-
house, a convenience store, the front door of a home, a parking lot, a soccer field),
all eerily vacant and mostly abandoned of other people yet architectural reminders
of a span of social classes. He or they walk (or occasionally drive) briskly onto the
scene, searching the corners and empty rooms but without hesitation or concern.
[fig. 5.7] Within the span of an approximately two-minute sequence, they find the
lone individual (occasionally two) they seek and without expression use a hand gun
or shotgun to kill the victim, as seemingly ordinary as it is shocking. Sometimes,
one shot concludes the killing; sometimes, the killer fires five or six shots into the
victim. After the killer quickly and calmly leaves the scene, the camera returns to
the unmoving body and holds for an inordinately long time take in which the following shot becomes a statically dead time, a frozen aftershock and afterimage.
[fig. 5.8] There are no witnesses, except for the impassive image as witness. Assas-
sins reveal nothing of their motives; places and buildings indicate little of political
or religious positions (Catholic or Protestant, rich or poor); and bodies of these
subjects speak no meaning across the long takes that tell only of the strain of time.
There is no suspense here, only reverberating shocks and surprises through simple

FIGURE 5.7   Marching time toward a killing (*Elephant*)

FIGURE 5.8   The long take as frozen aftershock and afterimage (*Elephant*)

variations and repetitions, extended as moments of stillness, even tranquility. In fact, Elephant *is a strangely silent film in which the vague sounds of daily activities (cars in the background, the rhythm of walking in the foreground) becomes suddenly shattered by the eruptive blasts of the gunfire.*

Here, walking is marching, not Herzog's walking on earth, but walking to time as a temporal inevitability. That march of inevitability accumulates momentum through the film and replaces anticipation and suspense in a manner that makes the final sequence a summary twist of the logic of the entire film. As two men exit a car and enter a vacant building, the sequence replicates the previous seventeen (although, at three and a half minutes, it is almost twice as long as earlier sequences): The two men walk casually but purposely side by side, and the long,

brisk walk through empty spaces suggests a common aim. When the two enter a
room where a third man awaits, however, one of the two supposed killers walks
freely away from his partner and moves calmly to face a white wall, at which point
the waiting third individual steps forward to execute him with a bullet to the back
of his head. [fig. 5.9]

If once Sean Thornton's actions and agency dramatized subjectivity as the
confident conquest of space, here experience becomes an undistinguished passivity
locked within temporal repetitions, a contemporary horror film without identifia-
ble characters or narrative suspense. Throughout the film, wide-angle, Steadicam
trackings give way to the stasis of long time takes, with the identification process—
of assassin and victim pair and viewers and character agents—stretched across a
moment between complicity and judgment. In the surprise of this final sequence,
the brightly lit factory seems ironically to underline the climax of a culture of
blindness, in which closure becomes complicity and complicity becomes closure.
This final sequence operates like a shocking version of Michel de Certeau's temporal
"occasions," whose "torsions" bring together "qualitatively heterogeneous dimen-
sions that are no longer only oppositions of contraries or of contradictions" and so
produce knowledge as a disruption and overturning of established hierarchies
(L'Invention 158–159).

Originally shown on BBC Belfast, this thirty-seven-minute essay film
strangely reinvests public experience with the excruciating temporality of every-
day Belfast, stretched between banal emergencies and attendant boredoms that,
in Ireland, have been vacated by the media's ritually repeated rhetoric surrounding
those events. What is so powerful about this film is, I think, how its structural
repetitions within a fragmentary length depict the daily matter that film and

FIGURE 5.9 The concluding sequence: the long passive walk to a self-execution (*Elephant*)

television have served to obscure, intensely mechanical repetitions that, in this film, refuse to repeat. As the inspiration for Gus Van Sant's own 2003 Elephant about the Columbine massacre of high school students in 1999, the film ultimately depicts not so much actuality in any documentary sense but experience as a daily, interminable encounter with the violent shocks and aftershocks of recognition.

As a conscious example of the use of the subjective shot so prevalent in video games, Van Sant's remade Elephant suggests, in fact, an important stylistic connection with the "first-person shooters" of video games, an especially resonant figure with which to consider Clarke's film. Alexander Galloway has examined the subjective perspective of this "first-person shooter" as it migrates from video games to films and becomes an intensification of the more common and traditional point-of-view shot that simply approximates a character's perspective. For Galloway, although rarely appropriated by films, this subjective shot creates what he calls "a gamic cinema" of "fully rendered actionable space" (62–63). As Van Sant's film makes clear, video-game violence is certainly a part of the formal migration of a gamic perspective, but for Galloway, it is the subjectively actionable space and "affective motion" that is the most significant part of the use (and misuse) of the figure in cinema: "The subjective camera is largely marginalized in filmmaking and used primarily to effect a sense of alienated, disoriented, or predatory vision. Yet with the advent of video games, a new set of possibilities were opened up for the subjective shot. In games the first-person perspective is not marginalized but instead is commonly used to achieve an intuitive sense of affective motion" that encourages rather than destabilizes the refashioning of identification itself (68–69).

While the tracking and following shots of Clarke's film never actually incorporate first-person subjective shots per se, the film does horrifically parody those video-game perspectives, immediately recalling the focus on the violence and killing that motivate some games. Reenforcing this connection, interior space in Clarkes's film becomes enfolded into the exterior spaces of Belfast as a disturbingly "fully rendered" world that consistently seems to exclude offscreen space as a knowable or recognizable historical context. Yet, in simultaneously approximating and subverting the "gamic perspective" of the "first-person shooter," the most disturbing formal paradox of Elephant might be that it suggests an actionable space in which affective motion is vacated of any subjectivity that might freely and affectively act on that space, that might actually alter its temporal patterns. [fig. 5.10] Especially for viewers in Belfast perhaps, the non-place of this gamic vision, depleted of an affective subjectivity, is, despite its recognizable shocks and repetitions, a game that has relentlessly demanded and has historically resisted actionable change.

FIGURE 5.10   A gamic perspective depleted of subjectivity and actionable space (*Elephant*)

One of the most potent and unusual dimensions to this essay film is thus the disappearance of the subjective voice or authorial persona that many claim is a hallmark of the essay film, a presence and a voice that is so pronounced in more obviously diaristic films like Moretti's Dear Diary. *What makes this film such an extreme but key example of the contemporary essay is that the subject of this essay is no subject or at best the blinded subject referenced in the title of the film as a subject unable to see or acknowledge an overwhelming reality at the center of the society. In* Elephant, *the essayistic subject, rather than dividing and dispersing across multiple positions as is typical, disappears radically into blind spots stretched across emergency and boredom. In Virilio's words, here "All that counts is the speed of the moving body and the undetectability of its path" ("The State of Emergency" 47). Turning the TV fantasy of "public life as private expression" inside out, that fantasy becomes exposed as the empty time and non-place that is television, the Internet, and many future vision machines emptied of an inner life and reexperienced as violently repeated shocks and surprises. Here, television becomes tapped and developed precisely in terms of its essayistic potentials: Televisual space becomes a public space uninhabited by temporal motivation, a space in which the private drifts, as in the final sequence, into a horrifying complicity with the undifferentiated action of killing, indistinguishably oneself or another, as a temporal logic or, in Virilio's words, a place where "non-distinction corresponds to political blindness" (51).*

Layering anticipation, repetition, and endurance, Elephant *delineates the boredom of killing and dying as temporal velocities eerily reflective of the television frame of BBC Belfast as a specific and localized experience of a total flow at a rhetorical degree zero, as reality TV in its most nakedly violent form. To watch*

Elephant *is to be subjected to a time slot made up only of temporal shapes vacated of temporal logics, in which subjectivity has been moved off the screen and in which the interstices that remain are only a series of temporal imperatives. To paraphrase one commentator about the film, with Clarke's brand of realism "there's a point of view but it's no point of view" (Director: Alan Clarke).*

With their extreme dissolution of the traditionally fragmented subject of the essay, Clarke's essay film is not typical of the practice. Its obsession with the timing of subjectivity as a definition of experience is, however, central to these times and the ways essay films might engage these times. More so than any practice, I believe, the essayistic lurking in many of these films, is the imperative of temporality to be engaged within the frame of public experience, across the trajectory where a thinking subjectivity makes something happen or not happen. "Who am I?" and "What motivates me" may no longer be the salient questions and may not even be crucial ones these days, just as the place "where I am" may often become less and less linked to our wandering identities. Instead, the questions "When am I?" "At what speeds and how often am I?" or "According to which temporal imperatives am I?" have, in many ways, assimilated these earlier queries to shape these essayistic diaries of self as the experiential crisis of acting within a public space stretched between boredom and emergency.

With Clarke's Elephant *in the background, as a self-conscious example of a public diary, Musil's* The Man without Qualities *reminds us of the critical temporal foundations of the essayistic. Perhaps as a temporal directive in the future tense of many contemporary experiences today where the glaring non-place of war disappears the realities of facts and subjects, Musil and his protagonist, Ulrich, reflect on that time zone between self and the world, between boredom and emergency, where thought leads to action: "What we cannot classify as either a fact or a subjective experience we sometimes call an imperative. But if one holds up an imperative for a long time without anything happening, the brain goes to sleep, just as the arm does that has held something up for too long" (274–275).*

6

Of the Currency of Events: The Essay Film as Editorial

ONE OF THE most prominent versions of the essayistic appears in different kinds of social and political essays. With a heritage that extends back as far as sermons and forward through contemporary newspaper editorials and Internet blogs, these versions of the essayistic often function as investigations into the truth and ethics of social events and behavior. One useful way to characterize this essayistic practice is as a kind of editorial intervention in the news of everyday history: Here, the "news" suggests the reporting of past, present, and future facts and events in a fashion that tends to blend and blur those three registers as "current events," and editorial intervention becomes both a subjective immersion in and disruption of that current. With an etymological origin in the fourteenth century, this idea of the editorialized news appears in its more modern form in eighteenth-century pamphlets and daily papers. Appearing early in the work of writers like revolutionary essayist Thomas Paine, these literary examples describe a history of social commentary that would later include Matthew Arnold's writings about education and Jacob Riis's photographic exposé of immigrant poverty in New York, *How the Other Half Lives* (1890). As polemics about hidden, missed, or critical events and people or about moral, political, or philosophical imperatives for understanding those people and events, these essays offer or demand ways of understanding and, more important, ways of personally and publicly reacting to the news of daily life. More exactly, they typically address and sometimes demonstrate the crucial work needed to discover an agency within the current events of history or what might be called the currencies of history. Although these kinds of essays can sometimes choose topics that are light or even trivial, more often than not they are attuned to crisis, frequently a crisis related to a social or communal collapse or trauma.

With essay films, this tradition has energetically continued in films as diverse as Morris's *The Thin Blue Line* (1988), Kluge's *The Candidate* (1980) and *Miscellaneous News* (1986), Spike Lee's *4 Little Girls* (1997), Zana Briski and Ross Kauffman's *Born into Brothels: Calcutta's Red Light Kids* (2004), and even Raoul Ruiz's parodic *Of Great Events and Ordinary People* (1979). As with most essay films, these films represent very different versions of the editorial essay and invariably overlap with other essayistic modes, as in Morris's investigation of the causes of the Vietnam War in his portrait of Robert McNamara in *The Fog of War* (2003) or Morgan Spurlock's tongue-in-cheek indictment of the MacDonald's food industry in his essay diary *Super Size Me* (2004).

Godard, the filmmaker perhaps most identified with personal vision and political imperatives, provides a concise statement of his version of this practice. In the 1960s, he defines this kind of filmmaking and its subjective encounter with current events this way: "If I have a secret ambition, it is to be put in charge of French newsreel service," he says. "All of my films have been reports on the state of the nation; they are newsreel documents, treated in a personal manner perhaps but in terms of contemporary actuality. . . . This is why I am so attracted by television. A televised newspaper made up of carefully prepared documents would be extraordinary. Even more so if one could get newspaper editors to take turns at editing these televised newspapers" (*Godard* 239). Decades later, in 2004, he traces the journey of two Israeli women in search of a politics of knowledge in *Notre Musique*. In this Dantesque investigation of the hell of war, the purgatory of Sarajevo, and the paradise of a beach guarded by Marines, Godard cryptically summarizes the crisis of postwar reportage, "We say that facts speak for themselves," but as Celine said in 1936 "not for much longer."

Unlike those films that are sometimes called investigative documentaries, editorial essay films unveil and analyze not only the realities and facts that are documented but also the subjective agencies (enmeshed in the films and their reception) of those realities and facts.[1] As reports on daily events, these essay films, like other kinds of editorials, foreground the necessary play of consciously and decisively mobile subjectivities within those reports, reports not only about facts, realities, people, and places discovered and revealed but also about the possibility of agency itself within a state of current affairs that is no longer transparent nor easily accessible.

Conventional news often claims a position of factual reportage through a singular agency "anchoring" the audience to the image through a celebrity or star personality (who implicitly replaces the traditional documentary voice of God). The editorial essay film, however, confronts exactly that assumed authority and its singularity and, brashly or obliquely, fragments it as part of the continuous work to disrupt that current of events from various angles and positions within the past, present, and future. Reporting history as current events thus spreads itself through a living experience that critically moves around and through events as different voices, places, and faces, insisting that those events are or should be a product of an active critical intelligence that responds to history especially as a series of crises. The essayistic works to create the unsettling state in which the subject recognizes him- or herself, often uncomfortably, as a participant in the configuration that is the news and its history, in short as a shifting and changing face in the space between the dates of a calendar. Through the history of the essay film, few crises have better mapped those movements than the calendar of events from World War II and the Holocaust to the West Bank today. Few, moreover, have better pinpointed the essayistic problematic and trouble in staking a decisive political position across the subjective flux of everyday events.

One of the most demanding and widely recognized essay filmmakers today, Harun Farocki has been characterized by a relentless investigation of the politics of everyday history.[2] One of his more recent and more insistent essays on the need to think through the unthinkable within the occasions of daily experience is his 2007 Respite, a film that is part silent historical report and part home-movie investigation of a Dutch transit camp for Jews, Westerbork. Built in 1939 by the Dutch for Jews who had fled Germany, Westerbork becomes, shortly after that, the "Police Transit Camp for Jews," run by the German SS. Shot by cinematographer-inmate Rudolf Breslauer but never completed, Respite is largely footage commissioned by the SS commandant of the camp, Albert Gemmeker, to counter the threat of the under-populated camp being closed, and Farocki's minimalist forty-minute reclamation of it, edited down from ninety minutes of found footage, becomes a tense reframing of the past with the language of the present. Appropriating some of the same footage from the Westerbork camp, Resnais's Night and Fog fully transforms the historical news report into an editorial investigation of current events as they forget the past of the Holocaust; Respite, however, turns and troubles similar but vastly different images of the past, as a way to make the silence of an everyday past speak within and out of itself, as a still-current event demanding a subject. Trains and transits define the essence of current events here, and Farocki's repeated visual recollection of a Lumière brothers' actuality, Train Arriving at the Station *(1895), offers a searing reverse-angle perspective on the movement of the actualities of the everyday. With recurrent camera angles and positions reminiscent of the Lumières' short film of a train's arrival, Farocki's more recent film focuses instead on departure as both a historical and a conceptual figure: "Tuesday morning a train left Westerbork, headed for Bergen-Belsen and Theresienstadt—to Auschwitz and Sobibor."*

The setting, subject, and activities of the film are an unsettling blend of the placid banalities of everyday life and the historically horrific, an overlay of the mundane local occasions of the camp and uncontainable tragedy of the Holocaust. Despite sometimes dreary still photos of the barren grounds, bleak buildings, and posed groups of inmates, there is only the rare shadow of death in the film; instead, the film mostly records the uncanny ordinary, as in shots of empty but clean and neat beds. Daily activities include the unloading and loading of train boxcars, the processing of ID cards, work in a laundry room by prisoners who serve "more than 10,000 inmates," gymnastics performed by smiling and laughing women, and orchestral and theatrical productions. "We expect other images from a camp of the German Nazis," an intertitle notes and then later describes the troubling overlay that resonates through these images: "Images that we know from other camps overshadow the ones from Westerbork." A futuristic knowledge located in the present thus visibly disrupts the transit from the past and becomes even more explicit when shots of workers lounging horizontally in the grass are intercut with a title that "ghosts" the reality of those past images with "afterimages": "Over the images of the afternoon break lies the image of the dead on the open grounds of Buchenwald." [fig. 6.1] In an excessively banal shot of individuals in white lab jackets sitting at a table, a simple intertitle reaches out and forward: "They are reminiscent of the human experiments in Auschwitz or Dachau."

An essayistic encounter with a home movie intended to be a propaganda film, Respite *moves between two frameworks of vision that interlock here as an*

FIGURE 6.1   Ghosted afterimages: the dead of Buchenwald haunt an afternoon work break (*Respite*)

engagement with a vanishing subjectivity swept up in everyday history: the insti-
tutional view of the commandant who (later) claims he wanted the film to be a
kind of documentary "for visitors to the camp" and that of Breslauer, a Jewish
inmate of the camp who, in 1944, was ordered to use two 16-mm cameras for two
months in his role as a different sort of man with a movie camera. The film shifts
almost imperceptibly between two views of the camp, struggling to negotiate the
gap between a false institutional objectivity and a mysteriously unknowable and
ultimately lost subjectivity. Producing ninety minutes of unfinished film material
"barely edited, sorted according to location," the commandant who "ordered these
images to be made" would claim in court that he was not aware of these images or
of Auschwitz. The other image producer of the film, Breslauer, would eventually
be deported to Auschwitz and killed. Ironically encapsulating the tension between
these two points of view is the filming of a variety show with musicians, dancers,
and comedians who "were allowed to remove the Yellow Star only on-stage."
When a freeze-frame stops the performance, the incident and Respite *itself*
interrupt the commandant's newsreel construction of daily events to insert,
almost incidentally, an offstage and offscreen view: "Suddenly a woman wearing
camp overalls appears on stage. . . . On her wheelbarrow appear the letters of the
Camp Police." The film then cuts to reveal a cart with the same lettering at the
ominous train platform.

Between the two silent views of events, of the seen and the barely seen, are
only titles and intertitles that comment on the images, an odd essayistic voice dis-
embodied and absented as a silent text. In a sense, the unsettling silence of the film
might be seen as ironically analogous to the vacant subjectivity of mainstream
news reportage, so commonly and oddly engaged as a respite from daily life. Coun-
terpointing that typically empty silence of the news, the center of Respite *is an*
essayistic enunciation that resides not in the common voice-over or dramatized
persona but as the in-between of the intertitles that visually interrupt the silence
of the images. As Elsaesser describes earlier versions of this two-part montage in
Farocki's films: "One is a sort of meta-commentary . . . like a steady murmur,
repeating the need to 'separate and join'. The other type . . . is embedded in the
movement of thought, as its structuring dynamic, but verbalized, if at all, only as
the cut, the gap of what becomes visible 'in-between'" ("Harun Farocki" 19).

At times, the intertitles alone create a minimal editorial inflection that sug-
gests less a position than the difficulty of taking a position. Describing the odd
passivity and complicity of the Jews at the camp, the title notes: "The SS was
hardly visible within the camp. Inmates themselves registered the new arrivals,
served in the Camp Police Corps, and helped make the lists of people to be deported."
At times, there is almost a perplexity in attempting to read these images with the

knowledge of the present: "SS soldiers stand around chatting. It seems as if nobody has to be afraid of them" or "Beatings and murder didn't happen at Westerbork." At other times, the titles describe the murmuring gap that resides within the images and where mere description seems like an anxious substitute for an interpretive interpellation. With footage of a soccer match, the intertitle drifts across the images, looking for an interpretive focus: "For this scene the title was supposed to appear: 'Roll Call on Sunday Afternoon' [presented in the original stylized script]. . . . In the background are the camp barracks. . . . In the background a watchtower." Finally, late in the film, in a sequence with extended shots of camp farm workers made apparently as propaganda to document the productivity of the transit camp, the commentary seems to struggle with its own perplexity as a retrospective reading of the footage: If these images appear to describe the inmates as animalistic slave labor, it reflects, they "can also be read differently. . . . As if they were developing something of their own, a new society perhaps."

Within this visual and verbal movement, Respite *becomes an investigation of the history of the minutiae of the camp, a discovery of fleeting truths and the transitory knowledge within the images of those past current events as a "form of intelligence" (Elsaesser, "Working at the Margins"). Here, truth and knowledge hide in the transitional current of everyday events, which the movement of the film image not only supports but also opens to the attentive viewer for possible interventions. In one remarkable sequence midway through* Respite, *the film repeats a shot of a sickly woman being wheeled to train cars filled with those to be sent to extermination camps. After freezing the frame with the cart, the film cuts to a close-up of her suitcase. The commentary notes an address on it, returns to the freeze-frame, and ruminates on the name and date as a hindsight analysis of the arrested image: "F. or P. Kroon can be read and the date: 26, 82, or 92? The official transport list notes the name Frouwke Kroon, born 9/26/1882. She was deported on May 19, 1944 to Auschwitz and murdered right after arriving. The writing on the suitcase makes it possible to determine the date of the film images: May 19, 1944." As the image cuts to another shot, the descriptions of seemingly incidental details, a child in a train window and a number on a boxcar changed to indicate not 74 but 75 persons inside, suddenly become charged with a perspective and history outside the image, probing that image: "On this day a child waved goodbye. A man helped close the door of the boxcar that carried him away. On May 19, 1944, a train with 691 people left Westerbork."*

In the shadow of trains arriving and departing, Respite *calmly but insistently examines events on film and the event of film as a crisis of transitions, transitions documented in the recurrent images of trains leaving the station for extermination camps, transitions within the conceptual current that blurs the past through the present, and transitions that produce anonymities that effectively erase those lost subjects. An official title from the original production celebrates these transitions with stunning specificity: "Ever since July, 1942, almost two years ago, the same image: Transit." Against footage of Jews loading and unloading from the trains, confusedly crossing the image pointing and looking, the commentary notes: "Most of the images we know from the camps were made after the liberation," when there is no possibility of hiding the brutality of the events. In* Respite, *however, that impending brutality of those events threatens to fade within the transitory anonymity of daily routines and travel, except when the singularity of those reverse shots of transit quietly anticipates that brutality as a future: "These are only images that exist of trains to the extermination camps. . . . About 100 trains left Westerbork. . . . About 100,000 people were deported from here."*

The transitions that describe the current of events here implicate film specifically as it works to erase the historical subject through the anonymity of the edited image. Women smiling at the camera become "moments of self-affirmation," and over footage of loading trains and trains leaving the platform, the film returns to the shot of the invalid woman in a cart and comments: "Perhaps the presence of the camera gave the deportees hope. . . . How could the destination be so terrible if the Nazis were letting the train's departure be filmed?" The irony here of course is that the camera elicits smiles and hope as a historical witness and affirmation made possible by the illusion of filmic presence and permanence, while, in fact, that original film works to eradicate the very historical presence of its real victims. As those subjects disappear into the passing boxcars and passing film image, Farocki pauses the movement, again with a freeze-frame, to isolate and rescue, with the aid of the Jewish cinematographer Breslauer, a subject and subjectivity from the vacant anonymity of the medium and long shots of the film: "Only once does the camera focus on a person's face," the title notes, as the film returns to an earlier shot of "ten-year-old Settela Steinbach, a Sinti, also murdered in Auschwitz. . . . In the girl's face is an expression of deathly fear or sense of death. . . . I think that is why the cameraman . . . avoided any further close ups." [fig. 6.2] A shocking and perhaps inadvertent rupture in the film presentation, this close-up of a face arrests the flow of images as vanishing subjective plea within the trauma of historical transit.

The news of history resides here as a knowledge to be discovered, within the respite of the everyday, to be rethought through the elided close-ups within the transit of daily events. The essayistic subject becomes dispersed here as a problem of knowing within the transitory movements of history and film. [fig. 6.3] Especially appropriate for this film is Farocki's description, in an interview with Elsaesser, of "the movement of thought" as a search for an image, "an image like a

FIGURE 6.2   The renowned close-up of a Sinti girl murdered at Auschwitz (*Respite*)

FIGURE 6.3   Transitions, junctures, and junctions of half-truths (*Respite*)

juncture, the way one speaks of a railway junction" (Harun Farocki 186). *The stir-*
ring question found at these junctures and junctions of Respite *becomes the inci-*
sively direct question that motivates many editorial essay films: "Are these images
comforting half-truths" about to leave the station? For this film, images are indeed
invariably half-truths that demand the essayistic necessity of intervening within
them at the juncture of their disappearance, where one discovers the other half of
those truths as they pass by, where one actively rethinks and reexamines those
images through the multiple perspectives of the present and future.

As Farocki reminds us with his other re-creation of a Lumière film, his 1995
Workers Leaving the Factory, the movies have been a forum for current events, views

of history, and the making of public opinion since the origins of film history. Beginning with the short presentations of "actualities" and "topicals" at the turn of the last century, film narratives and documentaries have famously and infamously run their course through propaganda, political countercinemas, documentary exposés, and postcolonial interventions. Summarized in Woodrow Wilson's astonishing description of *Birth of a Nation* (1915) as "history written in lightning," narrative cinema often aspires to purportedly factual views of past and current events, while other narrative films, like Sergei Eisenstein's *The Battleship Potemkin* (1925) or *District 9* (2009), about aliens segregated in South Africa, commonly use past or future events as commentaries on current events and contemporary public life.

When John Grierson coins the term *documentaries* in the 1920s, he names an alternative practice that would be devoted to "the creative treatment of actuality" for the next century and purportedly offer a more direct access to those actualities than that found in the reconstructions of narrative cinema, a practice exemplified in these first years by Grierson's own 1929 *The Drifters* and its presentation of the life of herring fishermen. This imperative to diffuse information in the present tense—social, ethnographic, political, and ecological—would continue through documentaries of the 1930s and develop into the more specific and continuous practice of political and war reportage seen in the *Why We Fight Series* and the more general news series *News on the March* of the 1930s and 1940s. With overtones that anticipate the essay film, Jonathan Kahana's study of American documentaries, *Intelligence Work*, follows the more politically and intellectually engaged of these early documentary traditions from the 1930s through the present as they activate "the role of the intellectual in mediating between dominant and oppressed groups, between state and people" (15).

After the watershed decade of the 1940s, documentary reportage changes directions, sometimes dramatically. As faith in the truth of the cinematic and documentary image erodes in the late 1930s, in the 1940s and early 1950s, the blurring of propaganda and documentary reportage raises persistent, if not permanent, questions about unmediated and unbiased representation of public events. Especially in the wake of the events of World War II, the most important and traumatic historical events frequently appear as unseeable and unspeakable current events (associated usually with past or future holocausts), threatening a kind of paralysis or silence before incomprehensible images.

In part a response to these and other regularly acknowledged blind spots that permeate postwar documentaries, the cinema vérité and direct cinema movements of Europe and North America respond to the increasingly fragile and indeterminate status of the documentary image by reporting the news as an interactive immediacy and public inquiry. In films such as *Chronicle of a Summer* (1961), lightweight technologies allow filmmakers to examine current events or social issues—about personal happiness, education, the war in Algeria—in a way that foregrounds the intervening perspectives and questions of the filmmakers, and so makes public events the product of a public and intersubjective dialogue with and investigation by the filmmakers. With different emphases, cinema vérité and direct cinema work to engage and establish documentary news (of social issues, politics, or popular culture) within an immediacy that highlights and confirms the authenticity of the various subjective agencies that shape them. For the editorial essay film, however, critical questions about the coherency and activity of this subjective agency are precisely what would distinguish it from these two other related practices, notably as the ideals of cinematic truth become remade by television news and its eventual paralysis of agency.

In the late 1950s, investigative television, as a mainstream variation on cinema vérité, represents some of the utopian potentials that television brought to the practice of documentary news, exemplified in the broadcasts of William Murrow. Through the next decades, the dialogic engagement of television with current events would become increasingly institutionalized around a celebrity agency that would redefine and undermine that investigation to know or to question the world of events and so reshape the legacy of cinema vérité as a "self-evident" current of the past disappearing into the present, the factual evidence for which is often the celebrity self that presents and anchors the report. Through television news especially but not exclusively, history becomes a flow of events whose currency depends on their materialization as consumable private events presented, like the found footage of a home movie but now depicting the world news, through a singularly reliable agent.

A central consequence of this anchored agency is the paralysis of agency within public events so that the viewer becomes, too frequently, the silent subject of a media history passively positioned before the unmalleable facts of the everyday. Jean Baudrillard's comments on the television coverage of the Gulf War are, in this regard, a powerful summary of what is most negative and problematic here: For him, this is "useless, instantaneous television" that only fills "a vacuum, blocking up the screen hole through which escapes the substance of events." This kind of television news is "promotional, speculative, virtual," the "emptiness of which fills our screens," and allows "no interrogation into the event itself or its reality" (101, 121). Or, in Fredric Jameson's formulation of "the media exhaustion of news": "One is tempted to say that the very function of the news media is to relegate such recent historical experiences as rapidly as possible into the past. The informational function of the media would thus be to help us forget, to serve as the very agents and mechanisms for our historical amnesia" ("Postmodernism" 1040–1041).

Indeed, a wry commentary on this state of contemporary media is Raoul Ruiz's 1978 television essay film *Of Great Events and Ordinary People* (1979): Commissioned to make a television documentary in his Paris arrondissement about a recent French election, the film parodies television's vérité structure and style (with an uncredited voice-over by Baudrillard) to create a film about current events in which the talking heads on the streets provide virtually no information and no knowledge about that election.

In this contemporary context, the editorial essay aims not only to activate a thinking subject before that empty screen but also to propel that thinking as an intellectual and concrete action within the historical unfolding of events.[3] Rather bluntly and awkwardly demonstrated in *An Inconvenient Truth* (2006), in which Al Gore lectures about the dangers of global warming (at best a mainstream version of an essay film), these films engage social events and institutions as not only about what is known or not known but also about how it is known, offering philosophical and political meditations on world events such as the Iraq war, the AIDS epidemic, and the devastation of New Orleans by Hurricane Katrina. Others initiate more circumscribed communal debates about social arenas or institutions such as the family crisis explored in essay films like *Capturing the Friedmans* (2003) and its deflected investigation of possible child abuse.[4] To editorialize as the subjective agent of the news here means to intervene and possibly to provoke, not as a way of delivering that news as facts but rather as a way of thinking about and exploring those events through various agencies. If portrait essays release and fracture the face of the subject within the flux of history, editorial essays seek out those many, often lost, subjects within the current of historical events, allowing those faces to emerge clearly as the multiple subjectivities on the street. If specific dates and times of events describe a vanishing sequence of abstract points in time, the essayist discovers beneath and between those dates the pronounced and graphic faces of different subjectivities in crisis.

One of the growing number of films that stretches the bounds of the essayistic into animation, Ari Folman's Waltz with Bashir *(2008) journeys through the crisis of the present to the crisis of the past in a struggle to know those events as simultaneously past and current. Built around recorded interviews with nine friends, it is an autobiographical investigation by an Israeli veteran of the First Lebanon War of 1982 that begins with his friend Boaz's anxious dream of twenty-six vicious dogs, a dream that is seemingly related to the Lebanon invasion and the buried questions about what actually happened then. In the dream, the dogs charge through streets past frightened bystanders while the dreamer watches from a window, high above the street: "I see all twenty-six of them. Here to take a life." For two years, the dream "always stops at the same point," when the dogs are killed to silence them, an oneiric flashback to when Israeli soldiers sometimes shot watchdogs to avoid detection. Buried beneath the dream is, we later discover, the massacre of Palestinian refugees by Christian Falangist militia at the Sabra and Shatila refugee camps, where hundreds of innocent people were murdered to avenge the assassination of Lebanese President Bashir Gemayel.*[5] *[fig. 6.4]*

The "waltz" with Bashir suggests, perhaps, a cryptic partnership and complicity between the Israeli army and the agents of the slaughter or, perhaps, a murkier complicity between individual soldiers, citizens, and even the media. The darker shadow that shades the animated report is whether the Israeli military forces enabled the slaughter by, if nothing else, their passivity. Within the current of those events and the general passivity before them, why did no one act, and how was one to act? A third suggestion in the title is dramatized in a memory of Ari's friend Frenkel, who seizes a gun and "waltzes" across an embattled intersection firing wildly before an audience of bystanders on a balcony, creating a surreal waltz with violence. Finally, a fourth connotation is Ari's own waltz as a psychological dance with those events, anchored in his only clear memory of a furrow when he sees a poster of Bashir. Less an investigative narrative than a conceptual, psychopolitical, and representational dance with wolves, the drawn-out imperative of the film is then to answer the silence that follows the death of the dogs, to unmask an aesthetics of violence, to address the cinematic and documentary passivity before historical events, and to make the present of current events a far more conceptually complex and vexed place for the subject experiencing that present as a past.[6]

FIGURE 6.4   Dancing with the dogs of war (*Waltz with Bashir*)

A dialogue with the dream of another, Waltz with Bashir *is an editorial investigation by an individual adrift in a historical trauma that has fragmented him both personally and socially, struggling with a repressed subjectivity that vibrates through a social network of former comrades. Early in one of the flashbacks that structure this investigation of memory, an attack on an Israeli tank ravages Ari's group, sending him fleeing into the sea, where his animated figure drifts aimlessly along the shore, searching for a safe place to emerge. Appearing early in the film, these images become a central metaphor for the subjective drift that structures the film, attempting to emerge from the current of its own history— not necessarily with a stable identity but at least with a self-knowledge of his past. At one point, one of his former comrades, Ronny Dayag, shows Ari a picture of himself animated against a real photographic background, and Ari remarks, "I don't recognize myself." Just as the animation troubles the indexical objectivity of the photograph, the recognition of self as part of a larger history describes the problematic struggle of the film. Pulled by a longing to forget, Ari is equally anxious to work against that current of forgetfulness and to actively know. "Tell me Frenkel, was I there too?" he asks, and Frenkel reminds him, "Sure . . . you were everywhere with me." As in many essayistic encounters, Ari begins to realize "maybe I'll discover things about myself I didn't really want to know."*

The problematic of this struggle to "discover things about myself" has led some viewers to criticize the film as an example of an Israeli "shoot-and-cry" posture, by which accountability for the violence in the Middle East becomes reformulated as a narrative of victimization.[7] *Whatever traces there are of this position,* Waltz with Bashir, *I would argue, confronts it as an effort to claim a personal responsibility through the struggle of memory to admit accountability, that is, as an essayistic restructuring of a public trauma as a personal responsibility. If memory commonly re-creates past events to protectively enfold the subject as a passive (and often victimized) agent of those events,* Waltz with Bashir *works to recover the memories of a historical trauma as a responsibility within the fabric of the present by documenting a representational history of everyday disassociations recovered and admitted as ethically associated responsibilities. Like daily news reports, Ari remembers his involvement in the war as a bland blend of barely reconcilable routines: Amidst bombings and killings, a rock song blares "I bombed Beirut today"; a daily routine means breakfast, "a quick swim, and then go after some terrorists"; everyday there is the "deposing" of the dead and wounded and a dull round of shooting and mechanical lining up of bodies. "We call them disassociative events," the therapist Zahava Solomon explains in the film. "A person experiences a situation and yet they perceive themselves as outside of it." To counter this experience of disassociated violence within the everyday demands an active rethinking*

*of that disassociated self, an aggressive remaking of that self within the turmoil of
the remembered as real and present. Solomon thus counters Ari's notion that passive dreams are active memories: "You've got it backwards: Our minds don't take
us to the places that we really don't want to go. They have a way of preventing us
from going into dark and totally dangerous recollections. Our memories will take
us only as far as we're capable of going." As those repeated images of Ari struggling
with his thoughts as he moves in and out of his memories suggest, the essayistic
memory actively demands a difficult intellectual and imaginative work to decipher
and to think through different selves and their relationship within the often-
opaque course of history, to acknowledge and to dismantle, in a sense, the collective dissociation of responsibility through the "shoot-and-cry" blur found in so
many recent film and media narratives of the Middle East wars.*

 *Possibly the most significant dream that is repeated throughout the entire
film is Ari's own flashback to the incident at the Sabra and Shatila refugee camps,
a dream of disruptions and disassociations. The dream—which, like others scattered throughout the film, is preceded by and accessed through a recollection of
past real events—is repeated three times over the course of* Waltz with Bashir.
*Against a sky filled with dark yellow flares, three nude men leave the calm ocean
waters and slowly approach the shore, where a trailing shot of their silhouettes
shows them dressing and retrieving their guns and approaching the city of Beirut.
[fig. 6.5] Shot in slow motion, the sequence quickly shifts from a yellow day to a
dark gray night, marking a representational and temporal disruption that is also
the visualization of a traumatic disassociation. After the shot circles Ari, the*

FIGURE 6.5 Ari emerges from sea as he begins to see (*Waltz with Bashir*)

sequence ends with a close-up of his blank face as the dream concludes, the memory of a self painfully attempting to comprehend himself as a subject of history emerging from a collective sea of forgetfulness and approaching the shock of knowledge that awaits him.

Within this crisis, the central representational strategies are to document history as a world that wavers between and blends realism and animation, a shifting space specifically related to other media representations in the film. In an occupied villa, an Israeli officer watches pornographic films while war and destruction rage around him. At a key moment in the film, amidst a sniper attack at the intersection of a large street, a reporter and cameraman walk mindlessly through the scene, while women and children at the balcony watch, making comments "as if they were just watching a movie." At another point in the film, a professor describes how this kind of media distraction is more fundamentally a crisis of documentary representation: "In 1983," he says, "a photographer [experienced the war] as if seeing it through an imaginary camera. Then something happened: his camera broke. He said that when the camera broke he stopped seeing the situation as something fantastic and it became traumatic for him." Here, the devastation of war begins to slip through the film frames and images, and without that objective distancing of a film frame or the humanizing strategies of a shot/countershot harmony, Ari begins to see dead horses with "real eyes," which becomes a horror that "consumed him."

When documentary immediacy becomes disassociated from the subjective experience in these scenes, animation encounters and counters documentary reality as an enunciation that re-creates historical events through an actively editorializing mind and imagination. Produced by three kinds of drawn-from-scratch animation and "flash animation," rather than rotoscoping, images throughout Waltz with Bashir *create a flexible and shifting media surface of changing subjectivities. Unlike rotoscoping, which smoothly superimposes animation on real footage, these images overlay and reanimate documentary reality as more visible disjunctions and disruptions that represent the disassociations that occur between the investigating subject, the subject's memory, and a resistant traumatic reality. As Garrett Stewart notes, the roughly recalibrated human movements of the animation produce "troubled bodies, heavy with dream and guilt, wading through a lurid quagmire of deflected memory." Along with its "hypercinematic gestures as warp-speed transitions" between different spaces and points of view, the animation results in a "surrogate cinema" in which its "photomechanical and electronic mediations" become what I would call an essayistic editorial that reveals the historical and psychological violence lost in the continuous flow of conventional documentary realism ("Screen Memory" 58, 59).*

Toward the conclusion of the film, the description of three concentric circles around the camp where the massacre occurs becomes a key metaphor for this essayistic and animated engagement with the history of current events in the film, for the layered effort "to find out what really happened." Within the innermost circle, the massacre that evades Ari's consciousness takes place out of sight; surrounding that center is a band of individuals from Israeli army intelligence who witness from afar the signs and sounds of the slaughter; beyond this band is the more distant world of the officers and politicians who merely receive reports on interior events at dinner parties. As Ari discovers through his interviews, he was positioned within the second circle with the Israeli soldiers who witnessed the massacre and did nothing but report it. Across the refrain "Did you see it?" and "What did you do?" Ari realizes what he did not see, but he passively participated in what was a genocide surrounded by concentric but disjoined circles of Israelis. As the climactically ironic turn of the screw, Ari's inquiry into his role and place in this history of events enfolds and rethinks those circles within the larger public history of the Holocaust. As the therapist Solomon points out, Ari was asked to "unload bodies mechanically": "You took on the role of a Nazi" in your mind, even though "you were firing flares and not killing people." No wonder that, as he approached the scene of the massacre the next morning, the camp looked like a "picture from the Warsaw ghetto." If the troubled shot/countershot ideology of the entire film visually and thematically allegorizes the space between the lulling oceanic drift of a memory without agency and the unseeable grief at the slaughtered camp, Ari ultimately must think himself into that in-between space of those concentric circles where, as Stewart points out, psychological and ideological separation is no longer tenable: "What memory has involuntarily spliced together of this sundered experience until then—the defensive sea dream and the terror that infiltrates it—is their final disjunction, where Folman must recognize himself not immersed in suffering but confronted by it from his own official if rapidly vanishing distance" ("Screen Memory" 61).

The concentric circles thus become specifically a spatial reconstitution of the linear and narrative figure of events; past history is now a broken current event encompassing the past, the present, and the future, a reconstitution that demonstrates the distinctive but shared space of the historical within current events and, most important, the imperative, to intervene in that current. Ari's investigation becomes an investigation of himself as social agent within that history of a public life in which to understand both is a matter of thought and choice. At the vacant Beirut airport, he wanders into an empty terminal where the residue of normal, everyday activity appears like an animated hallucination. Before a destination board announcing flights to London, Paris, and elsewhere—flights that will not *actually leave from this war zone—he realizes that he is "waiting to choose my destination" and "the choice of destination is all up to me. I am in control." Through the course of the film, Ari discovers that his involvement in the horrific truth of events must be, ultimately, his conscious destination and choice. [fig. 6.6]*

At the end of the film and the end of his investigation, Ari and the film choose to return to his destination of the once-forgotten crowd of weeping women approaching him at a guard post near the Sabra and Shatila camps. Suddenly, the image dramatically changes, for the first time in the film, to an enhanced documentary image of those actual inconsolable and traumatized faces on the street, followed by an extended series of silent images of slaughtered bodies. The living truth of events has surfaced through the subjective choices and inquiries of the essayist as he loses himself in and then emerges from the anonymous current of events that has sustained his denial within that floating current of events. In Stewart's words about this conclusion, applicable in different ways to many editorial essays, "Documentation dislodging fantasy turns fantasy itself into a document of disavowal, the superseding archival footage into a ghostly apparition-as much a haunting by history as its straightforward record" ("Screen Memory" 62). The howling dogs of a nightmare become the wailing human voices of real events. [fig. 6.7]

When past history is absorbed into the present, blurred through "the everyday" of a vacant media agency, how do you understand, think, and ultimately *act* on that history rather than be simply swept up in that current? For the essay film, the answer is to reclaim an active subjectivity as a kind of editor seeking a face, where

FIGURE 6.6   Choosing a destiny at the Beirut airport (*Waltz with Bashir*)

FIGURE 6.7 The concluding archival footage as a haunting of history (*Waltz with Bashir*)

to edit means to investigate or to open events with "an opinion," thought, or idea about history. Thinking through current events becomes the demonstration of an agency or a place for agency as it arrests and reconfigures itself within that current of events, both archeologically *down* through a past and *across* a moving present. In her striking essay "Thinking about Feeling Historical," Lauren Berlant puts it this way: "Thinking interrupts the flow of consciousness with a new demand for scanning and focus, not for any particular kind of cognitive processing. We are directed to see not an event but an emergent historical environment that can now be sensed atmospherically, collectively. To be forced into thought this way is to begin to formulate the event of feeling historical in the present" (5).[8]

Here especially, the risk that underpins the essayistic stands out since to risk a position within such a swirling tide of events often amounts to inserting a self in the unpredictable flux of material of history and the inevitable resistance of public events. As one indication and measure of the problem of politics in the essayistic, essayistic risk requires claiming a precarious position for the self as an agency of thought in which the private life questions the history it has inherited as the prelude to future action. In both the degree of risk and the measure of its achievement—what Nichols describes as a performative "magnitude" (*Blurred Boundaries* 106)—this subject must recognize its changing self as it struggles to construct or reconstruct its place in history.[9]

Visibly present sometimes in an individual in the film or the rhetorical position of the film's point of view, these editorial perspectives emerge from and intervene in representational mainstreams as a drama of reformation. With both public and private events, found footage or home movies commonly serve as material for that reformation, always marked by the traces of a past assimilated through a personal perspective. With found footage, the essay film typically activates or subjectively reactivates the events of history as "an aesthetic of ruins" and a "counter-history" which becomes "an often radical and experimental rethinking of context" (Danks 242, 251).[10] In "The Resurgence of History and the Avant-Garde Essay Film," Arthur connects found footage specifically with the essay, as it manifests itself in a variety of films from James Benning's *American Dreams* (1983) to Jean-Pierre Gorin's *Routine Pleasures* (1986), and demonstrates how the essayistic allows an avant-garde tradition to engage the present through documentary footage potentially lost in historical currents. Essays, he argues,

> tend to inscribe a central mediating consciousness that is itself engaged in active questioning of materials and the process of their ordering, able finally to secure only provisional truths. . . . Lacking the guarantees of a stable, self-assured narrator, the notion of a shared past is rendered fluid, plurivocal, riddled with the incursions of popular culture, high theory, and the vestiges of earlier avant-garde styles. . . . [In these films] a core of distant events—accessed through found objects, personal narratives, and/or direct camera observation—are subjected to a sinuous interaction of semiautonomous parts made up of different tenses, rhetorical voices, and visual styles. At their best, they can create collage effects that thicken and enliven our sense of historical time. (68)

In Linda Williams's description of the use of found footage in Morris's *The Thin Blue Line*, these "anti-vérité documentaries" dig "toward an impossible archeology" where "the contextualization of the present with the past . . . is the most effective representational strategy" since the event, "never whole, never fully represented," is always "a palimpsest of memory" (387, 388).

Contemporary essay films have addressed this perilous predicament of interpellating a subjective and investigative agency within the found footage of media events from a variety of angles. No doubt Michael Moore's films are the most visible and well known, as a remaking of the news across his own image and agency. Despite the sometimes shrill criticism of these films as distorting self-promotions, Moore's films are, I believe, not simply about a creating an oppositional view of current events but about dramatizing an always-present agency—which most news reportage works to disguise or makes invisible—engaged with the reconstruction of the news of history. Despite his often-outlandish and cartoonish posturing—or, more accurately, because of those poses—Moore and his films effectively mimic and ironize the strategies of conventional news reportage as efforts, I would argue, to return the ideological risks of subjective thinking to the streets of public events.

The most successful and highest-grossing documentary at the time of its release and the surprising and controversial winner of the 2004 Palme d'Or at the Cannes Film Festival, *Fahrenheit 9/11* (2004), for instance, targets a social crisis triggered by the questionable election of George W. Bush as the president of the United States and the subsequent launching of the war in Iraq. The real target of the film is, however, American news coverage of those events, signaled definitively in the opening sequences of the film. Following the "Florida Victory" rally for Al Gore, Moore's voice-over asks, "Was it all just a dream? Or was it real? Did the last four years really happen?" Moore then details the fiasco of the 2000 election coverage, when Fox News Channel's John Ellis, Bush's first cousin, "called the election in favor of the other guy" and "all of a sudden other networks said 'If Fox said it, it must be true.'" Although conservative criticism attacks Moore's lack of documentary objectivity, that assumed objectivity is precisely what Moore and other essay filmmakers recognize as no longer tenable or defendable in contemporary media and society, in which the facts and information now drift through the blurred regions of celebrity agencies, flaunting what Matthew Bernstein (following Arthur) refers to as Moore's "negative mastery" and ironic self-presentations of "uncontrolling antiheroes" (411).[11] If Moore's films are essay films of a sort, the more fundamental question is whether Moore simply re-creates those celebrity agencies that he attacks or does he ironize and parody them to provoke the unstable thinking of selves in public that describes essayism.

Other essay films undertake pronouncedly more theoretical, rigorous, and open-ended investigations of how and where ethical and political agencies might enter the stream of current event and the news of them. Perhaps the preeminent archeologist of the found footage and imagistic ruins of twentieth-century media history, Kluge and his films have embodied this essayistic agenda to the extent that Kluge has himself assumed, for a time, a place within the German television industry, recognizing that that machinery is not the primary problem but the lack of alternative positions that would provide and provoke a complex interaction with that machinery and the so-called facts of history.[12] His film *Miscellaneous News* (1986) is explicit: It satirizes and deconstructs a conventional television news format and its talking-head agencies and delivers perhaps its most incisive editorial cut: "Saturday, April 26, 1986, 10 pm," the date of the meltdown of a nuclear reactor in Chernobyl, followed immediately by the curious face of a child. The closing quotation of his open-ended essay on nuclear war, *War and Peace*

(1982), locates what is for Kluge the crucial task of activating the film "inside the spectator's head" in an effort to editorially dismantle the imagistic news of history, delivered through those anonymous celebrity agents of that history: "The nearly unsolvable problem is how to avoid being struck dumb, whether through the power of others, or through one's own paralysis."

As with many of the richest suggestions about the essayistic and film, Benjamin describes and anticipates the conceptual place of the essayistic subject as he or she might intervene in these currents of history. Writing in the late 1930s in his monumental "The Work of Art in the Age of Its Technological Reproducibility," Benjamin briefly shifts his attention from film to newspapers to suggest how, as an analogy for film's performative audiences, the public circulation of the news offers editorial possibilities and potential to any and all individuals. He explains here that the potential "testing" of experience through which audiences critically engage films has first been demonstrated by newspapers. "With the growth and extension of the press," he notes,

> an increasing number of readers . . . [have] turned into writers. It began with the space set aside for "letter to the editors" in the daily press, and has now reached a point where there is hardly a European engaged in the work process who could not, in principle, find an opportunity to publish somewhere or other an account of a work experience, a complaint, a report, or something of the kind. Thus, the distinction between author and public is about to lose its axiomatic character. . . . At any moment, the reader is become a writer. (262).

Characteristic of Benjamin's work, this sociological observation about newly activated subjects of the news springs from a philosophical foundation about how knowledge can be produced within the currents of history, specifically as a critical act of "recognition." For him, the assimilation of the past into the present as a current of events disguises a more fundamental dialectical relationship between these two figures of history, a relationship revealed, for him, in a flash of recognition that crystallizes, in a conceptual image, a "constellation" of thought:

> It is not that what is past casts its light on what is present, or what is present its light on what is past; rather image is that wherein what has been comes together in a flash with the now to form a constellation. In other words, image is dialectics at a standstill. For while the relation of the present to the past is a purely temporal, continuous one, the relation of what-has-been to the now is dialectical: is not progression but image, suddenly emergent. (*The Arcades Project* 462)

Recalling Chris Marker's space between two shots, Benjamin's constellation image also recalls Farocki's image at the juncture/junction of movement and Folman's tensely animated documentary images, identifying the act of recognition as a moment of active and sometimes violent construction of a dialectical image: "To thinking belongs the movement as well as the arrest of thoughts. Where thinking comes to a standstill in a constellation saturated with tensions—there the dialectical image appears. It is the caesura in the movement of thought. Its position is naturally not an arbitrary one. It is to be found, in a word, where the tension between dialectical opposites is greatest. Hence, the object constructed in the materialist presentation of history is itself a dialectical image. The latter is identical with the historical object; it justifies its violent expulsion from the continuum of historical process" (*The Arcades Project* 475). Within Benjamin's larger philosophical scheme, thinking in history becomes a temporally fragile and thus risky recognition that recovers or rescues the meaning of events from a "homogenous empty time" ("On the Concept of History" 396) through a freeze-frame of insight described as "The Now of recognizability": "The dialectical is an image that emerges suddenly, in a flash. What has been is to be held fast—as an image flashing up in the now of its recognizability. The rescue that is carried out by these means—and only by these—can operate solely for the sake of what in the next moment is already irretrievably lost" (*The Arcades Project* 473).

Following Benjamin, I would characterize essayistic agency within the current of historical events as the difference between witnessing events and recognizing events where the act of recognition is both a rescue and an expectation that reframes the act of witnessing. Again extrapolating from Benjamin, the editorial agent of history might be said to engage the current of events as a merging of all three of Benjamin's temporal agents: the gambler, the flaneur, and the active host. "Rather than pass the time, one must invite it in," Benjamin says. "To pass the time (to kill time, expel it) is the act of the gambler. Time spills from his every pore"; "To store time as a battery stores energy" is the act of the flaneur; and the third type is "he who waits. He takes in time and renders it up in altered form—that of expectation" (*The Arcades Project* 107). At once expelling, storing, and waiting, the essayist enters the current of events balancing multiple stances toward those events as risky moments of recognition that are also intellectually insistent acts of expectation.

Lynne Sachs's States of UnBelonging *(2006) begins in a private life suffused by global television images, visible on a screen in the background of a living room in New York City. A young girl (Sachs's daughter) plays on the left side of the frame, while Sachs sits at a table on the right side, watching a news report that shows*

scenes of war and protest in the Middle East. Over the clicking of an e-mail cor-
respondence, Sachs writes to her Israeli friend Nir: "Did you ever have the feeling that
the history you are experiencing has no shape? Even as a teenager I was obsessed
with history's shifts and ruptures. Wars helped us order time." She writes Nir about
a news report in New York Times that describes the terrorist murder of Israeli filmmaker Revital Ohayon and her two children living in Kibbutz Metzer on the West
Bank. As she later talks with Nir on the telephone about the incident, a close-up of
Sachs's hands cuts out the newspaper article while the blurred television image continues in the background. She folds and turns the material of the newspaper article
and then a map of Israel, through a series of superimposed images. Introducing a
kind of home movie of current events, these first, dense, and layered images locate
the film against the background of television news and the difficult understanding of
history through the crisis of war. [fig. 6.8] Here, a seemingly never-ending crisis
becomes the quintessential contemporary current of events that, in this essay, must
be engaged and rewritten as a caesura across global geographies, an imagistic constellation rather than an indefatigable historical flow. Over television images of street
violence in Israel late in the film, Sachs's daughter Maya later asks her, "Is there a
war in Israel, mom?" "No, not today" is Sachs's reply, ironically but accurately introducing an essayistic longing to arrest those events within the layers of history.

Through the course of the film, this current of events changes directions constantly, as the film stops, redirects, and reverses the movement of those events.
Reminiscent of Marker's Sunless with its rapid and unexpected global movements,
States of UnBelonging disperses perspectives and voices across different individuals and material representations. A multitechnological epistolary exchange
between New York City and Israel across e-mails and phone conversations, the film

FIGURE 6.8   Editing the world news as a home movie (*States of UnBelonging*)

ultimately culminates in a series of face-to-face meetings in Israel, meetings with the living and the dead. At one point, Sachs searches for information on the Internet in foreground, while watching a video in background of the weeping Avi Ohayon, husband of Revital, and at the same time speaking to Nir on the telephone. Even global geographies fluctuate and overlap within this global current of crises: When Sachs interviews Revital's brother, Yossi, and asks why, after 9/11, did she live so close to danger, he replies that his sister may have wondered why Sachs would live in New York with two daughters. Exact dates announce moments and movements—November 12, 2002; December 10, 2002; February 27, 2005; March 1, 2005—but rather than indicate a chronological movement of history, the dates suggest ruptures and gaps in the difficult effort to comprehend the everyday of a present through the ruins of a past. Like dates of a daily newspaper, these dates threaten to become only fragments of the past.

Materialized as found footage, old home movies, and rebroadcast television news, history surfaces in the course of the film as the shifting and superimposed constellations of different geographies, textualities, time zones, and imagistic fabrics. News broadcasts of war, home movies of Revital and her son, videos of the daycare center the day after the death of two children, Nir's filmed interview of Avi, and clips of Revital's own films Young Poetry *and* It Happens So Often *together create a fractured montage of the past and the present, the public and the personal, which even images of the luxurious beauty of abundant olive groves and Sachs's readings of Biblical histories are unable to harmonize and resolve as anything but clashes across a geography that "drives people mad" and where individuals "on both sides of the Green Line, on the other side of the Wall" live with death minute to minute. Here the everyday waivers and cracks: Shots of a soldier walking the streets are slowed and disrupted by small jump cuts, and street scenes tilt out of focus or tip within canted frames. Like an endless war, these states of unbelonging offer no place in which a self can be situated and clearly articulated. It is rather a state of perilous expectations or, as Revital's husband describes it, a place of such intense longing that there is simply nowhere to locate the extreme sorrow of that longing. Even film practice is, it seems, tautly drawn between unbelonging and longing, between the news and knowledge: "Did you know that this week is the Jerusalem Film Festival?" Nir writes, "Parallel to it is the Ramallah International Film Festival. Ramallah is a big city on the Palestinian side of the border. I wish I could visit to show my films and also to see film in a theater over there. I would have a drink in the local Palestinian café. See a life that is so close to me and yet so far away. Separated and strange. It exists as the Palestinian town from the news. I can only imagine, of course, since I have never visited myself. It is quite impossible for me as an Israeli to experience Ramallah. Ramallah Dreaming."*

In this current of longing and unbelonging, however, Sachs simultaneously discovers and creates an image of recognition, the image of an agency that is in fact the face and history of the film itself. Early in the film, her voice-over describes a hesitant, fearful, and divided self, doubled in fact as the reflection of Rivetal, that other woman, mother, and filmmaker. Throughout this first part of the film, Sachs's presence assumes, despite its centrality, almost a marginal position. Watching, commenting, reading, she is ubiquitously there, but the film never provides a full image of her, only parts of her (hands, hair, and partial glimpses). Gradually, though, she begins to emerge as a recognizable presence and body, first in a café interview with Revital's brother, Yossi. Later, a full shot of her shows her adjusting her camera, and then a close-up focuses on her as she places the rock on the grave of Revital, a gesture that, while an act of mourning, also describes, I believe, an act of mutual recognition. [fig. 6.9]

Sachs's gradual assumption of an agency here, as part of a recognized bond with Revital, depends on and provokes two related actions: her turning off the television and her decision to go to Israel. They are complimentary actions, suggesting, first, her refusal to participate in the empty and homogeneous media flow of events and, second, her choice to enter the current of real events. Unlike Revital, whom Yossi describes as living in "a bubble" on her kibbutz, not reading or watching the news and not wanting to know, Sachs chooses ultimately to "know" as an investigation beyond the news, and her words and voice quickly assume a declarative rhetoric that confronts the alienating collage of abstracted images of the televised streets in Israel. Two titles on the screen describe at once her hesitation and decision: "I don't think there's any way I can go to Israel," immediately followed by, "I don't think there's any way I cannot go to Israel." On March 1, 2005, she

FIGURE 6.9   The emergence of Sachs at the grave of Revital (*States of UnBelonging*)

announces, "I've stopped watching television all together. I have a rock to put on her grave."

What is most significant about this transition is, I believe, that it is an act of will and mind to overcome the paralysis and distance of world events and to know those events by inhabiting them the way one would know the physical land. In that sense, that actual land, so often abstracted through borders, maps, and news broadcasts, becomes an anchor within the current of events through which the subject can feel and live those events as personal experience. "This is the land that devours it own, I've read and read again in the Bible," Sachs says of the Middle East. "The land of hyenas and jackals and doves, perpetually dry or consumed by water. It is a land I know now, but only anciently. At last, I can follow the green line with my finger, but I have yet to feel its actual bumps and crevices." Earlier, Avi observes that "when you see those pictures coming from Israel every day, you stop seeing it as something that's happening to people and you start approaching it as a big event in the corner of the world," as part of a "geographic farness [that] makes you numb." It is precisely that numbness before the geographic farness of media events that Sachs engages and chooses to physically and mentally overcome. Remarking on a world of bombs and explosions constantly flowing across the news from Israel to Istanbul to Iraq, Sachs thinks out loud in a flash of recognition and participation that is a visceral experience: "Any shake up on the surface of the earth dislodges my equilibrium. Newspapers drape us with the news of another person's death. When scanning a page of horrors, . . . an open window onto the spectacle of killing. A gust of wind and I almost smell it." As she leaves for the Middle East, she is thus determined not be "a war photographer," and unlike the endless stream of news reports, she is "not going to Israel to shoot a film." Hers is a decision, rather, to experience that world as an active agency, outside images and as almost physical experience, in search of knowledge, a knowledge that will presumably extend her beyond the boundaries of not only New York or Israel but also her own self and her own film. Avi remarks earlier that for Revital "no matter what choice you make it's the right choice," and here Sachs's choice becomes, not too far from that of Ari in Waltz with Bashir, the critical choice to be the changing agent and editor of her own destiny, which is inextricably also the destiny of her children.

If recognition, expectation, and choice are the cornerstones of essayistic investigations, their agency becomes positioned in State of UnBelonging through Sachs to the many children in the film as the emblems of choice and anticipatory expectation. Sachs's identification with Revital as a filmmaker most obviously functions as a point of subjective transference and transformation by which she remakes the filmmaker's death and the found footage of Revital's films as she

FIGURE 6.10   Giving the dates of history a physiognomy (*States of UnBelonging*)

incorporates them into herself and her own film. A second, and probably more important, point of identification, though, occurs with Revital's children and Sachs's two daughters, who appear in the opening and closing sequences and sporadically through the film. Images of these and other children and their loss suffuse the film: a videotape of the daycare center where young boys and girls work to process the death of their former classmates and a child playing in the extreme foreground of an image while Jewish children play in the street on a large monitor in the background. In one shot, a corner of an otherwise black image contains only the image of a terrified child.

In the final sequence, these images of children crystallize in an almost-naïve flash of insight and awareness, as the film returns to the New York living room that opened the film, now brightly lit. Before the television news in background, a daughter's voice recounts the tale of Abraham and the casting out of Ishmael that she and her sister heard from Sachs that morning. When Sachs asks her daughters how they think the two separated brothers in the tale felt, one daughter responds that she thinks they could have learned to live together. The daughter then continues with a simple question that is the kind of question rarely asked of those current events whose past moves relentlessly through the present into the future: "Who sent them into the desert?" The film then cuts to a high-angle shot of the daughter sitting down in front of a silent television, pens and paper before her on the table. [fig. 6.10] In this crisis of knowing and acting, States of UnBelonging, *like Benjamin, concludes with the recognition that "to write history means giving dates a physiognomy"* (The Arcades Project 476).

7

About Refractive Cinema: When Films Interrogate Films

ART ABOUT ART—or better put, art through art—is a tradition as long as artistic and literary history itself, extending back through many centuries of literature and visual representation and forward into film history, from well before John Keats's ode on an urn to well after Buster Keaton's comedies about a film projectionist and cameraman.[1] Like its forerunners, versions of this reflexivity in film both create and participate in their own aesthetic principals, overlapping their representations of other artistic and aesthetic experiences with their own cinematic processes and frequently reflecting those processes as a reflection on film itself. This particular kind of reflexivity commonly appears within narrative fiction films, such as Godard's *Contempt* (1963) or Robert Altman's *The Player* (1992), the first a darkly ironic story of cinematic adaptation weaving multilayer issues about fidelity and the second a wry, bitter comedy about contemporary film production. As often, however, this tradition has eschewed narrative fiction and instead followed the practices of literary essays that address and evaluate art and literature as critical engagements outside rather than inside the aesthetic tropes and positions that are their subjects.[2] Sometimes, these essay films encounter other artistic forms, as in Shari Berman and Robert Pulcini's look at underground cartoonist Harvey Pekar in *American Splendor* (2003), in which the artistic object, figure, or practice documented becomes a vehicle to reflect on the film medium itself. Other times, however, these films address films themselves, either by focusing on the figure of the filmmaker or some other dimension of the cinematic process, such as

the history of cinema or a specific technology. In these reenactments of the cinematic, the best of these films about art and film do not simply describe or document filmic or other aesthetic practices but specifically engage them within an
essayistic arena that abstracts the very activity of thinking through a cinematic
process. These particular kinds of essay films are not, I would insist, simply films
that incorporate metaphors of the cinematic as part of a narration about, for
instance, human love and loss but are films that enact and disperse the critical act
of thinking cinematically itself.

Even a cursory list of these films is overwhelming in the range and kinds of
topics they cover and how they represent them. Films that reflect on art, literature,
or other artistic practices as oblique engagements with cinematic practice would
include, to name only a few well-known examples, Resnais's *Van Gogh* (1948);
Henri-Georges Clouzot's *The Mystery of Picasso* (1956); Peter Watkins's *Edvard
Munch* (1974); Welles's *Filming "Othello"* (1978) and *F for Fake* (1975); Ruiz's *Hypothesis on a Stolen Painting* (1979); Francois Girard's *Thirty Two Short Films about Glenn
Gould* (1993); Sally Potter's *The Tango Lesson* (1997); Alexander Sokurov's *Russian
Ark* (2003); and Banksy's *Exit through the Gift Shop* (2010). Those films that engage
in a more ostensibly direct relationship with another film or filmmaker include the
traditional films about the making of a film, such as Fax Bahr and George Hicken-
looper's account of the production of *Apocalypse Now* (1979) in *Hearts of Darkness:
A Filmmaker's Apocalypse* (1991) or *Burden of Dreams* (1982), which documents the
making of Herzog's *Fitzcarraldo* (1982). More complex and essayistic versions of
these films about films are not as common but are increasingly visible in contemporary film culture: Wender's *Tokyo-Ga* (1985); Varda's *Jacquot de Nantes* (2001);
Kiarostami's *Close-Up* (1990), *Five Dedicated to Ozu* (2004), and *Ten on 10* (2004);
Marker's *One Day in the Life of Andrei Arsenevich* (1999); Lars Von Trier's *The Five
Obstructions* (2004); and Takeshi Kitano's *Glory to the Filmmaker* (2007). This type
of essay film might even occasionally aspire to theoretical debates as in Sophie
Fiennes and Slavoj Žižek's *The Pervert's Guide to Cinema* (2006) or Godard's
Histoire(s) du Cinema (1997–1998) with its emblematic motif that cinema is "a form
that thinks and thought that forms."

As an intensified version of those more wide-ranging films about art and literature, essay films about films distill, I want to argue, the fundamental inadequacy
and triumph of the essayistic, asserting that, even in the experience of the essay
film "as like" an aesthetic experience, its essential aim is anti-aesthetic, in a way
that aims to return the film to the world and ideas about the world.[3] Unlike reflexive
narrative fiction films, these essay films depend on the force and pressure of a
presumed public experience or, more precisely I think, a *public circulation* of experience
that troubles and comments on the aesthetic experience and the subjectivity that

articulates it. This does not mean that essay films about art and film necessitate a documentary style or format, as Potter's *Tango Lesson* makes clear in its deft manner of fictionalizing and personalizing the director-protagonist's relationship with the famed dancer Pablo Veron. Yet, even as partly or wholly fictionalized dramas, these films turn away from the structures of narrative and fictive identification and turn to questions of aesthetic value and judgment within other semantic contexts of public experience, such as economics, politics, technology, reception, or cultural and historical differences. Rather than mimic aesthetic terms and questions, they refract and deflect them. Rather than acting as artistic commentaries, what I will call refractive cinema reenacts art as open-ended criticism.[4] If Marker's films, notably his 1958 *Letter from Siberia*, stand out so monumentally in the early history of the essay film tradition and so broadly and intricately represent many of the strategies and subjects of this practice, his 1993 film *The Last Bolshevick* and its meditation on Russian filmmaker Aleksandr Medvedkin turns that essayistic look onto film itself where, as the commentator of that film notes, "my work is to question images."

An enigmatic example of refractive cinema, Raoul Ruiz's Hypothesis on a Stolen Painting *(1978) concentrates and ironizes many of its terms. Presented like a somber, tongue-in-cheek parody of an essayistic precedent, the academic lecture, the film is an aesthetic puzzle, presented across a series of seven paintings by a nineteenth-century painter, Frederic Tonnerre—with only six of the paintings available since the fourth has hypothetically been stolen. As an exaggerated version of the dialogic structure of the essay, the film employs an insistent direct address that jars, redirects, irritates, and confuses. At times addressing the film's spectator and at times testily in conversation with an unseen "Commentator," a "Collector" acts as the focal point of a wandering and wryly tormented subjectivity, wandering through gloomy rooms and shabby passageways of a large mansion located off a Parisian street, discussing the paintings and elusive meanings they both offer and hide. [fig. 7.1]*

Across this quest and inquest, Hypothesis *is about hermeneutics, about discovering a meaningful link between art and the world, and implicitly about film as a heuristic medium—all frustrated by a figurative aesthetic gap, the missing painting, that might provide a critical link in the investigation. The quest for the significance of the missing painting (which may or may not even have existed) as the missing link in a photogrammatic series of paintings involves five registers of images within the film, each suggesting different analytical dimensions of film form: the paintings themselves as two-dimensional representations, the tableaux vivant reenactments of the paintings by actors who give the images three-dimensional*

FIGURE 7.1 The Collector reflects on the elusive meaning of the painting (*Hypothesis on a Stolen Painting*)

depth, the movement within those otherwise motionless reenactments as the actors change scenes or accidentally shift their positions, the movement of the camera frame around these representations, and finally, the stick figures that the Collector retrieves from his desk drawer to re-create abstract rearrangements of the figure positions in the paintings. That the series of seven paintings approximates a series of film shots, scenes, or even photograms underlines the apparently reflexive relation between the subject of the film and the film itself, exacerbated and complicated further by the difficulty—for the collector, the commentator, and viewer—of finding continuity or connections to link this montage of painterly images.

The chief hermeneutical path here is visual or, more precisely, the effort to follow sight lines and lighting directions to discover explanatory links that bind the images as a movement of meaning. The film thus takes the form of an investigation into not only the meaning and history of the paintings but also the mechanisms for understanding and judging these paintings, becoming a kind of debate and trial conducted by the Commentator and Collector with the viewers of the film, who are situated as an aesthetic jury. Indicative is an early sequence of two scenes that begins when the Collector looks, with binoculars, through an open window at a tableaux vivant of the first painting in the garden below. [fig. 7.2] Alongside the actors playing the mythical Acteon and Diane, what he sees is a third figure (there "simply to watch the watcher") who holds a mirror reflecting the ray of the sun into a basement room. When Collector follows that ray, he discovers another tableaux vivant in which two Templars from the Crusades play chess, a page "with a secret smile" sits in the foreground, and another crusader in the background "interrupts" the scene of this second painting. The refracted ray of

FIGURE 7.2 Following sight lines and rays of light in search of a missing painting (*Hypothesis on a Stolen Painting*)

FIGURE 7.3 The refraction of light leads to the tableau vivant of the Templars (*Hypothesis on a Stolen Painting*)

the sun directed from the garden through the window now becomes identified as the paradoxical second source of sunlight witnessed earlier in the painting, opposite the sunlight from another window and responsible for the "theatrical composition" of this new image and painting. [fig. 7.3] The Commentator argues that "the narrative element, the arrangement of objects, and even the object of the character's point of view" are the way to understand the scene but then claims that it may be the refraction of light as a movement resembling the curve of a crescent that holds the real meaning of the images and that connects this painting to the others: "Perhaps one may now venture the hypothesis of a group of paintings whose interconnection is ensured by a play of mirrors," he says, whereby "one might see the painter's oeuvre as a reflection on the art of reproduction." But, even this interpretation becomes unsustainable for the Collector, who retorts "Absolutely not! That is not the way to look at this painting. . . . Or we shall become ensnared in the trap set for us."

To avoid that heuristic trap means to continually suspend and refract the temptation of interpretive judgment. Both the Collector and Commentator pursue the lure of numerous critical entryways, ranging from mathematical and narrative analyses of the images to allegorical and historical readings of myths, including references to a roman à clef published at the time. Yet, the continual movement across and through the staged images, alternately lost in chiaroscuro shades or redirected by specific highlighting, discovers only elusive lines of light, thinking, and meaning, refractive eye-line matches played out through a chain of mirrors, the curve of gestures, and an unresolved argument concerning images about images or images about the secrets of a world. The Collector remarks about one scenario for which he offers an elegant reading about the gestures of "the characters slowly completing a circle": "What we have here are really curves which form circles of unequal diameter if completed by imagination. And these circles may be classified roughly in three groups" forming spheres "which we can imagine as combined or not but which still evoke spheres" since "any movement effected by a human being leaves an imaginary trace comparable to a sphere."

Both the composition and course of this film are then to refract and destabilize a point of view, within the framework of the cinematic movement, redirecting it outside itself toward a field demarcated as "scandal." What specifically motivates the visual and hermeneutical movement of the film is, that is, a scandal that the film at times associates with, first, a "scandalous painting rejected by the Salon in 1887" and, second, through the analysis of the paintings, certain sexual missteps and hostilities in an aristocratic family, their connection with a secret society as ancient as the Crusades, and possibly that society's murderous "ceremony of the androgyny" whose figurehead is "Baphomet, an androgynous demon, the principle of nondefinition."[5] [fig. 7.4] Indeed, more than those vague and wry speculations about the meaning of the paintings that drift through the Collector's analyses (in fact collecting all those speculations), this fundamental principle of "nondefinition" locates, like the missing painting, the central truth of this essayistic investigation as unlocatable. Here, thinking through the aesthetic becomes not about establishing a definitive meaning or truth but about the ceremonial experience of nondefinition as metaphorically figured in Baphomet, not about recognizing meaning but about recognizing a forum for thinking about meaning. "What a terrible revelation," the Collector remarks, "The paintings did not allude, they showed. The paintings were the ceremony."

FIGURE 7.4   Scandal and the "ceremony of the androgyny" (*Hypothesis on a Stolen Painting*)

Viewers are positioned here as critical jurors of the paintings and by exten-
sions of the scandal; in the end, however, these viewer-jurors are left only with gaps
and a clutter of tableaux scattered through an abandoned mansion. In the last
sequence, an exhausted Collector sits meditating at his desk, doubting his own
interpretive powers and reminding us that these are just some fragmentary "ideas"
that the paintings have inspired. He returns to the fifth register of images (or in
fact a sixth) in the film as he removes photos of the plastic stick figures from the
desk drawer, and his own unsettled rhetoric identifies, ever so tentatively, that
elusive and self-annihilating flow that is thinking about art: "All that these paint-
ings represent is the ceremony whose solemn expression signifies the mutual anni-
hilation of the celebrants . . . no, I don't think so. . . . And yet I know that something
will be retained. The paintings are beginning to fade. . . . The paintings vanish, so
that all that remains is the isolated gestures." Or, as Ruiz notes about the larger
play between hermeneutics, aesthetics, and meaning, "Every time that a general
theory . . . is elaborated I have the impression that . . . there is a painting stolen, a
part of the story or puzzle missing. The final explanation is no more than a conven-
tional means of tying together all the paintings. It's like the horizon: once you
reach it, there is still the horizon" (Elsaesser, "Raoul Ruiz's L'Hypthesis du Tab-
leau Vole" 254). As "the collector courteously shows us the door," returning us to
the opening shot of an empty Parisian side street lined with cars, the hermetic and
hermeneutical investigations of the inside return to the vanishing points of the
outside where essayistic thought eventually resides.

If the tradition of films about aesthetic objects, practices, and figures can be
described as commentaries in the most flexible sense of the term, refractive essay
films, across their spectrum of differences, describe the move toward criticism. In

this sense, refractive cinema is the essence of the essayistic dynamic, a dynamic that Michel Foucault marks historically when he locates a sea change in Western thought in the sixteenth century, evidenced specifically in the writings of Montaigne. From those beginnings, essayistic knowledge emerges, according to Foucault, as it positions itself between the commentaries described in early responses to biblical and philosophical texts and the critical responses of scientific systems that would drive analysis in the modern era. At this transitional period in history, Foucault claims, "commentary yields to criticism," so that language no longer simply glosses a text but now intervenes to investigate, decipher, and interpret the possibilities and limits of that language. With an argument that could gloss Ruiz's film, he observes:

> For the enigma of a speech which a second language must interpret is substituted the essential discursivity of representation. . . . When this discourse becomes in turn an object of language, it is not questioned as if it were saying something without actually saying it, as if it were a language enclosed upon itself; one no longer attempts to uncover the great enigmatic statement that lies hidden beneath its signs; one asks how it functions: what representations it designates; what elements it cuts out and removes; how it analyzes and composes; what play of substitutions enables it to accomplish its role of representation. (*The Order of Things* 79–80)

In contrast to these critical endeavors, Foucault quotes Montaigne on the redundancies of commentary for which "it is more of a job to interpret the interpretations than to interpret the things" (81). Instead, criticism "questions language as if language were a pure function, a totality of mechanisms, a great autonomous play of signs; but, at the same time, it cannot fail to question it as to its truth or falsity, its transparency or opacity" (80). Rather than supplement a primary text or truth with a redundancy of commentary, criticism creates a subjective encounter with and through another representational language or medium as a questioning of the possibilities and limitations of that discourse. When commentaries yield to criticism, it generates a proliferation of interpretive points of views and positions theoretically unable to close the proliferations of discursive meaning. With the essayistic as the essence of criticism, this questioning becomes a critical thinking of discourse as that instability of discourse engages the experience of a self at the crossroads of aesthetics and the world.[6] With essay films, the commentaries of cinematic reproduction (essentialized perhaps in genre films and genre commentary) give way to the essayistic criticism of refractive cinema.[7]

A common, if rarely acknowledged, twentieth-century forum for this distinction between commentary and criticism on art, literature, and film has been the practices and theories of film adaptation. In this context, many adaptations, especially before 1945, might usefully and productively be seen and described as commentaries. Early cinematic adaptations of Shakespeare's plays and other literatures, such as *Uncle Tom's Cabin* (1903) or *Faust* (1904), are not simply cinematic representations of the text or images of a play or book but are better understood, I think, as commentaries on those works, often functioning in an important sense as visual annotations and illustrations. In the first quarter of the century, these adaptations appear as creative commentaries that, at one extreme, reenact that primary text through sometimes numerous versions that simply record a staged production (as with the radically abbreviated forms of many early adaptations of Shakespeare) or, at the other extreme, aim to reclaim and fully mimic as much as possible an original text (as with the singularly massive and precise adaptation of Frank Norris's *McTeague* as Erich von Stroheim's 1924 film *Greed*). In their different ways, these adapting commentaries gloss a primary text as a way of acknowledging its determining cultural and canonical truth, so that, not surprisingly, adaptations as commentary typically align with different senses of fidelity, just as the essayistic as criticism aligns with scandal.

With faithful commentaries at one end of the spectrum and what I am calling essayistic criticism at the other, Linda Hutcheon offers an especially rich way to consider adaptation along a "continuum model" that "positions adaptations specifically as (re-) interpretations and (re-) creations" (172). At the opposite end of this continuum from fidelity, adaptation appears, for Hutcheon, as various forms of "expansion," according to which a film like *"Play It Again Sam* (1972) . . . offers an overt and critical commentary on another prior film (in this case, *Casablanca* [1942])" and so positions these forms of expansion near "academic criticism and reviews of a work" (171). For my argument, this movement toward adaptation as critical expansion describes numerous modern narrative films, notably beginning in the 1940s, in which the activity and thematic of adaptation expands from narration to a definitively critical and, at least partially, essayistic mode. Examples include the defining transition from the stage of the recreated Globe Theater to the openly scenic and cinematic spaces of Laurence Olivier's *Henry V* (1944); Godard's meditation on love, commerce, and *The Odyssey* in *Contempt* (1961); R. W. Fassbinder's self-analytic deconstruction in his epilogue for his nearly sixteen-hour adaptation of *Berlin Alexanderplatz* (1980); and Spike Jonze and Charlie Kaufman's convoluted struggle to remake Susan Orlean's extended essay, *The Orchid Thief*, as the film *Adaptation* (2002). In each of these cases, adaptations aggressively reshape, distort, condense, extend, and reposition literary texts not as objects of faithful commentary but as the focus of critical testings of those texts and, concomitantly, testings of the filmic itself.

Informing this postwar move from adaptation as commentary to adaptation as criticism is the more pronounced version of "expansive" adaptations that I am calling refractive essays, a shift most famously signaled by Resnais's 1948 *Van Gogh*, a portrait film less about the Dutch painter than a cinematic interpretation of his paintings. That same year, Bazin in "Adaptation, or the Cinema as Digest" would introduce the notion of refraction as a model for a kind of adaptation that he would compare to André Malraux's imaginary museum (the centerpiece of a book that appeared a year earlier), a photographic museum that "refracts the original painting into million of facts thanks to photographic reproduction" (19). Three years later, Bazin returns to this key term in explaining Robert Bresson's adaptation of a *Diary of a Country Priest* (1951) as a "dialectic between cinema and literature" that includes "all that the novel has to offer plus . . . its refraction into the cinema" ("Stylistics of Robert Bresson" 142–143).[8] He insists here that there "is no question here of translation. Still less is it a question of free inspiration with the intention of building a duplicate. It is a question of building a secondary work with the novel as foundation. . . . It is a new aesthetic creation, the novel so to speak multiplied by the cinema" (142). With Resnais's *Van Gogh* as his primary example, adaptation as refraction becomes a symbiotic multiplication of two forms that has nothing to do with the popularizing commentaries of conventional adaptations but rather puts into play a productive interaction of two kinds of "aesthetic biology" (142).[9] In his "Painting and Cinema," Bazin returns to *Van Gogh* and similar essayistic films like Luciano Emmer's *Guerrieri* (1942) and continues to pursue the logic of cinematic refraction as a centrifugal action unlike the centripetal focus of paintings. As a "strange method of cultural dissemination . . . based on the destruction of its very object," these films "fragment" and "abstract" paintings to recirculate those works "within the range of everyday seeing." In the "dangerous" and "risky business" of "pulling the work apart, in breaking up its component parts," Bazin concludes, the films enact the subjectively critical play of refractive cinema similar to "a certain type of literary criticism which is likewise a recreation— Baudelaire on Delacroix, Valery on Baudelaire, Mallarme on Greco" (166–169).

In extending and readapting Bazin's term *refractive* and describing it as a practice of deflection or dispersal at the center of this particular kind of essay film, I am differentiating these films from the common characterization of them as (self) "reflexive" or "reflective" cinema in which works typically turn back on themselves to comment on their own making. Most essay films work with a large degree of reflexivity since, whatever the primary topic, the essayistic calls attention to a representational exchange between a presiding subjectivity, public experience, and cinematic thinking. As Christa Blümlinger describes one approach to these films, essay films in general might be described as "autobiographical inventories of filmic perceptions," and what I am calling refractive films, like Godard's *Scenario of the Film Passion* (1982) and *Letter to Freddy Bauche* (1982), according to Blümlinger, are simply more concentrated "essays on the cinema" (57). More precisely, refractive essay films concentrate the representational regime of the essayistic on the cinematic itself in order to distill and intensify the essayistic by directing it not, for instance, at portraits of human subjectivity or the spaces of public life but at the aesthetics or, more exactly, the anti-aesthetics of representation that always hover about essay films as a filmic thinking of the world.

Refractive suggests a kind of "unmaking" of the work of art or the film or, as we will see, its failure or "abjection." Like the beam of light sent through a glass cube, refractive cinema breaks up and disperses the art or object it engages, splinters or deflects it in ways that leave the original work scattered and drifting across a world outside. Rather than the mimetic idea of a mirror reflecting a world, these films set up a chain of mirrors, as so archly dramatized in *Hypothesis of a Stolen Painting*, that disperses the image through a social space. Whether the object is other artistic media or other films, these films interrogate first and, most important, their own representational regime not so much to call attention to themselves in a more or less binary relationship but to call attention to the world as a multidimensional field where film must ultimately be thought. If one finds in refractive cinema variations on the activities and thematics of other kinds of essay films—the testing of time and temporality in the arena of experience, for instance—refractive essay films focus explicitly on some version of the aesthetic experience in and of itself, undermining representational stability by confronting one aesthetic practice with that of another, anti-aesthetic practice. At the heart of many of these films—especially essay films about film—is then a critical reenactment of the cinematic representation itself as a way of reconceptualizing that process as an open-ended encounter with the world, as an act of criticism rather than commentary.

These films ask us not to think so much about the aesthetics of film—the genius behind it, artistic strategies, or its emotional and imaginative communications. Rather, refractive cinema tends, in a variety of ways, to draw attention to where film fails or, more precisely, where and how the cinematic can force us beyond its borders and our borders, can force us to think about a world and ourselves that necessarily and crucially exist outside the limits of the cinema.

While a film like *Hypothesis of a Stolen Painting* is a somewhat rarified and concentrated example, refractive cinema embraces and defines a large and diverse category of cinematic practices that are increasingly central to film and media culture today. As noted, the most commonplace version of these essay films take the form of a film about the making of a feature film, whose formulaic structure can often be creatively challenged and stretched as in *Lost in La Mancha* (2002), a documentary about Terry Gilliam's failed attempt to adapt *Don Quixote* as *The Man Who Killed Don Quixote*. The more contemporary, less-obvious, and increasingly ubiquitous twist on essayistic refraction appears as DVD supplements. Beside the more prosaic examples of these incorporations of critical commentary, more dramatic versions of DVD supplements can feature alternative perspectives of production personnel (directors or cinematographers, for instance), whose explanations and interpretations may differ or even contradict each other (as on the commentary tracks of the 2000 *American Beauty* DVD).[10] Of a different kind, the 1992 short *Gillo Pontecorvo: The Dictatorship of Truth* appears on the Criterion edition of *The Battle of Algiers* and features Edward Said in an extended dialogue with director Pontecorvo and others involved in that 1967 film and later projects. Although there is little that could be called essayistic in this review of a director's life and work, its emplacement as part of a critical perspective surrounding the primary film calls attention to the interactive and dialogic shape of its essayistic relation to the Pontecorvo film.

A tongue-in-cheek version of cinema vérité, Lars von Trier's The Five Obstructions, *describes an encounter between von Trier and legendary Danish filmmaker Jorgen Leth in which von Trier proposes that Leth remake and adapt the latter's avant-garde classic* The Perfect Human *(which features the minimalist movement, aesthetically stylized living patterns of a "perfect human") according to five precisely defined requirements or "obstructions." [fig. 7.5] Von Trier quite literally*

FIGURE 7.5 Leth's original perfect human (*Five Obstructions*)

"tests" Leth by asking him to remake or adapt that landmark 1967 film according to specific experiential and aesthetic limits proposed by von Trier. Leth then attempts to adapt The Perfect Human *to these five obstructions: (1) in Cuba with no take longer than 12 frames; (2) in "the most miserable place in the world," for Leth the red light district of Bombay; (3) either as a return to Bombay to remake his failed first effort or as a film without rules; (4) as an animated film; and (5) as a text composed by von Trier and read by Leth.[11] Through these critical tests, von Trier aims to break down Leth's aesthetic view of the human so that he must abandon certain artistic distances and shields through which, according to von Trier, Leth distances himself from the world: to overcome "the highly affective distance" Leth maintains from the world and so test "the ethics of the observer." "I want to put your ethics to a test," von Trier claims, and this refractive exercise will be "like therapy" or "a laboratory experiment," whose ultimate aim is to "banalize" Leth.*

The film interrogates Leth's and by implication the representational system of film to adequately engage a world beyond its prescribed borders. Appropriately a product of a Dogme95 director with a flare for announcing rules meant to break established rules, each of the obstructions or systemic "laws" tests and exposes, "goads" and "examines" the aesthetic principles of Leth's original film. Von Trier, for instance, rejects the film made according to the second set of obstructions for not following his instructions when it showed a crowd of Indian onlookers. He then insists Leth remake it with "complete freedom" by returning to Bombay. [fig. 7.6] Leth, however, wants and needs rules, and the film becomes punctuated by the

FIGURE 7.6   Leth and the rejected Bombay film (*Five Obstructions*)

*director wandering, confused or dumbfounded, caught in his own long takes (in a
Brussels hotel, overhearing sexual shouts, and inadvertently stuck in a remake of
Eric Rohmer's* La Collectioneuse*). With each failure, von Trier demands that
Lethe needs to make a film that "leaves a mark on you."*

Highlighting again the second-person address so common in the essayistic,
The Five Obstructions *takes the form of a critical dialogue that, according to
Susan Dwyer, explores "the possibilities of intersubjective communication," that
fundamental fault line of the essayistic. By "exposing" personal artistic vision to the
dialogic structure of a public experience, the film dramatizes "the extent to which
the individual's self-understanding depends on the availability to that person of a
genuinely second-person perspective" (5) and thus "brilliantly re-presents . . .
questions about the moral significance of the asymmetry between observed and
observer at the meta-level" (2–3). One of the aesthetic terms prominently challenged and exposed here is the power and control of auteurism and its association
with the Romantically coherent subjectivity of authorship. [fig. 7.7] The last obstruction accordingly becomes an explicit showdown and blending of the two auteurs as
a testimony to productive loss, a kind of self-destructive ventriloquism of voices and
texts. Over a montage of shots from the earlier obstructions, Leth reads von Trier's
words as if they were a letter from Leth to von Trier about the entire project of the
film. Through the series of tests and encounters, "Nothing was revealed," Leth says
with von Trier's words. "The dishonest person was you, Lars. You only saw what*

FIGURE 7.7   Leth and von Trier: the confrontation and undoing of two auteurs as a "laboratory
experiment" (*Five Obstructions*)

you wanted to see. . . . You exposed yourself. . . . This is how the perfect human falls." In the end, with this last obstruction particularly, the film testifies to both Leth's and von Trier's "abject" failure, the failure of the auteur and the failure of cinematic representation.

What is particularly important about this film and others like it is not their reflexivity but that they open up the central and essential space of essay films: a kind of abstracted zone for thinking through and about film as a critical experience in itself, thinking through the very terms of cinematic thinking. Many essay films with other modal emphases—on portraiture, travel, diaryistic time, or current events—often highlight similar reflexive moments within their explorations, but the refractive essay film distills and crystallizes that moment as the experience of the cinematic itself distorted and revealed as part of a public circulation. Rather than the typical essayistic formulation of something like "thoughts occasioned by" or "thoughts on" a particular public experience, refractive cinema proposes something like "thoughts on the experience of cinematic thinking in a world that resists" and in this way remakes the reflective self. Perhaps a more theoretical way of rephrasing what numerous critics and scholars have identified as the central metaphors of The Five Obstructions, as something between a game and a therapy session, is Hector Rodriguez's formulation of the central thematic of the film: The Five Obstructions is "a hall of mirrors, shot through with ambiguities"(53) that aims "to open the cinema to the outside, to the flesh-and-blood richness of human life" (40), and so becomes a "work of thinking as problematising" (55). Or in von Trier's words, it is a film that asks its makers and audience "to see without looking, to defocus!" (Hjort xvii).

If von Trier's project is to adapt "a little gem that we're now going to ruin," that "plan is to proceed from the perfect to the human." In this game, there is no conclusion, and at this trial there is ultimately no verdict—except that that the human always exceeds the aesthetic. A critical refrain in both the original film and von Trier's critical essay is "I experienced something today that I hope I understand in a few days," and the relentless urging of that understanding to consider rigorously the aesthetics of experience and the experience of aesthetics is all that remains when one is forced to see oneself finally as Leth does as an "abject" human being, constantly "obstructed" and excluded from the world, where the essence of knowledge may be only, as the conclusion of the film indicates, "how the perfect human falls." If the commentator of Leth's original perfect human concludes by wondering "What is the perfect human thinking?" and von Trier's film opens with the query "What was I thinking?" the unspoken question that lingers at the end of von Trier's film might be "How now do we rethink the imperfect filmmaker through the resistant medium that is our world?"

Because refractive cinema is an adaptive practice that is essentially critical reflection rather than assimilative commentary, the centerpiece of this type of essay film is reenactment. As both *Hypothesis* and *The Five Obstructions* demonstrate, reenactments can productively be described as refractions, adaptive strategies that create a critical repositioning of real events, people, places, or objects that insist on subjective and social evaluations or reevaluations of those precedent texts or realities. Common and central to contemporary documentary films and essay films in general, reenactments are key structures in refractive essays and another indication of how this particular kind of essay film tends to highlight and concentrate key strategies in all essay films. As in a judicial trial in which reenactments are also standard strategies, there are two layers of cinematic reenactment, one that illustrates the event or subject reenacted and the other that demands rethinking that event or subject through its adaptive framework. In its most basic form, this thinking or rethinking through reenactments works to determine the truth, falsity, or simply the meaning of the event. In the more subtle and complex versions of cinematic reenactments (especially in refractive essays), thinking through representational reenactment becomes an unresolved end in itself.

Bill Nichols and Ivone Margulies, among others, have both written incisively about reenactments across film culture, providing sophisticated theoretical frameworks for their importance to the essay film and refractive films specifically.[12] Nichols emphasizes the psychoanalytic movement and "fantasmatic power" of reenactments, and Margulies calls attention to their social and ethical evaluative force. As part of his discussion, Nichols provides a historical lineage of reenactments from the 1922 *Nanook of the North* through Caveh Zahedi's 2005 *I Am a Sex Addict*, sketching the background to his argument that reenactments "retrieve a lost object in its original form even as the very act of retrieval generates a new object and a new pleasure." Encountering reality in this way, the "viewer experiences the uncanny sense of a repetition of what remains historically unique" whereby a "specter haunts the text" with its "fantasmatic power" ("Documentrary Reenactment" 73). Especially pertinent to the essayistic in Nichols's argument is his analysis of this psychoanalytical dimension as a gray zone of subjectivity, specifically as presented in *Capturing the Friedmans* (2003) and *Chile, Obstinate Memory* (1997), films that act out a "desubjectivization" of the subject in "a gap between the objectivity/subjectivity binary and the workings of the fantasmatic" (77), a variation on what I have emphasized through this study as essayistic desubjectivization. "Facts remain facts," he points out "but the iterative effort of going through the motions of reenacting them imbues such facts with the lived stuff of immediate and situated experience" (77–78). The experience of these now-fantasmatic facts as a lived experience creates a gap of a troubled subjectivity, and in manner that anticipates my return in this discussion to Lukacs's essay on essayism, a reenactment, for Nichols, "complicates the literal, linear, and binary logic of the judicial system" and "reinscribes the ambiguity of perspective, and voice, that separates such judicial determinations from the plain of fantasy" (77).

Margulies takes a different path in her discussion of reenactments, a path that points to the public life of the essay. She identifies the ability of reenactments to make Nichols's fantasmatic a definitively public experience that engages a tradition of "exemplarity" in which reenactments construct ethical stages requiring a kind of evaluative judgment.[13] For her, "reenactment films conflate repetition and moral revision, and their main outcome is exemplarity" ("Exemplary Bodies" 217). The repetitious exemplarity of reenactments "converts" the spectator because they produce "an improved version of the event" as "modern morality tales" (220): "Inflected by a psychodramatic (or liturgical) belief in the enlightening effects of literal repetition, reenactment creates, performatively speaking, another body, place, and time. At stake is an identity that can recall the original event (through a second-degree indexicality) but in doing so can also re-form it" (220).

Together, Nichols's and Margulies' positions graft onto my argument about refractive essay films. As a reenactment incorporates the lived experience of aesthetics, it creates both a subjectively fantasmatic and a socially exemplary reformation of the aesthetic by which the viewer straddles and vacillates between the instability of a haunted subjectivity (as a lived experience) and the imperatives of a social ethics (as the possibility of a rediscovered value); that viewer subsequently actualizes a juristic position in a developing trial of artistic and cinematic value itself. For this viewer as juror, reenactments become adaptations as acts of anti-aesthetic criticism, not aesthetic commentary, always demanding a judgment, not a verdict.

This turn toward the relation of the refractive essay to a judicial position returns the question—with a teleological and historical irony typical of what Adorno refers to as the heresy of the essay—to George Lukacs and his well-known "On the Nature and Form of the Essay" (1910). Rooted in nineteenth-century idealism, Lukacs's version of the essay presents an unmediated immediacy that directs its questions to "life problems" (3). While embracing many types of essays, Lukacs's model especially emphasizes how the essay generates "ideas" about art and literature in its critical responses to those practices, just as refractive essays engage different ideas of the aesthetic as part of their critical and creative dynamic. For him, the essay becomes an "intellectual poem" (18) that opens the aesthetic to multiple positions and incarnations. As the refractive films of Ruiz and von Trier exemplify in a sometimes extreme and sometimes comical manner: "The essayist speaks of a picture or a book, but leaves it again at once—why?

Because, I think, the idea of a picture or book has become predominant in his mind, because he has forgotten all that is concretely incidental about it, because he has used it only as a starting point, a springboard" (15–16). Rather than a simple gloss or commentary on an aesthetic object, the essay becomes the springboard to thought: The "title of every essay is preceded in invisible letters, by the words 'Thoughts occasioned by. . . .' The idea is the measure of everything that exists, and that is why the critic whose thinking is 'occasioned by' by something already created, and who reveals its idea, is the one who will write the truest and most profound criticism" (16). Critical evaluations and values thus double back or reflect back on the art object itself only as a provisional but profound redirecting of that object into the worldly life of ideas. For Lukacs, the center of the essay is a certain irony that, for me, describes the refractive and reenactment process of essay films about art, literature, and other films. This irony consists in the critic "always speaking about the ultimate problems of life, but in a tone which implies that he is only discussing pictures and books, only the inessential and pretty ornaments of real life. . . . Thus, each essay appears to be removed as far as possible from life, and the distance between them seems the greater, the more burningly and painfully we actually sense the actual closeness of the true essence of both" (9).

For Lukacs, that provisional and constant movement of ideas through the essayistic then aligns all good essays but, for me, especially the refractive kind with the shifting and deflective measurements of the judicial and its play of reenactments: "The essay is a judgement, but the essential, the value-determining thing about it is not the verdict (as is the case with the system) but the process of judging" (18). This is far from Kant's four reflective judgments of the agreeable, the sublime, the beautiful, and the good and in fact encompasses all these judgments when refractive essays bring into play the activity of judging as analogous to thinking itself, opening up the experience to the the world rather than foreclosing it as the verdict of one or more systemic perspectives.

Essayistic reenactment as a focus for refractive cinema becomes therefore a particular modern and postmodern variation on or incorporation of Lukacs's more philosophical reflections on the essay. Concentrated on particular events or practices, essayistic reenactment suggests a kind of restaging of the process of subjective thinking through public experience. With refractive essay films specifically, that public experience and process shifts its focus from the more recognizable topics of public personas, experiential activities in time and space, and the politics of news and instead aims at where aesthetic experience unwinds at the intersection of public and private life, where reenactments engage thinking through film as a judicial testing of aesthetic value and meaning itself.

Abbas Kiarostami's Close-Up *(1990) circulates, refocuses, and redirects questions about cinematic representation across the image of self in close-up and more broadly across the social and cultural world of contemporary Iran that surrounds that image. A documentary essay about a naïve Iranian poseur, Hossein Sabzian, the film describes how Sabzian happens to meet an upper-middle-class woman on a bus and then, almost accidentally, pretends to be the celebrated Iranian director Mohsen Makhmalbaf. He then insinuates himself into the Ahankhah family under the pretense of making a film with and about them, and when discovered and brought to trial, he delivers a wordy apology in which he defends his action as the result of his love of cinema. If the film at first seems driven by a reporter's journalistic inquiry into a fraudulent theft of a famous filmmaker's name, image, and agency, it culminates in a lengthy trial about the power of the cinema and cinema spectatorship, a trial less about a verdict than about the complex action and play of judgment and the suspension of judgment when a worldly compassion trumps aesthetic authority or the authority of aesthetics.*[14]

If Hypothesis *measures the multiple and shifting layers and movements of the aesthetic image and* The Five Obstructions *tests the film image as it circulates through the world, Kiarostami's film examines and exposes the cinematic image as a slippery social and psychoanalytic figure whose instability and dependence on contingencies necessarily undermines its power. Traditionally, a close-up might suggest what Balázs has called a "physiognomy of expression" that reveals the authentic meaning of an object or person, the film image binding an interior or subjective reality and its exterior or objective appearance. In* Close-Up, *however, this presumed essence of the cinematic comes undone, refracted and deflected through levels and streams of reenactments, beginning with Sabzian's fraudulent reenactment of Makhmalbaf's identity and continuing through the film's reenactment of various scenes that recount the supposed crime. As with other versions of refractive cinema, the adaptation of an image in this case becomes a critical reenactment that does not simply identify the differences between the original and its simulation but more importantly deflects those questions of aesthetic fidelity to a humanistic and social realm that requires a viewer to experience the unstable relationship between the cinematic image and life. Kiarostami's film ultimately humanizes the aesthetic of the close-up not as a coherent cinematic figure of personal subjectivity but as part of a complex social and technological system of beliefs and desires.*

That Close-Up *dwells (for an inordinately long time) on the trial of Sabzian recalls the juridical shape of reenactments and refractive essays specifically, drawing out the extended implications of essayistic refraction as a trial in which Sabzian's reenacts his "crime" of representation as a meditative thought process. [fig. 7.8]*

FIGURE 7.8   Sabzian on trial for his love of cinema (*Close-Up*)

Bordering on a casuistic defense of his actions, Sabzian claims: "Legally it might be
an appropriate charge but morally it is not. . . . All this arose from my love of the
arts" and specifically his love of Makhmalbaf's films. As the sequence cuts between
Sabzian and the reactions of a community of judges (including the investigative
journalist Farazmand, the Ahankhahs, and the police authorities), Sabzian insists
that he was in fact only reenacting a role, performing a part like a director performs a
film ("I like interpreting the character. . . . I started to believe I was a director"), but
when the judge confronts him by asking "Are you not acting for the camera right
now?" his reply recalls an experiential divide that informs this and other essay
films that strain the relation among the subject, a social reality, and its meaning:
"I'm speaking of my suffering, that's not acting."

  Besides the central trial within the film, the whole of Close-Up *becomes a*
trial on and of film. In this larger trial, the play between image and its reenact-
ments extends beyond individual identities as the film maps a mise-en-scène that
alternates interiors and exteriors in which spectators inhabit subjective and social
disjunctions and gaps where they must struggle with judgments about the capa-
bilities of the cinematic to accurately describe the human complexities of the world.
Paralleling the alternating use of two camera lenses in the trial sequence, one for
close-ups and one for long shots, a key episode in the film, for instance, takes place
twice, from two different perspectives dramatizing those gaps as reenactments in
which viewers are critically positioned. At the beginning of the film, soldiers enter
the Ahankhah home to arrest Sabzian, while outside a reporter idly spends a some-
what protracted wait shuffling about; at one point, he kicks a can down the street,
and the shot follows its lengthy incidental and meandering roll, a particularly
undramatic counterpoint to Sabzian's dramatic desires and crisis. [fig. 7.9] Later,

FIGURE 7.9   As the journalist awaits the arrest, the incidental and meandering roll of the can in the street (*Close-Up*)

after the trial, the film returns to the arrest but now reenacts it from inside the house where the family listens to—and reenacts for Kiarostami's film—Sabzian's scheme while awaiting the soldiers to arrive to arrest him. As a countershot reenactment of the event in which the family only simulates their belief, the viewer not only witnesses a theatrical mise-en-âbyme concerning the fraud but also occupies a deferred and deflected space—in Gilberto Perez's words, a place "in suspension but not exactly suspense" (264)—between the earlier representation of the exterior street with its randomly rolling can and the painful interior reenactment of the arrest in which both Sabzian and the Ahankhah family play out the arrest with clear discomfort and representational confusion. Margulies comments about this important sequence as it recollects the earlier sequence in the street:

> *Its placement after the trial, its bitter expressions of disappointment, and its quality as a repetition of an event grant it a special function: instead of creating a distancing effect, the reenactment of the arrest co-opts the representational mise-en-âbyme as a dramatic effect. Here reenactment magnifies the drama of deceit. We watch the family's agitation as the father first receives the reporter, etc. Because this scene shows us the drama that was unfolding inside the house as we waited with the cab driver in the street at the beginning of the film, it retroactively feeds dramatic momentum into a rather banal, gratuitous moment—the kicking of the can by the cab driver. By showing this scene from two different perspectives—one in which we know nothing, another in which we know too much—Kiarostami turns witnessing into a clear, costly embarrassment. ("Exemplary Bodies" 237)*

What "embarrassment" suggests here, for me, is not only social discomfort but also an intellectual and aesthetic unease—between knowing nothing and knowing too much—in which witnessing evokes a noncommittal judging of the ethical and aesthetic refractions that move across public event, trial, and private performance. The film dramatizes this dialectic, in Margulies' words,

> *as a comparative paradigm, a series of repeated situations . . . that alternate on the screen. These versions, equally framed, are then placed one after the next so they can be compared. Framing here refers not only to the cinematic composition and mise-en-scene but to the sense of scrutiny [or ways of understanding] enforced upon a given behavior or situation, as these are repeated with significant differences, which then become the object of comparison. ("Exemplary Bodies" 238)*

As an intensified version of the judicial positioning of the viewer throughout the film, this play of perspectives, suspended between the social crime of cinematic fraud and its exposure as a subjective performance, describes a refracted shift between the anonymous, desubjectivized exteriors of the streets and the overly self-conscious, overly subjectivized interiors of the home as a failure to reenact adequately, as an adaptation that is quintessentially and positively critical. The "predicament of judging" thus provides "so many vicissitudes in arguing that the rigidity of form breaks down" that it becomes "a humanistic gauge in which selfish drives and desires are all but excused under a benign, understanding gaze" (238).

In the concluding sequence of the film, the invisible emblem of aesthetic authority throughout the film, the auteur Makhlambaf, enters the reality of the streets to reconcile with his reenacted double. As Sabzian leaves the police station, Makhlambaf meets him and whisks him through the streets of Tehran on his motorbike for a final reconciliation with the Ahankhahs. Here, within the exponentially refracted terrain of reenactment in the film, the real filmmaker momentarily bonds with Sabzian and temporarily bridges the rift between the fantasmatic of reenactment and a social ethics. Rather than replicating the artistic and juridical authority traditionally assigned to the subjectivity of the auteur, Makhlambaf becomes a figure of mediation with the fraudulent reflection on the back of his motorbike, so that the authorized subject and his criminal double are now adapted partners. If the suspended trial that is the film takes place partly within mise-en-âbyme close-ups of reflected identities, the final sequence refracts again that collapse as a long shot darting through the streets where the aesthetic subject and its anti-aesthetic counterpart are interlocked. As the soundtrack cuts in and out during the sequence, the operator complains about the faulty mechanics of the shot (hardly accidental) in a way that metaphorically suggests a larger point: "We lost him. We can't retake this. We've lost sound." Filmed through a broken windshield and obstructive glass, the film documents here the limitations, if not failure, of the cinematic to retain an authorized subject in a fundamentally uncinematic world where Makhlambaf and Sabzian can barely be distinguished. [fig. 7.10] At the gate of the Ahankhah home, that gateway between the drama of interiors and exteriors, self and world, a final reconciliation occurs as what Margulies calls the film's "redemptive reenactment" that recovers the dizzying refractions of the film as "a benign, understanding gaze" (238), as what I would call a judgment without verdict by which, to paraphrase Deleuze, a thinking cinema aims to restore our belief in the world.

If Hypothesis of a Stolen Painting *refracts the search for artistic meanings across numerous imagistic registers and* The Five Obstructions *critically tests and retests the experiential shortcomings of film as adaptation,* Close-Up *reflects on and deflects the power of the cinema and cinephilia to offer illusions of systemic representational authority and authenticity into a crowd of human reenactments that inhabit the streets. Not far from* The Five Obstructions, *in the end, the incidental figure of the elusively human here falls inevitably back into the world and falls out of that systemic circuit of the cinema, as a kind of celebration of cinematic failure. Whereas* The Five Obstructions *can be described as a refractive film that underlines the gaps and distances within cinematic representations of life,* Close-Up *maps the collapse and then expansion of those gaps and distances to show Makhlambaf, Kiarostami, and Sabzian circulating and overlapping as imperfect individuals in an essayistic world.*

FIGURE 7.10 Makhlambaf and Sabzian: elusive figures on the street where the aesthetic and the anti-aesthetic bond (*Close-Up*)

Close-Up *returns us to my first essayistic mode, the portrait film, but now, more reflexively, to investigate not the portraits or self-portraits of other subjectivities but the portrait of auteurs and cinephiliac viewers whose passion for bonding with movies becomes remade as part of a cinematic thinking of public life. Indeed, for portrait essays and refractive essays, as Lukacs reminds us, the truth of the essay, like "likeness" in a portrait, "is a struggle for truth, for the incarnation of a life which someone has seen in a man, an epoch or a form" (11), an irony of likeness that may suffuse all essay films. In all their variations, as Lukacs notes, essays appear "to be removed as far as possible from life, and the distance between them seems the greater, the more burningly and painfully we actually sense the actual closeness of the true essence of both" (9). Or, as Kiarostami puts it in his personal version of Socratic filmmaking as a suspended trial, in a phrase that he could have borrowed from Montaigne, "the shortest way to truth is a lie."*

INTRODUCTION

1. The first full-length study in English of the essay film, Rascaroli's *The Personal Camera: Subjective Cinema and the Essay Film*, appeared in 2009 while I was completing this book, and while I find many points in common with her book and consider our different foci complimentary in many ways, there are enough differences (and perhaps disagreements) to energize further discussion.

2. One of the first scholars to wrestle with this topic, Michael Renov persuasively emphasizes the "documentary context" of the essay film in his examination of Jonas Mekas's *Lost, Lost, Lost* (1976) in his essay "*Lost, Lost, Lost*: Mekas as Essayist." His defining categories for the film essay are (1) to record, reveal, and preserve; (2) to persuade or promote; (3) to express; and (4) to analyze or interrogate. Renov consistently addresses key topics and variations on the essay film, often connecting the practice with variations on documentary forms, as in his "Domestic Ethnographies" in *The Subject of Documentary*, where he perceptively links Su Friedrich's *Sink or Swim* (1990) to that documentary heritage.

3. Perhaps the best-known effort to characterize traditional and contemporary documentaries are Bill Nichols's five modes: expository, observational, interactive, reflexive, and performative (*Blurred Boundaries*). See also Stella Bruzzi's 2006 work on documentary cinema as it reconsiders and challenges some of Nichols's positions, most importantly how it identifies the subjective voice and vision of documentaries.

4. Especially in recent years, more narrative films, such as Terrence Malick's *The Thin Red Line* (1998), can be said to incorporate the essayistic within their narrative structure, much as many twentieth-century novels like Robert Musil's 1930 *Man without Qualities* refashioned narrative fiction around the essayistic. See Leo Bersani's *Forms of Being* on Malick's film and Thomas Harrison's *Essayism* for a discussion of Musil's novel.

5. See José Moure's "Essai de definition de essai au cinema."

6. See, for instance, Nora Alter's keen expansion of essayistic practice to include installation art in her "Translating the Essay into Film and Installation," and Michael Renov's "The Electronic Essay" and "Video Confessions" in *The Subject of Documentary* (182–215).

7. Pertinent are Bensmaïa's remarks: "Among all the terms that relate to literary genres, the word Essay is certainly the one that has given rise to the most confusion in the history of literature. . . . A unique case in the annals of literature, the Essay is the only literary genre to have resisted integration, until quite recently in the taxonomy of genres. No other genre ever raised so many theoretical problems concerning the origin and the definition of its Form: an atopic genre or, more precisely, an eccentric one insofar as it seems to flirt with all the genres without ever letting itself be pinned down, the literary essay such as the Montaigne bequeathed to posterity has always had a special status. . . . The Essay appears historically as one of the rare literary texts whose apparent principal task was to provoke a 'generalized collapse' of the economies of the rhetorically coded text" (95–99).

8. For discussion of the literary (specifically German) essay in these terms, see John A. McCarthy's *Crossing Boundaries: A Theory and History of Essay Writing in German, 1680–1815.*

CHAPTER 1

1. Whereas Marker is consistently associated with the beginnings of the essay film, other films historians and scholars identify other key films in the formation of the practice. Michael Renov, for instance, discusses Jonas Mekas's *Lost, Lost, Lost* (1969/1976) as an early and key example of the essay film. Arguing that "the foundations of the essay film derive from three landmark documentaries," Paul Arthur ("The Resurgence of History" 65–66) places Alain Resnais's *Night and Fog* (1955) and Jean Rouch's *Les Maitres fous* (1955) alongside *Letter from Siberia*. Alter follows Jay Leyda and aligns the essay film with an earlier history, beginning with Richter's 1928 *Inflation* ("Hans Richter in Exile").

2. See Reda Bensmaïa's *The Barthes Effect*.

3. Here he champions writing's ability to avoid the servility and power implicit in language, where the one alternative is "to cheat with speech, to cheat speech" through a practice of writing, "by the play of words of which [speech] is the theater" (462).

4. Victor Burgin's discussion of Barthes's essays in *In/Different Spaces* (161–178) has been especially helpful to my argument.

5. Historically, this is an essentially Romantic formulation as a "personal essay."

6. A highly recommended contemporary reading of Montaigne's work is Lawrence D. Kritzman's *The Fabulous Imagination: On Montaigne's Essays*.

7. Thomas Harrison's *Essayism: Conrad, Musil, & Pirandello* is a smart investigation of how certain twentieth-century writers merged the novel and the essay to create a hybrid essayistic novel.

8. An incisive examination of this relationship among subjectivity, the verbal, and the visible in the early nineteenth century is William Galperin's 1993 study *The Return of the Visible in British Romanticism*.

9. This tension and dialogue between the verbal and the visual becomes particularly pronounced in the nineteenth century in ways that adumbrate the rise of the essayistic and film representation more generally. J. Hillis Miller identifies some of the precedents for this practice in his *Illustration*; he examines precursive examples such as the photographic frontispieces that accompany Henry James's *The Golden Bowl* (1904).

10. See Martha Rosler's "The Bowery in Two Inadequate Systems of Descriptions."

11. Thanks to Jonathan Kahana for this insight.

12. Developed over a series of books, Nichols has come closest to setting a standard framework for documentary practices with his five categories of expositional, observational, interactive, reflexive, and performative documentaries, each representing a variation on "representing reality" that calls increasing attention to the acknowledged place of the filmmaker or perceiving subject. While Nichols defines these categories as "modes," they also map an historical movement from the more objective assumptions of early documentaries, such as Pare Lorentz's *The Plow that Broke the Plains* (1936), to the more contemporary foregrounding of subjective interaction, such as Marlon Riggs's *Tongues Untied* (1989).

13. Recent studies, such as those of Nichols and Stella Bruzzi, have partially shifted the focus of documentaries to the subjective articulation or performance of different realities and referents, yet even with these important theoretical adjustments, there is a tendency to enlist with a documentary imperative that defers to the more or less stable activity of the subjective vision organizing a public experience.

14. A streamlined version of Habermas's argument would forefront how his bourgeois public sphere, as it developed at the end of the eighteenth century, separated itself from the civil state, defining itself as an open dialogue between the private individual and public concerns. Not coincidentally, as a historical movement, it gives birth to the idea and place of culture within society—a bracketed sphere that, in the idealism of the late eighteenth and early nineteenth century and its foundation resting on property and family, both could influence and remain separate from the various economic and political pressure of that society.

15. For me and others, Kluge is one of the most important theoreticians and filmmakers associated with the essay film. Especially useful for this part of my argument is Hansen's "Alexander Kluge, Cinema and the Public Sphere: The Construction Site of Counter-History."

16. Lopate's argument represents a common tack to associate the essayistic with a strong and coherent personal voice, which is very much contrary to my argument about essayistic subjectivity.

17. In his compelling book *Filmosophy*, Daniel Frampton surveys the many positions that have overlapped models of subjectivity and the activity of cinematic thinking. His own position sometimes comes close to mine in its resistance to locating filmic thinking within an analogously homocentric mind. For him, "Cinema is the projection, screening, showing of *thoughts of the real*" (5): "Film acts out an interaction with a world, which thus becomes a mirror for us to recognize *our* interaction with *our* world. . . . The creation of this film-world is set and immovable and thus untouchable, unchangeable—it is unwavering intention, decision, choice, belief: a filmic kind of thought" (6). Thinking is not only verbal or linguistic but also spatial, temporal, tactile, and so forth, involving imagination and fantasy and denaturalizing the world as a kind of thought. Notably, while the notion that filmind "intends" the world as a kind of thinking and provides a way to account for the poetics of most films, the thinking of essay films, I would contend, hesitates before the entirety of the power of intention and tends productively to "balk" before the world as an experience of subjectivity creating, to use Frampton's term, a less-coherent or -stable "filmind."

18. This quotation and the ideas that resonate around it are explored in Gregory Flaxman's edited collection *The Brain Is a Screen: Deleuze and the Philosophy of Cinema.*

19. Sobchack comments elsewhere: "Experience comes to description in acts of reflection: consciousness turning reflexively on itself to become conscious of consciousness. And it is in reflection that experience is given formal significance, is spoken and written. . . .

Experience . . . seeks and is fulfilled by language even as language and experience are categorically incommensurable" (*The Address of the Eye* xvii).

20. While *Bright Leaves* and other essay films unmistakably draw on the figure of the home movie, many other essay films make that figure less obvious but, I think, no less suggestive. My use of it is less to claim an "amateurish" point of view in these films and more to suggest a kind of reception.

21. Besides Lupton's recent book, there is Alter's exceptional study *Chris Marker*, which addresses many of these issues around Marker. Also of note is the two-part series on Marker in *Film Comment* in 2003 (see, for instance, Paul Arthur's "Essay Questions").

22. Despite these political reminders, the book focuses largely on North Korea.

23. Telling of the critical relation between the photo-essay and the essay film, two of Marker's own photo-essays are in fact companion pieces to specific films: "China's Light: A Film in the Guise of a Greeting Card," a series of photos and commentaries published in *Esprit* to accompany his film *Sunday in Peking* (1956) and the 1982 companion piece to *Sunless*, the photo-essay *Abroad*. Lupton notes that in these cases the "film and the photo-text publication are not designed to explain or absorb each other, but as an open-ended relay that invites fresh perspectives on their shared subject matter" (62).

24. In *Between Film and Screen: Modernism's Photo Synthesis*, Garrett Stewart describes *The Jetty* as a "text of decelerated process" where "Marker's plot is a perfect allegory of this devitalization" (103).

25. See Ross Gibson, "What Do I Know? Chris Marker and the Essayist Mode of Cinema." *Filmviews* (Summer 1988): 26–32.

26. That Marker seems to regard his work preceding *La Jolie mai* (1962) and *The Jetty* as juvenilia suits one line of my argument that the essayistic (and its association with the "short film") represents a testing and exploration of new practices.

27. Deleuze's three relations of thought to the image are "critical thought," "hypnotic thought," and "action thought" (*Cinema 2* 157–163). It is worth considering Garrett Stewart's strong counterargument to Deleuze bipartite of the movement image and the time image, particularly as he insists a much broader photogrammatic tension in film practice that encompasses the "movement-image" as well as the "time-image." He writes: "Everything Deleuze resists attributing to the movement-image as an already textured or textualized imprint of the scopic field seems displaced onto the time-image, where betweenness, stratigraphic layering, interstitial and lacunary process . . ., where the whole process opalescent faceting of indeterminancy takes place" (*Between Film and Screen* 89).

CHAPTER 2

1. It is important to recall that the idea of a "documentary film" was hardly currency in 1929.

2. For a relatively early discussion in English of Godard as essayist, see Louis Giannetti's "Godard's *Masculine-Feminine*: The Cinematic Essay." More in line with my perspective on the essayistic and specifically Godard's manner of employing it is Kaja Silverman's "The Author as Receiver" which demonstrates the way Godard deconstructs his own enunciative presence as part of a second-person address to himself.

3. See André Gaudreault and Germain Lacasse's *The Moving Picture Lecturer*. Also see Rick Altman's "From Lecturer's Prop to Industrial Product: The Early History of Travel Films" in *Virtual Voyages: Cinema and Travel*.

4. As Gunning points put, these are "Films that 'mean something,' picture-sermons that 'help those who see them,' [are] phases [that] encapsulate the narrative ambitions of Griffith in 1909" ("A Corner in Wheat" 135). Not coincidentally, a significant mount of writing about film in this era, from Vachel Lindsay to Béla Balázs, suggests that films of all types offer the possibilities for replicating and initiating thought and social action.

5. At the center of precursive essay films are larger debates about the mass cultural status of the movies and their social and intellectual potential as a representational confrontation between the technological image and language as expression. If film form has always reflected modernist concerns with spatial fragmentation and temporal motions, according to some historians, early association with mass culture tended to undermine film's radical potentials for subjective expression and interpretation and reshape them as realist transparencies or later versions of propaganda films.

6. In "The Voice of Documentary," Nichols suggests five documentary styles or structures in the use of voice: direct address or commentary (voice of God or expository), transparency (observational), interview oriented (interactve), reflexive, and performative.

7. See Jonathan Kahana's *Intelligence Works* for a discussion of the critical dialogue between American documentaries and a literary culture in the 1930s.

8. See Vincent Pinel's *Introduction au Ciné-club: histoire, théorie, pratique du Ciné-club en France.*

9. See the entire Chapter 3 of Richard Abel's *French Cinema: The First Wave.*

10. In 1924, in "The Expressive Techniques of the Cinema," Germaine Dulac (in Abel *French Film Theory*) also identifies the film experience with a kind of thinking and thought: "What is more mobile than our psychological life with its reactions, its manifold impressions, its sudden movements, its dreams, its memories? The cinema is marvelously equipped to express these manifestations of our thinking" (310).

11. Directors of the essayistic *The Hour of the Furnaces* (1968), Fernando Solanas and Octavio Getino, are also authors of "Towards a Third Cinema," one of the best-known and most political rearticulation of the cine club tradition as a forum for active debate, social thought, and political action.

12. The definitive study of this movement is Edward Lowry's *The Filmology Movement and Film Study in France.*

13. An excellent discussion of Richter's career and work and its relation to the avant-garde is Alter's "Hans Richter in Exile: Translating the Avant-Garde."

14. Compare Bazin's comments in "The Evolution of the Language of Cinema": In "the silent days, montage evoked what the director wanted to say; in the editing of 1938, it described it. Today we can say that at last the director writes in film. The image—its plastic composition and the way it is set in time, because it is founded on a much higher degree of realism—has at its disposal more means of manipulating reality and of modifying it from within. The filmmaker is no longer the competitor of the painter and the playwright, he is, at last, the equal of the novelist" (39–40).

15. It is worth saying again that those in the so-called Left Bank of the French New Wave (Marker, Resnais, Varda, and others) figure more logically in the formation of the essay film because of their consistent interest in the interdisciplinary connections of film with literature and the other arts, yet a wide range of other filmmakers, inside and outside France, respond to the possibilities of the essay films.

16. These in turn anticipate one of the most fertile and productive forums for the essayistic and its relation to the sketch: anthology films, such as *Far from Vietnam* (1967) and *Germany in Autumn* (1978).

17. Indeed, these two dimensions align the essay film with that important other literary precedent, the British essayist Francis Bacon, whose pithy essays counterpoint Montaigne at about the same point in history but pursue a more scientific inquiry into the ethics of living.

18. As a theoretical marker of the relation of the essay film to the short film and the larger issue implied, Jacque Aumont's study of "the film sketch" in "The Variable Eye" reminds us of this representational overlap between the temporality of the nineteenth-century essay and a temporality in the cinema engaged by the essayistic cinema of the 1950s. Around 1800, significant changes in the status of the image as "sketch" specifically anticipate photography and film: "The crux of these changes may be dated to the period between 1780 and 1820, when a veritable revolution occurred in the status of the nature sketch: the ébuache, an attempt to register a reality predetermined by the project of a future painting, gave way to the étude, an attempt to register reality 'just as it is' and for no other reason" (232–234).

19. Rivette's positive description of Rossellini's film as an amateurish "sketch" within a neorealistic tradition again calls attention to and importantly differentiates the essay film from its contemporaneous counterparts found in cinema vérité (and later American direct cinema), documentary practices so central to the essay film, which inform the essay film and act as a platform for its distinctions. An often-voiced dissatisfaction with these two traditions coincides with the foregrounding of the essay film. There is, for instance, Godard's remark about Richard Leacock's direct cinema: "There's no point in having sharp images if you've got fuzzy ideas. Leacock's lack of subjectivity leads him ultimately to a lack of *objectivity*. He doesn't even know he's a *metteur-en-scene*, that pure reportage doesn't exist" (quoted in Roud *Godard*, 139).

20. See Arthur's "The Resurgence of History and the Avant-Garde Essay Film."

21. Kelley Conway first recognized this connection between the cine clubs and *Two Years Later* in "'A New Wave of Spectators': Contemporary Responses to *Cleo from 5 to 7*."

CHAPTER 3

1. In her study of the "the personal camera," Laura Rascaroli distinguishes between essay films proper and autobiographical films, where the latter only tangentially "belong to the field of essayistic cinema": "Whereas essay films are necessarily subjective and personal, but may not be autobiographical, diaries notebooks, travelogues, and self-portraits always are [autobiographical], though not necessarily with the same degree of intensity" (106).

2. Self-expression, like Michel Foucault's writing of an authorial self, "is now linked to sacrifice and to the sacrifice of life itself" ("What Is an Author?" 117)

3. See George F. Custen's detailed study *Bio/Pics: How Hollywood Constructed Public History*. A more recent study of the contemporary biopic is Dennis Bingham's *Whose Lives Are They Anyway?*

4. As part of observations made in 1945, Balazs later identifies a troubling of that ontology when facial expression becomes a mask, disguising and complicating the exchange between subjective interiors and facial masks. As an illustration, he describes a powerful scene featuring Asta Nielsen in which she feigns love for a man she then begins to love and in which the play of her features creates not a core subject but a multiple layered images of self: "We can see all this clearly in her face, over which she has drawn two different masks. At such times an invisible face appears in front of a real one, just as spoken words can by association of ideas conjure up things unspoken and unseen, perceived only by those to whom they are addressed" (64–65).

5. From a different theoretical angle, Deleuze describes the expressive image produced by this gaze, the face, as the center of an "affection image" of the cinema: "The face is in itself close-up, the close-up is by itself face and both are affect, affection-image" (*Cinema 1* 88) whose two poles, "facefication" and "faceicity," describe the outline and movement of expression as "the expressed" (97). The expressive face as "the affection-image occupies the interval between incoming perception and an outgoing action." The face becomes "expression of a power which passes from one quality to another" (90–91), and the combination of the two traits is "the expressed." See David Rodowick's *Gilles Deleuze's Time Machine* (pp. 66–67).

6. The proliferation of so-called autobiographical films in the 1960s and 1970s is a belated sign of this shift, in some cases indicative of the problem of representing an authentically expressive identity, such as Jim McBride's parodic self-portrait *David Holtzman's Diary*, and in others representing a an almost nostalgic longing, I would argue, for an autonomous, interior, and coherent self, such as Jerome Hill's *Film Portrait* (1972). See especially Jim Lane's chapter "Autobiographical Portraiture" in *The Autobiographical Documentary in America* (pp. 94–144). Other studies of autobiography and film include John Katz's *Autobiography: Film/Video/Photography* and Elizabeth Buss's "Eye for I: Making and Unmaking Autobiography in Film." Most pertinent to my discussion is Rascaroli's chapter "The Self-Portrait Film: Michelangelo's Last Gaze" in *The Personal Camera*.

7. Indeed, two contemporary biopics might be described as engaging Bazin's warning and criticism by deconstructing and reconstructing the practice of biopics and heroic documentaries to harmonize subjectivity and public history: A fake documentary portrait of a man in the 1920s who completely changes identities to reflect changing surrounding and communities, Woody Allen's 1983 *Zelig* parodies and inverts the notion that the image of the singular individual can assimilate history. Todd Haynes's 2007 *I'm Not There: Suppositions on a Film Concerning Bob Dylan* refashions the biopic—as the title and the use of multiple actors to play Dylan suggests—along the lines of an essay in which historical identity becomes a series of contingent performances.

8. Nichols suggests that two recent documentary traditions employ the interview as direct address and as self-reflexive address in "The Voice of Documentary." As a broader sociological/psychological study, also suggestive in this context is Erving Goffman's description of facial interaction as a "face work" along a "line" of social interaction. According to Goffman, "Every person lives in a world of social encounters, involving him either in face-to-face or mediated contact with other participants. In each of these contacts, he tends to act out what is sometimes called a *line*—that is, a pattern of verbal and nonverbal acts by which he expresses his view of the situation and through his evaluation of the participants, especially himself" (5).

9. See especially Phil Rosen's *Change Mummified* and Ivone Margulies' collection *Rites of Realism: Essays on Corporeal*, which explicitly takes up the heritage of Bazin as part of the various arguments in the volume.

10. Many of Russell's insights line up with mine about how mortality and subjectivity are represented in many contemporary films, but I argue, as some of her examples also suggest, that often this relationship demands a confrontation with or a departure from narrative that, for me, can lead specifically to the essayistic.

11. See especially Peter Wollen's "Blue" for an extended discussion of the history and aesthetic background that inform the film, as well as Derek Jarman's *Chroma: A Book of Colors*. Two good studies of Jarman's work and this film specifically are Rowland Wymer's *Derek Jarman* and Jim Ellis's *Derek Jarman's Angelic Conversations*.

12. Murray borrows the last phrase from Simon Field and Michael O'Pray's interview with Jarman (55).

13. After experiments with different film processes (including loops), James Mackey produced the astonishing blue gels used for the film.

14. Another important reference is Gainsborough's painting *Blue Boy* since for a British audience it is the most iconic blue body. Further, as Kevin Harty pointed out to me, AZT, the first antiviral AIDS drug, was a white capsule with a central blue band, a shade that in the gay community simply became known as AZT blue.

15. According to Watney, these spectacles have reduced the social scale of the AIDS crisis to some version of family space (55).

CHAPTER 4

1. I would even describe Kristof Kieslowski's series of ten essays within a single housing complex, *The Decalogue* (1989), as a strange and remarkable set of travel essays in which, shadowed by the Ten Commandments, exploration and travel are also ethical trips.

2. I am indebted to Margulies for assistance in many ways and for her magisterial study of Akerman, *Nothing Happens*.

3. See Jeffrey Ruoff's collection *Virtual Voyages: Cinema and Travel*, especially Lauren Rabinovitz's "From Hale's Tours to Star Tours: Virtual Voyages, Travel Ride Films, and the Delirium of the Hyper-Real."

4. Besides Naficy's chapter in *An Accented Cinema*, "The Epistolarity and the Epistolary Narrative," other important discussions of the epistolary include Jacques Derrida's *The Post Card: From Socrates to Freud and Beyond*, Linda Kauffman's *Special Delivery: Epistolary Modes in Modern Fiction*, and Janet Altman's *Epistolarity: Approaches to a Form*.

5. For excellent readings of *Sunless*, I recommend Alter's *Chris Marker* and Lupton's *Chris Marker: Memories of the Future*.

6. Several good studies of Keiller's films are as follows: Paul Dave's "Representations of Capitalism, History and Nation in the Work of Patrick Keiller"; David Martin-Jones's "Patrick Keiller"; and Ian Sinclair's "London: Necropolis of Fretful Ghosts."

7. Other suggestive categorizations of spatial arrangements include those of Victor Burgin: fantastic spaces, inner spaces, and outer spaces (*In/Different Spaces*).

8. Currently, the most complete discussion of Herzog's films in English is Brad Prager's *The Cinema of Werner Herzog*.

9. As Deleuze says of *Heart of Glass*, "The search for the alchemical heart and secret, for the red crystal, is inseparable from the search for cosmic limits, as the highest tension of the spirit and the deepest level of reality" (*Cinema 2*, 74–75).

10. To call attention to the work of ideas in Herzog's films is not to equate them with the essay films of Godard, for instance—whom, by the way, Herzog refers to as an intellectual counterfeit. Rather, it is to make manifest that wide variety of what I refer to as essayistic thinking as different conceptual and figural engagements with the world.

11. This perceptive analysis of the film through the framework of Bazin's notion of becoming animal summarizes this movement toward a kind of thought this way: "Through a belated advent made possible by two cameras, a ghost is called forth, triggering our becoming-ghost. Subordinating film language to the animal scream, Herzog has given us room to think about the relation between animal and human death, about the (im)possibility of becoming-animal, about the quasi-presence of ghosts, about the ontology of the cinematic image and

about the other real worlds immanent in all these conundrums. He has, in short, cleared room to think about the unthinkable" (12).

CHAPTER 5

1. In terms of David James's distinction between a film diary and a diary film, the essay diary aligns mostly with the latter and its self-reflexive and public address. See James's "Film Diary/Diary Film: Practice and Product in *Walden*" in *To Free the Cinema*.

2. Bruzzi offers typically sharp readings of *Seven Up* (1964) and *Hoop Dreams* (1994) as another example of "making documentaries over time" (85–97).

3. See Charney and Schwartz's *Cinema and the Invention of Modern Life*.

4. Some of the most celebrated positions on this relationship of subjectivity to a theatrics of vision and and ideology of property include the work of Metz, Michael Fried, Stephen Heath, and Fredric Jameson.

5. See Maureen Turim's *Flashbacks in Film: Memory and History* and Metz's "Fiction Film and Its Spectator" in *The Imaginary Signifier: Psychoanalysis and the Cinema*.

6. Besides Wahlberg's work, see Rascaroli's discussion of "the musealization of experience" in *The Personal Camera*.

7. If different timings and velocities may have been a cinematic potential since the nineteenth century, traditional narrative and documentary cinemas have largely worked to naturalize and recuperate these through predictable schemes that serve homogeneous or uniform spaces. The change after World War II is signaled most notably in Deleuze's two-volume argument in *Cinema 1* and *Cinema 2* about a movement from a cinema of action and movement to one of temporality.

8. As early as 1915, Vachel Lindsay remarks that what differentiates film from theater is "*splendor* and *speed*" (193). In his essay "Speed and the Cinema," Peter Wollen explores the attraction of this velocity from the 1920s through the present and notes how the thrills produced through high speed "*exposes* the viewer to unfamiliar situations . . . far removed from the zones of safety and normality" (265). Yet, in that exposure, the experiences of cinematic speed are consistently counterpointed by the viewer's distance from and control of those virtually violent thrills.

9. Besides Petro's chapter "Aftershocks: Between Boredom and History" in *Aftershocks*, see also Patricia Meyer Spacks's *Boredom: The Literary History of a State of Mind*.

10. Note how Virilio expands on these points: "Today it is impossible to talk about the development of the audiovisual without also talking about the development of virtual imagery and its influence on human behaviour, or without pointing to the new *industrialization of vision*, to the growth of a veritable market in synthetic perception and all the ethical questions this entails. This should be considered not only in relation to control of surveillance, and the attendant persecution mania, but also primarily in relation to the philosophical question of the *splitting of viewpoint*, the sharing of perception of the environment between the animate (the living subject) and the inanimate (the object, the seeing machine). . . . Once we are definitively removed from the realm of direct or indirect observation of synthetic images created *by the machine for the machine*, instrumental virtual images will be for us the equivalent of what a foreigner's mental pictures already represent: an enigma" (59–60).

11. A useful collection of interviews from different participants in Clarke's films is Richard Kelly's 1998 publication *Alan Clarke*.

CHAPTER 6

1. In this sense, editorial essay films are a consciously unstable blend of Nichols's binary of social issue documentaries and personal portrait documentaries (*Introduction* 166–167).

2. Thomas Elsaesser's collection *Harun Farocki: Working on the Sight-Lines* is perhaps the best English collection of essays on Farocki's films. Besides Elsaesser's introductory "Harun Farocki: Filmmaker, Artist, Media Theorist" and his "Working at the Margins: Film as a Form of Intelligence," two other contributions to this volume are especially pertinent as they examine Farocki's films as essay films: Christa Blümlinger's "Slowly Forming a Thought While Working on Images" and Nora Alter's "The Political Im/perceptible: *Images of the World*." Antje Ehmann and Kodwo Eshun's 2010 collection *Harun Farocki: Against What? Against Whom?* features several essays, by Alter, Elsaesser, and Sylvie Lindeperg, on *Respite*. Laura Rascaroli's *Personal Cinema* also features a discussion of Farocki as essayist and his film *Images of the World and the Inscription of War* (1989).

3. See Thomas Benson and Brian Snee's *The Rhetoric of the New Political Documentary* for a collection that concentrates on various interventionist efforts in contemporary documentaries.

4. The argument of Patricia Zimmermann's *States of Emergency: Documentaries, Wars, Democracies* overlaps with and significantly expands some of my suggestions here, examining both the dangerously repressive climate of global media after 1989 and some of the strongest and most creative interventions by independent documentaries.

5. Two significantly more conventional films about the Lebanon war are Samuel Moaz's *Lebanon* (2010) and Joseph Cedar's *Beaufort* (2007), the first an autobiographical account of a tank crew and the second about soldiers defending an outpost soon to be abandoned.

6. Thanks to Ruth Perlmutter for the suggestive notion of a "waltz with wolves." The implicit contrast in that metaphor with the film *Dances with Wolves* (1990) dramatizes the massive aesthetic and political distance of *Waltz with Bashir* from that Hollywood narrative of war and colonization.

7. Filmmaker Eran Preis is the first person I heard use this phrase in criticizing the film.

8 Thanks to Lynne Sachs for sending me this essay.

9. It is worth quoting Nichols at length about this rich term: "Social subjectivity will remain beyond the horizon of a text that affirms the personal vision and subjective experience of individual, poetic consciousness but little more. This question of magnitude as a domain of social subjectivity and historical engagement is what distinguishes performative documentary from a large portion of the traditional film avant-garde with which it otherwise shares so much.

And yet the passage from a transcendental but individual consciousness to a dialectical and social one is further compounded by the absence of a specifically political frame within which performative documentary might be received. The formalists' claim that there is no 'there' there becomes joined to the Marxists' lament that there is no Left left. This is not quite true, though. It would be more accurate to say that the Left has taken a dispersed, decentered form, and that its absence is only perceptible when what we seek is the traditional Left of vanguard parties, united front politics, and a correct line. Political affinities are already dispersed across a wide field of organizations and issues; they overlap and coalesce in unpredictable and unstable ways. There is great cause for optimism in this movement toward a new magnitude of political organization and process, to which performative documentary contributes significantly, but an aura of nostalgic loss and misrecognition may also loom. This is, after all, a time of multinational if not global capitalism, of a new world order of command and control, of interactive but hierarchically organized communications, of a "late" capitalism that continues to discover ways to transform and perpetuate itself.

As this economic lion, or perhaps paper tiger, grows larger and larger, more globally interconnected and less locally responsible, the contrast between its power and scope and the apparent power of identity politics, makeshift alliances, and cyborg affinities may seem dwarfed out of all proportion. This is a perception that performative documentary sets out to revise. By restoring a sense of the local, specific, and embodied as a vital locus for social subjectivity, performative documentary gives figuration to and evokes dimensions of the political unconscious that remain suspended between an immediate here and now and a utopian alternative (*Blurred Boundaries* 106).

10. See especially Catherine Russell's "Archival Apocalypse: Found Footage as Ethnography."

11. Bernstein incorporates Arthur's essay "Jargons of Authenticity (Three American Moments)" as a part of an argument that is more dubious about Moore's persona and strategies.

12. A good English-language study of Kluge's films is Peter C. Lutze's *Alexander Kluge: The Last Modernist*.

CHAPTER 7

1. Paisley Livingston has coined the term *nested art* to describe this widespread practice in various aesthetic realms.

2. During the first half of the twentieth century, films about art and artists, about painting or music, or even films about films normally become, for the most part, narrative commentaries, incorporating aesthetic figures into plots about individual encounters and development to supplement the original figure, text, or discourse as a primary referent. From biopics about artists to avant-garde blendings of different artistic experiences, the aesthetic tends to function mainly as a vehicle or background for subjective development rather than as an experience that productively resists subjectivity.

3. I am using the phrase *anti-aesthetic* in a much more specific way than the way it ranges through Hal Foster's important collection *The Anti-Aesthetic: Essays on Postmodernism*. However, just as the essayistic engages, for Lyotard and others, some of the fundamentals of postmodernism, my use of anti-aesthetic does overlap some of the arguments in Foster's volume.

4. In a work that does bear on some of my argument here, John Mullarkey's *Refractions of Reality: Philosophy and the Moving Image* employs the idea and figure of refraction in a broadly philosophical and expansive way to discuss how all films "think" and in turn refract as many different kinds of critical engagements: "Cinematic thought or philosophy," he writes, "is never about reflection . . . but about resistant refraction, a freedom that resists definitions of essence" (190).

5. Inspired by the novelist and theorist Pierre Klossowski, the film was originally intended to be a documentary profile of Klossowski for French television and was influenced by Klossowski's final novel *La Baphomet*.

6. For Walter Benjamin, *Denkbild* describes the necessity of criticism to negotiate a dialect between proximity and distance, experience and thought, a negotiation that must be continually reconsidered through experience and thought ("The Storyteller").

7. It is worth recalling in this context Derrida's observation that the essayistic is antigeneric.

8. In his essay on "Adaptation," Dudley Andrew retrieves Bazin's term to help explain his category of adaptation as "intersecting."

9. Bazin continues: "The fidelity of Resnais to Van Gogh is but the prior condition of a symbiosis of cinema and painting. That is why, as a rule, painters fail utterly to understand the whole procedure. If you see these films as nothing more than an intelligent, effective, and even a valuable means of popularizing painting—they are certainly that too—you know nothing of their aesthetic biology" (142).

10. Deborah and Mark Parker's *The DVD and the Study of Film* is one of the first books to look thoroughly at how DVD supplements have become their own form of criticism.

11. An engaging and consistently insightful collection of essays on *The Five Obstructions* is Mette Hjort's *Dekalog 01: On the Five Obstructions*

12. *Framework* 50 (Fall 2009) is devoted entirely to cinematic reenactments. Titled "What Now? Re-enactment in Contemporary Documentary Film, Video, And Performance Dossier," the issue demonstrates how varied and important the topic and practice are to contemporary film culture.

13. Needless to say, perhaps, this relationship between reenactment and a judicial structure is also found in celebrated essay films like *The Thin Blue Line* (1988) and *Capturing the Friedmans*.

14. As is clear in my reading, my analysis of *Close-Up* is generally and specifically indebted to Margulies' superb reading of the film in *Rites of Realism*.

Aron, Raymond. *Dix-huit leçons sur la société industrielle*. Paris: Flammarion, 1986.

Abel, Richard (ed.). *French Film Theory and Criticism: A History/Anthology, 1907–1939, Volume 1: 1907–1929*. Princeton, N.J.: Princeton Univ. Press, 1988.

———. *French Cinema: The First Wave: 1915-1929*. Princeton Univ. Press, 1987.

Addison, Joseph. *Addison's Essays from the Spectator*. London, Adamant Media, 2001.

Adorno, T.W. "The Essay as Form." In *Notes to Literature*, Vol. 1. New York: Columbia Univ. Press, 1991. 3–23.

Agee, James and Walker Evans. *Let Us Now Praise Famous Men*. Cambridge, MA: Houghton Mifflin, 1939.

Alter, Nora. "The Political Im/perceptible in the Essay Film: Farocki's *Images of the World and the Inscription of War*." *New German Critique* 68 (1996): 165–192.

———. "Documentary as Simulacrum: *Tokyo-Ga*." In *The Cinema of Wim Wenders: Image, Narrative, and the Postmodern Condition*. Ed. Roger F. Cook and Gerd Gemunden. Detroit: Wayne State Univ. Press, 1997. 136–162.

———. "Mourning, Sound, and Vision: Jean-Luc Godard's *JLG/JLG*." *Camera Obscura* 15.2 (2000): 75–103.

———. *Chris Marker*. Urbana: Univ. of Illinois Press, 2006.

———. "Hans Richter in Exile: Translating the Avant-Garde." In *Caught by Politics*. Ed. S. Eckmann and L. Koepnick. New York: Palgrave, 2007. 223–243.

———. "Translating the Essay into Film and Installation." *Journal of Visual Culture* 6.1 (2007): 44–57.

———. "The Political Im/perceptible: *Images of the World*." *Harun Farocki: Working on the Sight-Lines*. Amsterdam: Amsterdam Univ. Press, 2004. 211–236.

Altman, Janet. *Epistolarity: Approaches to a Form*. Columbus: Ohio State Univ. Press, 1982.

Altman, Rick. "From Lecturer's Prop to Industrial Product: The Early History of Travel Films." *Virtual Voyages: Cinema and Travel*. Ed. Jeffrey Ruoff. Durham: Duke Univ. Press, 2006. 61–78.

Andrew, Dudley. "Adaptation." *Concepts in Film Theory*. NY: Oxford Univ. Press, 1984.

Arendt, Hannah. *The Human Condition*. Chicago: Univ. of Chicago Press, 1958.

Arthur, Paul. "Jargons of Authenticity (Three American Moments)." In *Theorizing Documentary*. Ed. Michael Renov. New York: Routledge, 1993. 108–134.

———. "Essay Questions." *Film Comment* 39.1 (2003): 53–62.

———. "No Longer Absolute: Portraiture in American Avant-Garde and Documentary Films of the 1960s." In *Rites of Realism: Essays on Corporeal Cinema*. Ed. Ivone Margulies. Durham, N.C.: Duke Univ. Press, 2003. 93–118.

———. "The Resurgence of History and the Avant-Garde Essay Film." In *A Line of Sight: American Avant-Garde Film Since 1965*. Minneapolis: Univ. of Minnesota Press, 2005. 61–73.

Astruc, Alexandre. *Du stylo à la caméra . . . Et de la caméra au stylo, Écrits (1942–1984)*. Paris: L'Archipel, 1992.

———. "L'Avenir du cinema." *Trafic* 3 (Summer 1992): 151–158.

———. "The Birth of a New Avant-Garde: La Caméra-Stylo." In *Film and Literature: An Introduction and Reader*. Ed. Timothy Corrigan. Upper Saddle River, N.J.: Prentice-Hall, 1999. 158–162.

Aumont, Jacque. "The Variable Eye, or the Mobilization of the Gaze." In *The Image in Dispute: Art Cinema in the Age of Photography*. Ed. Dudley Andrew. Austin: Univ. of Texas Press, 1997. 231–259.

Bacon, Francis. *Complete Essays*. NY: Dover, 2008.

Balázs, Béla. *Theory of Film: Character and Growth of a New Art*. NY: Dover, 1970.

Baldwin, James. *Collected Essays*. New York: Library of America, 1998.

———. "I'll Make Me a World." PBS broadcast, February 2, 1999.

Barthes, Roland. *S/Z*. New York: Farrar, Straus, Giroux, 1974.

———. *Roland Barthes by Roland Barthes*. New York: Hill and Wang, 1977.

———. "The Third Meaning." In *Image-Music-Text*. New York: Hill and Wang, 1977. 52–68.

———. *La chamber claire*. Paris: Seuil, 1980.

———. "Inaugural Lecture, College de France." In *A Barthes Reader*. Ed. Susan Sontag. New York: Hill and Wang, 1982. 457–478.

———. "Leaving the Movie Theater." In *Rustle of Language*. New York: Hill and Wang, 1986.

Baudrillard, Jean. "The Gulf War: Is It Really Taking Place?" In *The Jean Baudrillard Reader*. Ed. Steve Redhead. New York: Columbia Univ. Press, 2008. 99–125.

Bazin, André. "In Defense of Mixed Cinema." In *What Is Cinema?* Vol. 1. Berkeley: Univ. of California Press, 1967. 53–75.

———. "*Le Journal d'un Curé de Campagne* and the Stylistics of Robert Bresson." *What Is Cinema?* Vol. 1. Berkeley: Univ. of California Press, 1967. 125–143.

———. "The Ontology of the Photographic Image." In *What Is Cinema?* Vol. 1. Berkeley: Univ. of California Press, 1967. 9–16.

———. "Painting and Cinema." In *What Is Cinema?* Vol. 1. Berkeley: Univ. of California Press, 1967. 164–172.

———. "The Evolution of the Language of Cinema." *What Is Cinema?* Vol. 1. Berkeley: Univ. of California Press, 1967. 23–40.

———. *What Is Cinema?* Vols. 1 and 2. Berkeley: Univ. of California Press, 1967.

———. "The Stalin Myth in Soviet Cinema." In *Movies and Methods*. Vol. 2. Ed. Bill Nichols. Berkeley: Univ. of California Press, 1985. 29–40.

————."Adaptation, or the Cinema as Digest." In *Film Adaptation*. Ed. James Nareomore. New Brunswick, N.J.: Rutgers Univ. Press, 2000. 19–27.

————. "Death Every Afternoon." In *Rites of Realism: Essays on Corporeal Cinema*. Ed. Ivone Margulies. Durham, N.C.: Duke Univ. Press, 2002. 27–31.

————. "Bazin on Marker." Trans. Dave Kehr. *Film Comment* 39.4 (2003): 43–44.

Beaujour, Michel. *Poetics of the Literary Self-Portrait*. New York: New York Univ. Press, 1992.

Benjamin, Walter. *The Arcades Project*. Cambridge, Mass.: Belknap Press, 1999.

————. "On the Concept of History."*Selected Writings. Vol. 4: 1935–1938*. Ed. Howard Eiland and Michael W. Jennings. Cambridge, Mass.: Belknap Press, 2002. 389–401.

————. "The Work of Art in the Age of Its Technological Reproducibility." *Selected Writings. Vol. 4: 1938–1940*. Ed. Howard Eiland and Michael W. Jennings. Cambridge, Mass.: Belknap Press, 2003. 251–284.

————. "The Storyteller: Observations on the Works of Nikolai Leskov." *Selected Writings. Vol. 3: 1935–1938*. Ed. Howard Eiland and Michael W. Jennings. Cambridge, Mass.: Belknap Press, 2002. 143–166

————. *The Origin of German Tragic Drama*. London: Verso, 1977.

Bense, Max. "Über den Essay und seine Prosa." *Merkur* 1.3 (1947): 414–424.

Bensmaïa, Réda. *The Barthes Effect*. Minneapolis: Univ. of Minnesota Press, 1987.

Benson, Thomas and Brian Snee, ed. *The Rhetoric of the New Political Documentary*. Carbondale: Southern Illinois Univ. Press, 2008.

Berlant, Lauren. "Thinking about Feeling Historical." *Emotion, Space and Society* 1.1 (2008): 4–9.

Bernstein, Matthew. "Documentaphobia and Mixed Modes: Michael Moore's *Roger and Me*." In *Documenting the Documentary: Close Readings of Documentary Film and Video*. Ed. Barry Keith Grant and Jeannette Sloniowski. Detroit: Wayne State Univ. Press, 1998. 397–415.

Bersani, Leo. *Forms of Being: Cinema, Aesthetics, Subjectivity*. London: BFI, 2008.

Bertolucci, Bernardo. "The Boundless Frivolity of People about to Die." In *Nick's Film: Lightning over Water*. Ed. Wim Wenders and Chris Sievernich. Frankfurt: Zweitausendeins, 1981. 5.

Bingham, Dennis. *Whose Lives Are They Anyway? The Biopic as Contemporary Film Genre*. New Brunswick, N.J.: Rutgers Univ. Press, 2010.

Blanchot, Maurice. "Everyday Speech." *Yale French Studies* 73. New Haven, Conn.: Yale Univ. Press, 1987. 12–20

Blümlinger, Christa. "Lire entre les Images." In *L'Essai et le cinéma*. Ed. Suzanne Liandrat-Guigues and Murielle Gagnebin. Paris: Champs Vallon, 2004. 49–66.

————. "Slowly Forming a Thought While Working on Images." *Harun Farocki: Working on the Sight-Lines*. Amsterdam: Amsterdam Univ. Press, 2004. 163–176.

Bruno, Guiliana. *The Atlas of Emotion: Journeys in Art, Architecture, and Film*. New York: Verso, 2002.

Bruzzi, Stella. *New Documentary: A Critical Introduction*. 2nd ed. London: Routledge, 2006.

Burch, Noël. *Theory of Film Practice*. Princeton, N.J.: Princeton Univ. Press, 1981.

Burgin, Victor. *In/Different Spaces: Place and Memory in Visual Culture*. Berkeley: Univ. of California Press, 1996.

Buss, Elizabeth. "Eye for I: Making and Unmaking Autobiography in Film." In *Autobiography: Essays Theoretical and Critical*. Ed. James Olney. Princeton, N.J.: Princeton Univ. Press. 298–320.

Caughie, John. "Humphrey Jennings." *Encyclopedia of European Cinema*. Ed. Ginette Vincendeau. London: BFI, 1995, 231.

———. "Derek Jarman." *Encyclopedia of European Cinema.* Ed. Ginette Vincendeau. London: BFI, 1995, 229.

Chapman, William, ed. *Films on Art 1952.* New York: American Federation of Arts, 1953.

Charney, Leo and Vanessa R. Schwartz, ed. *Cinema and the Invention of Modern Life.* Berkeley: Univ. of California Press, 1995.

Chion, Michel. *The Voice in Cinema.* NY: Columbia Univ. Press, 1999.

Coleridge, S.T. *Biographia Literaria: Biographical Sketches of my Literary Life & Opinions.* Princeton: Princeton Univ. Press, 1985.

Conway, Kelley. "'A New Wave of Spectators': Contemporary Responses to *Cleo from 5 to 7*." *Film Quarterly* 61.1 (2007): 38–47.

Covert, Nadine, ed. *Art on Screen: A Directory of Films and Videos About the Visual Arts.* New York: Metropolitan Museum of Art, 1991.

Custen, George F. *Bio/Pics: How Hollywood Constructed Public History.* New Brunswick, N.J.: Rutgers Univ. Press, 1992.

Danks, Adrian. "The Global Art of Found Footage Cinema." In *Traditions in World Cinema.* Ed. Linda Badley, R. Barton Palmer, and Steven Jay Schneider. New Brunswick, N.J.: Rutgers Univ. Press, 2006. 241–253.

Dave, Paul. "Representations of Capitalism, History and Nation in the Work of Patrick Keiller." In *British Cinema, Past and Present.* Ed. Justine Ashby and Andrew Higson. London: Routledge, 2000. 339–352

de Certeau, Michel. *L'Invention du quotidien.* Paris: Union Général d'Edtions, 1980.

———. *The Practice of Everyday Life.* Berkeley: Univ. of California Press, 1984.

Defore, Daniel. *Tour through the Whole Island of Great Britain.* New Haven: Yale Univ. Press, 1991.

———. *Robinson Crusoe.* NY: Oxford Univ. Press, 1999.

Deleuze, Gilles. *Cinema 1: The Movement-Image.* Minneapolis: Univ. of Minnesota Press, 1986.

———. *Foucault.* Minneapolis: Univ. of Minnesota Press, 1988.

———. *Cinema 2: The Time-Image.* Minneapolis: Univ. of Minnesota Press, 1989.

Deluc, Germaine. "The Essence of Cinema: The Visual Idea." In *The Avant-Garde Film: A Reader of Theory and Criticism.* Ed. P. Adam Sitney. New York: Anthology Film Archives, 1987. 36–42

———. "The Expressive Techniques of the Cinema." In *French Film Criticism and Theory: A History/Anthology, 1907–1939. Vol. 1: 1907–1929.* Ed. Richard Abel. Princeton, N.J.: Princeton Univ. Press, 1998. 310.

de Obaldia, Claire. *The Essayistic Spirit: Literature, Modern Criticism, and the Essay.* New York: Oxford Univ. Press, 1995.

Derrida, Jacques. *The Post Card: From Socrates to Freud and Beyond.* Chicago: Univ. of Chicago Press, 1980.

"Director: Alan Clarke." *The Alan Clark Collection.* 1979-1996. *Blue Underground.* 2004. DVD.

Doane, Mary Ann. *The Emergence of Cinematic Time: Modernity, Contingency, the Archive.* Cambridge, Mass.: Harvard Univ. Press, 2002.

Donald, James, Anne Freidberg, and Laura Marcus, eds. *Close Up, 1927–1933: Cinema and Modernism.* Princeton, N.J.: Princeton Univ. Press, 1998.

Duffy, Edna. *The Speed Handbook: Velocity, Pleasure, Modernism.* Durham, N.C.: Duke Univ. Press, 2009.

Dumont, Francois. *Approches de l'essai.* Quebec: Éditions Nota bene, 2003.

Dwyer, Susan. "Romancing the Dane: Ethics and Observation." In *Dekalog 01: On the Five Obstructions.* Ed. Mette Hjort. London: Wallflower Press, 2008. 1–14.

Ehmann, Antje and Kodwo Eshun. *Harun Farocki: Against What? Against Whom?* London: Koenig Books, 2010.

Eisenstein, Sergei. "Notes for a Film of 'Capital.'" Trans. Maciej Sliwowski, Jay Leuda, and Annette Michelson. *October* 2 (1976): 3–26.

Ellis, Jim. *Derek Jarman's Angelic Conversations.* Minneapolis: Univ. of Minnesota Press, 2009.

Elsaesser, Thomas, ed. *Harun Farocki: Working on the Sight-Lines.* Amsterdam: Amsterdam Univ. Press, 2004.

———. "Working at the Margins: Film as a Form of Intelligence." *Harun Farocki: Working on the Sight-Lines.* Ed. Thomas Elsaesser. Amsterdam: Amsterdam Univ. Press, 2004. 95–104.

———. "Harun Farocki: Filmmaker, Artist, Media Theorist." *Harun Farocki: Working on the Sight-Lines.* Ed. Thomas Elsaesser. Amsterdam: Amsterdam Univ. Press, 2004. 11–42.

———. "Raoul Ruiz's *L'Hypothesis du Tableau Vole*." In *European Cinema: Face to Face with Hollywood.* Amsterdam: Amsterdam Univ. Press, 2005. 251–254.

———. *New German Cinema: A History.* New Brunswick: Rutgers Univ. Press, 1989.

Field, Simon and Michael O'Pray. "On Imaging October, Dr. Dee and Other Matters: An Interview with Derek Jarman." *Afterimage* 12 (1985): 41–57.

Fihman, Guy. "L'Essai cinématographique et ses transformations expérimentales." In *L'Essai et le cinéma.* Ed. Suzanne Liandrat-Guigues and Murielle Gagnebin. Paris: Champs Vallon, 2004. 41–48.

Flaxman, Gregory, ed. *The Brain Is a Screen: Deleuze and the Philosophy of Cinema.* Minneapolis: Univ. of Minnesota Press, 2000.

Flitterman-Lewis, Sandy. "Documenting the Ineffable: Terror and Memory in Alain Resnais's Night and Fog." In *Documenting the Documentary: Close Readings of Documentary Film and Video.* Eds. Barry Keith Grant and Jeannette Sloniowski. Detroit: Wayne State Univ. Press, 1998. 204–222.

Foster, Hal, ed. *The Anti-Aesthetic: Essays on Postmodernism.* Seattle: Bay Press, 1983.

Foucault, Michel. *The Order of Things: An Archeology of the Human Sciences.* New York: Pantheon, 1970.

———. "What Is an Author?" In *Language, Counter-Memory, Practice: Selected Essays and Interviews.* Ed. Donald Bouchard. Ithaca, N.Y.: Cornell Univ. Press, 1980. 113–138.

Frampton, Daniel. *Filmosophy.* London: Wallflower Press, 2006.

Frears, Stephen. "Interview in 'Director: Alan Clarke'." *The Alan Clark Collection.* 1979-1996. *Blue Underground.* 2004. DVD.

Gaines, Jane and Michael Renov, eds. *Collecting Visible Evidence.* Minneapolis: Univ. of Minnesota Press, 1999.

Galperin, William. *The Return of the Visible in British Romanticism.* Baltimore: Johns Hopkins Univ. Press, 1993.

Galloway, Alexander R. *Gaming: Essays on Algorithmic Culture.* Minneapolis: Univ. of Minnesota Press, 2006.

Gass, William. *On Being Blue: A Philosophical Inquiry.* NY: David A. Godine, 1991.

Gaudreault, André and Germain Lacasse, eds. *The Moving Picture Lecturer.* Special issues of *Iris* 22 (1999).

Giannetti, Louis. "Godard's *Masculine-Feminine*: The Cinematic Essay." In *Godard and Others: Essays on Film Form.* Rutherford, NJ: Fairleigh Dickinson Press, 1975.

Gibson, Ross "What Do I Know? Chris Marker and the Essayist Mode of Cinema." *Filmviews* (Summer 1988): 26–32.

Godard, Jean-Luc. *Godard on Godard.* Trans. Tom Milne. New York: Viking, 1972.

————. *Histoire(s) du cinema*. Paris: Gallimard-Gaumont, 1998.

Goffman, Erving. *Interaction Ritual: Essays on Face-to-Face Behavior*. New York: Pantheon, 1967.

Good, Graham. *The Observing Self: Rediscovering the Essay*. London: Routledge, 1988.

Gras, Vernon and Marguerite Gras. *Peter Greenaway Interviews*. Jackson: Univ. of Mississippi, 2000.

Grierson, John. *Grierson on Documentary*. Berkeley: Univ. of California Press, 1966.

Grundmann, Royt and Cynthia Rockwell, "Truth Is Not Subjective: An Interview with Errol Morris." *Cineaste* 24.3 (2000): 4–9.

Gubern, Roman. "Cent ans de cinema." In *Historia general del cinema, vol. XII: el cine en la era del audiovisual*. Madrid: Catedra, 1995. Quoted in Liandrat-Guigues, Suzanne and Murielle Gagnebin, 2004, 27.

Gunning, Tom. "A Corner in Wheat." In *The Griffith Project, Volume 3*. Ed. Paolo Cherchi Usai. London: British Film Institute, 1999. 130–41.

Habermas, Jürgen. *The Structural Transformation of the Public Sphere: An Inquiry into a Category of Bourgeois Society*. Cambridge, MA: MIT Press, 1991.

Hampl, Patricia. "Memory's Movies." In *Beyond Document: Essays on Nonfiction Film*. Ed. Charles Warren. Hanover, N.H.: Wesleyan Univ. Press, 1996. 51–78.

Hansen, Miriam. "Alexander Kluge, Cinema and the Public Sphere: The Construction Site of Counter-History." *Discourse* 4 (Winter 1981/1982): 57–58.

————. *Babel & Babylon: Spectatorship in American Silent Film*. Cambridge, Mass.: Harvard Univ. Press, 1991.

Harrison, Thomas. *Essayism: Conrad, Musil, & Pirandello*. Baltimore: Johns Hopkins Univ. Press, 1992.

Hazlitt, William. "On Going on a Journey." In *Selected Essays of Willliam Hazlitt*. Ed. Geoffrey Keynes. London: Nonesuch Press, 1970. 71–82.

Herzog, Werner. *Of Walking in Ice*. New York: Tanam, 1980.

————. "Minnesota Declaration." 1999. http://www.wernerherzog.com/52.html#c93.

Hjort, Mette. *Dekalog 01: On the Five Obstructions*. London: Wallflower Press, 2008.

hooks, bell. "Blue." *Artforum* 33.3 (November 1994): 10.

Hutcheon, Linda. *A Theory of Adaptation*. New York: Routledge, 2006.

Huxley, Aldous. "Preface to *The Collected Essays of Aldous Huxley*." In *Aldous Huxley Complete Essays. Vol. 6, 1956–1963*. Ed. Robert Baker and James Sexton. Chicago: Dee, 2002. 329–332.

James, David. *To Free the Cinema: Jonas Mekas and the New York Underground*. Princeton, N.J.: Princeton Univ. Press, 1992.

Jameson, Fredric. "Reading without Interpretation: Postmodernism and the Video-Text." In *The Linguistics of Writing: Arguments between Language and Literture*. Ed. Derek Attridge, Alan Durant, Nigel Fabb, Colin MacCabe,. Manchester, UK: Manchester Univ. Press, 1987. 199–223.

————. "Postmodernism and Consumer Society." In *Critical Visions in Film Theory: Classic and Contemporary Readings*. Ed. Timothy Corrigan and Patricia White. New York: Bedford/St. Martin's, 2011. 1031–1040.

Jarman, Derek. *Blue*. New York: The Overlook Press, 1994.

————. *Chroma: A Book of Colors*. Minneapolis: Univ. of Minnesota Press, 2010.

Jeong, Seung-Hoon and Dudley Andrew. "Grizzly Ghost: Herzog, Bazin and the Cinematic Animal." *Screen* 49.1 (Spring 2008): 1–12.

Kahana, Jonathan. *Intelligence Work: The Politics of American Documentary*. New York: Columbia Univ. Press, 2008.

Kamper, Birgit and Thomas Tode, eds. *Chris Marker: Filmessayist*. Munich: CICIM, 1997.

Katz, John. *Autobiography: Film/Video/Photography*. Ontario: Art Gallery of Ontario, 1978.

Kauffman, Linda S. *Special Delivery: Epistolary Modes in Modern Fiction*. Chicago: Univ. of Chicago Press, 1992.

Kelly, Richard, ed. *Alan Clarke*. London: Faber and Faber, 1998.

Keiller, Patrick. "The Visible Surface." *Sight and Sound* (November 1994): 35.

———. *Robinson in Space/and an Interview with Patrick Wright*. London: Reaktion Books, 1999.

———. "Architectural Cinematograph." In *This Is Not Architecture*. Ed. Kester Rattenbury. New York: Routledge, 2002.

———. "The Future of Landscape and the Moving Image." 2008. http://thefutureoflandscape. wordpress.com/.

Klossowski, Pierre. *La Baphomet*. NY: Marsilio, 1998.

Kluge, Alexander et al. "Word and Film." In *Film and Literature: An Introduction and Reader*. Ed. Timothy Corrigan. Upper Saddle River, N.J.: Prentice-Hall, 1999.

Kluge, Alexander and Oskar Negt. *Public Sphere and Experience: Toward an Analysis of the Bourgeois and Proletarian Public Sphere*. Minneapolis: Univ. of Minnesota Press, 1993.

Koch, Gertrud. "Blindness as Insight: Visions of the Unseen in *Land of Silence and Darkness*." *The Films of Werner Herzog: Between Mirage and History*. Ed. Timothy Corrigan. London: Methuen, 1986.

Kritzman, Lawrence D. *The Fabulous Imagination: On Montaigne's Essays*. New York: Columbia Univ. Press, 2009.

Lacan, Jaques. *The Four Fundamental Concepts of Psycho-Analysis*. Trans. Alan Sheridan. New York: Norton, 1978.

Lane, Jim. *The Autobiographical Documentary in America*. Madison: Univ. of Wisconsin Press, 2002.

Leach, Jim. "The Poetics of Propaganda: Humphrey Jennings and Listen to Britain." In *Documenting the Documentary: Close Readings of Documentary Films and Video*. Ed. Barry Keith Grant and Jeannette Sloniowski. Detroit: Wayne State Univ. Press, 1998. 154–170.

Lefebvre, Henri. *The Production of Space*. Oxford, UK: Basil Blackwell, 1991.

Liandrat-Guigues, Suzanne and Murielle Gagnebin, eds. *L'Essai et le cinéma*. Paris: Champs Vallon, 2004.

Lindsay, Vachel. *The Art of the Moving Picture*. NY: Liveright, 1970.

Livingston, Paisley. "Nested Art." *Journal of Aesthetic and Art Criticism*, 61 (2003): 233–245.

Lopate, Phillip. "In Search of the Centaur: The Essay Film." In *Beyond Document: Essays on Nonfiction Film*. Ed. Charles Warren. Hanover, N.H.: Wesleyan Univ. Press, 1996. 243–270.

Lowry, Edward. *The Filmology Movement and Film Study in France*. Ann Arbor:UMI Press, 1985.

Lukacs, Georg. "On the Nature and Form of the Essay." In *Soul and Form*. Cambridge, Mass.: MIT Press, 1974. 1–19.

Lupton, Catherine. *Chris Marker: Memories of the Future*. London: Reaktion Books, 2005.

Lutze, Peter C. *Alexander Kluge: The Last Modernist*. Detroit: Wayne State Univ. Press, 1998.

Lyotard, Jean-Francois. *The Postmodern Condition: A Report on Knowledge*. Minneapolis: Univ. of Minnesota, Press, 1984.

Malraux, André, *Esquisse d'une psychologie du cinéma*. Paris: Gallimard, 1946.

———. *Le Musée imaginaire*. Geneva: Skira, 1947.

Margulies, Ivone. *Nothing Happens: Chantal Akerman's Hyperrealist Everyday*. Durham, N.C.: Duke Univ. Press, 1996.

————. *Rites of Realism: Essays on Corporeal Cinema. Rites of Realism: Essays on Corporeal Cinema*. Ed. Ivone Margulies. Durham, N.C.: Duke Univ. Press, 2002.

————. "Exemplary Bodies: Reenactment in *Love in the City, Sons,* and *Close Up*." In *Rites of Realism: Essays on Corporeal Cinema*. Ed. Ivone Margulies. Durham, N.C.: Duke Univ. Press, 2002. 217–244.

Marker, Chris. *Giradoux par lui-meme*. Paris: Editions du Seuil, 1952.

————. *Le Coeur net (The Forthright Spirit)*. Paris: Editions de Seuil, 1949.

————. *Coréennes*. Paris: Editons du Seuil, 1959.

Martin-Jones, David. "Patrick Keiller." *Journal of Popular British Cinema* 5 (2002): 123–132.

Mazierska, Ewa and Laura Rascaroli. *The Cinema of Nannia Moretti: Dreams and Diaries*. London: Wallflower, 2004.

McCarthy, John A. *Crossing Boundaries: A Theory and History of Essay Writing in German, 1680–1815*. Philadelphia: Univ. of Pennsylvania Press, 1989.

Mekas, Jonas. "The Diary Film (A Lecture on Reminiscences of a Journey to Lithuania)." In *Avant-Garde Film: A Reader, Theory and Criticism*. Ed. P. Adams Sitney. New York: New York Univ. Press, 1978.

Metz, Christian. *The Imaginary Signifier: Psychoanalysis and the Cinema*. Bloomington: Indiana Univ. Press, 1982.

Miller, J. Hillis. *Illustration*. Cambridge, MA: Harvard Univ. Press, 1992.

Milne, Tom, ed. *Godard on Godard*. New York: Viking, 1971.

Minh-ha, Trinh T. "Documentary Is/Not a Name." *October* 52 (Spring 1990): 76–98.

————. *Cinema Interval*. New York: Routledge, 1999.

————. "Altérité: The D-Image Effect." In *Subtitles: On the Foreignness of Film*. Ed. Atom Egoyan and Ian Balfour. Cambridge, MA: MIT Press, 2004. 193–209.

Mitchell, W.J.T. *Picture Theory*. Chicago: Univ. of Chicago Press, 1994.

Monaco, James. *The New Wave: Truffaut, Godard, Chabrol, Rohmer, Rivette*. New York: Oxford Univ. Press, 1976.

————. *Alain Resnais*. New York: Oxford Univ. Press, 1978.

Montaigne, Michel de. *The Complete Works of Montaigne*. Trans. Donald M. Frame. Stanford, CA: Stanford Univ. Press, 1948.

Morris, Errol. "Not Every Picture Tells a Story." *The New York Times* (November 20, 2004), A31.

Moure, José. "Essai de definition de essai au cinema." In *L'Essai et le cinema*. Ed. Suzanne Liandrat-Guigues and Murielle Gagnebin. Paris: Champs Vallon, 2004.

Mullarkey, John. *Refractions of Reality: Philosophy and the Moving Image*. New York Palgravc MacMillan, 2009.

Murray, Timothy. *Like a Film: Ideological Fantasy on Screen, Camera and Canvas*. London: Routledge, 1993.

Musil, Robert. *The Man without Qualities, I*. New York: Knopf, 1995. New Edition.

Naficy, Hamid. *Accented Cinema: Exile and Diasporic Filmmaking*. Princeton, N.J.: Princeton Univ. Press, 2001.

Nichols, Bill. *Blurred Boundaries: Questions of Meaning in Contemporary Culture*. Bloomington: Indiana Univ. Press, 1994.

————. *Introduction to Documentary*. Bloomington: Indiana Univ. Press, 2001.

————. "The Voice of Documentary." In *New Challenges for Documentary*. 2nd ed. Ed. Alan Rosenthal and Jorn Corner. Manchester, UK: Univ. of Manchester Press, 2005, 17–33.

————. "Documentary Reenactment and the Fantasmatic Subject." *Critical Inquiry* 35.1 (2008): 72–89.

Norris, Frank. *McTeague: A Story of San Fransisco*. NY: Signet, 1964.

O'Pray, Michael. *Derek Jarman: Dreams of England*. London: BFI, 1996.

Ostrowska, Dorota. *Reading the French New Wave: Critics, Writers and Art Cinema in France*.

Panofsky, Erwin. "Style and Medium in the Motion Pictures." In *Film Theory and Criticism*. 7th ed. Ed. Leo Braudy and Marshall Cohen. New York: Oxford Univ. Press, 2009.

Parker, Deborah, and Mark Parker. *The DVD and the Study of Film: The Attainable Text*. New York: Palgrave, 2011.

Perez, Gilberto. *The Material Ghost: Films and Their Medium*. Baltimore: Johns Hopkins Univ. Press, 1998.

Petro, Patrice. *Aftershocks of the New: Feminism and Film History*. New Brunswick, N.J.: Rutgers Univ. Press, 2002.

Pinel, Vincent. *Introduction au Ciné-club: histoire, théorie, pratique du Ciné-club en France*. Paris: Editions Ouvrieres, 1964.

Porcile, Francois. *Defense du court metrage*. Paris: Les Editions du Cerf, 1965.

Porton, Richard. "Language Games and Aesthetic Attitudes: Style and Ideology in Jarman's Late Films." In *By Angels Driven: The Films of Derek Jarman*. Ed. Chris Lippard. Wiltshire, UK: Flicks Books, 1996. 135–160.

Potamkin, Harry. *The Compound Cinema: The Film Writings of Harry Alan Potamkin*. Ed. Lewis Jacobs. New York: Teachers College Press, 1977.

Prager, Bad. *The Cinema of Werner Herzog: Aesthetic Ecstasy and Truth*. London: Wallflower, 2007.

Rabinovitz, Lauren. "From Hale's Tours to Star Tours: Virtual Voyages, Travel Ride Films, and the Delirium of the Hyper-Real." In *Virtual Voyages: Cinema and Travel*. Ed. Jeffrey Ruoff. Durham, N.C.: Duke Univ. Press. 2006. 42–60.

Rascaroli, Laura. *The Personal Camera: Subjective Cinema and the Essay Film*. London: Wallflower, 2009.

Renov, Michael. *Theorizing Documentary*. London: Routledge, 1993.

———. *The Subject of Documentary*. Minneapolis: Univ. of Minnesota Press, 2004.

———. "*Lost, Lost, Lost*: Mekas as Essayist." *The Subject of Documentary*. Minneapolis: Univ. of Minnesota Press, 2004. 69–92.

Richter, Gerhard. *Thought-Images: Frankfurt School Writers' Reflections from Damaged Life*. Stanford, Calif.: Stanford Univ. Press, 2007.

Richter, Hans. "Der Film Essay: Eine neue Form des Dokumentarfilms." *Nationalzeitung* (May 25, 1940). Reprinted in *Schreiben Bilder Sperechen*, Ed. Christa Blumlinger and Constantin Wulff. Vienna: Sonderzahl, 1992. 194–197.

Riis, Jacob. *How the Other Half Lives*. Ed. David Leviatin. Boston: Bedford/St. Martin's, 1996.

Rivette, Jacques. "Letter on Rossellini." In *Cahiers du cinéma. The 1950s: Neo-Realism, Hollywood, New Wave*. Ed. Jim Hillier. Cambridge, Mass.: Harvard Univ. Press, 1985. 192–204.

Rodowick, David. *Gille Deleuze's Time Machine*. Durham, N.C.: Duke Univ. Press, 1997.

Rodriguez, Hector. "Constraint, Cruelty, and Conversation." In *Dekalog 01: On the Five Obstructions*. Ed. Mette Hjort. London: Wallflower Press, 2008. 38–56.

Rosen, Philip. *Change Mummified: Cinema, Historicity, Theory*. Minneapolis: Univ. of Minnesota Press, 2001.

Rosenbaum, Jonathan. "Orson Welles's Essay Films and Documentary Fictions." In *Discovering Orson Welles*. Berkeley: Univ. of California Press, 2007. 129–145.

Rosler, Martha. "The Bowery in Two Inadequate Systems of Descriptions." In *Martha Rosler, 3 Works: 1. The Restoration of High Culture in Chile; 2. The Bowery in Two Inadequate Descriptive*

Systems; 3. In, Around, and Afterthoughts (on Documentary Photography). Novia Scotia: Press of the Nova Scotia College of Art and Design, 2006.

Roud, Richard. "The Left Bank." *Sight and Sound* (Winter 1962–1963): 24–27.

———. *Godard*. New York: Doubleday, 1968.

Ruoff, Jeffrey, ed. *Virtual Voyages: Cinema and Travel*. Durham, N.C.: Duke Univ. Press, 2006.

Russell, Catherine. *Narrative Mortality: Death, Closure, and New Wave Cinema*. Minneapolis: Univ. of Minnesota Press, 1995.

———. "Archival Apocalypse: Found Footage as Ethnography." In *Experimental Ethnography: The Work of Film in the Age of Video*. Durham, N.C.: Duke Univ. Press, 1999.

Sadoul, George. *The French Film*. London: Falcon, 1953.

Shaviro, Steven. *The Cinematic Body*. Minneapolis: Univ. of Minnesota Press, 1993.

Silverman, Kaja. "The Author as Receiver." *October* 96 (2001): 17–34.

Sinclair, Iain. "London: Necropolis of Fretful Ghosts." *Sight and Sound* (June 1994): 12–15.

Smith, Gary, ed. *Benjamin: Philosophy, Aesthetics, and History*. Chicago: Univ. of Chicago Press, 1989.

Sobchack, Vivian. *The Address of the Eye: A Phenomenlogy of Film Experience*. Princeton, N.J.: Princeton Univ. Press, 1992.

———. "Toward a Phenomenology of Nonfictional Film Experience." In *Collecting Visible Evidence*. Ed. Jaine M. Gaines and Michael Renov. Minneapolis: Univ. of Minnesota Press, 1999. 241–254.

Solanas, Fernando and Octavio Getino's "Towards a Third Cinema." In *Critical Visions in Film Theory: Classic and Contemporary Readings*. Ed. Timothy Corrigan and Patricia White, with Meta Mazaj. Boston: Bedford/St. Martin's, 2011. 925–939.

Spacks, Patricia Meyer. *Boredom: The Literary History of a State of Mind*. Chicago: Univ. of Chicago Press, 1996.

Stewart, Garrett. *Between Film and Screen: Modernism's Photo Synthesis*. Chicago: Univ. of Chicago Press, 1999.

———. "Screen Memory in *Waltz with Bashir*." *Film Quarterly* 63.3 (2010): 58–62.

Thomson, David. *The New Biographical Dictionary of Film*. New York: Knopf, 2002.

Turim, Maureen. *Flashbacks in Film: Memory and History*. New York: Routledge, 1989.

Van, Mai Thu. *Vietnam: un people, des voix*. Paris: Pierre Horay, 1992.

Virilio, Paul. "Video Letters: An Interview with Atom Egoyan." In *Atom Egoyan*. Ed. Carole Desbarats et al. Paris: Editions Dis Voir, 1994. 105–110.

———. *The Vision Machine*. Bloomington: Indiana Univ. Press, 1994.

———. "The State of Emergency." *The Virilio Reader*. Ed. James De Derian. Malden, MA: Blackwell, 1998.

Wahlberg, Malin. *Documentary Time: Film and Phenomenology*. Minneapolis: Univ. of Minnesota Press, 2008.

Warner, Michael. *Publics and Counterpublics*. New York: Zone Books, 2002.

Warren, Charles, ed. *Beyond Document: Essays on Nonfiction Film*. Hanover, N.H.: Wesleyan Univ. Press, 1996.

Watney, Simon. *Practices of Freedom: Selected Writings on HIV/AIDS*. Durham, N.C.: Duke Univ. Press, 1994.

Williams, Linda. "Mirrors without Memories: Truth, History, and *The Thin Blue Line*." In *Documenting the Documentary: Close Readings of Documentary Film and Video*. Ed. Barry Keith Grant and Jeannette Sloniowski. Detroit: Wayne State Univ. Press, 1998. 379–396.

Willumson, Glenn G. *W. Eugene Smith and the Photographic Essay*. Cambridge: Cambridge Univ. Press, 1992.

Wolf, Christa. *The Author's Dimension: Selected Essays*. New York: Farrar, Straus, Giroux, 1993.

Wollen, Peter. "Blue." *New Left Review* 6 (November–December 2000): 120–133.

———. "Speed and the Cinema." In *Paris Hollywood: Writings on Film*. London: Verso, 2002. 264–274.

Woolf, Virginia. "Street Haunting: A London Adventure." In *The Art of the Personal Essay: An Anthology from the Classical Era to the Present*. Ed. Phillip Lopate. New York: Anchor Books, 1995. 256–265.

Wymer, Rowland. *Derek Jarman*. Manchester, UK: Manchester Univ. Press, 2005.

Zimmermann, Patricia R. *States of Emergency: Documentaries, Wars, Democracies*. Minneapolis: Univ. of Minnesota Press, 2000.